Leadership
That
Matters

THE CRITICAL FACTORS
FOR MAKING A DIFFERENCE
IN PEOPLE'S LIVES
AND ORGANIZATIONS' SUCCESS

Marshall Sashkin
Molly G. Sashkin

BERRETT-KOEHLER PUBLISHERS, INC.
San Francisco

Berrett-Koehler Publishers, Inc.
235 Montgomery Street, Suite 650
San Francisco, CA 94104-2916
Tel: (415) 288-0260   Fax: (415) 362-2512   www.bkconnection.com

ORDERING INFORMATION
Quantity sales. Special discounts are available on quantity purchases by corporations,
associations, and others. For details, contact the "Special Sales Department" at the
Berrett-Koehler address above.

Individual sales. Berrett-Koehler publications are available through most bookstores.
They can also be ordered direct from Berrett-Koehler: Tel: (800) 929-2929;
Fax: (802) 864-7626; www.bkconnection.com

Orders for college textbook/course adoption use. Please contact Berrett-Koehler:
Tel: (800) 929-2929; Fax: (802) 864-7626.

Orders by U.S. trade bookstores and wholesalers. Please contact Publishers Group West,
1700 Fourth Street, Berkeley, CA 94710. Tel: (510) 528-1444; Fax (510) 528-3444.

Berrett-Koehler and the BK logo are registered trademarks of Berrett-Koehler Publishers, Inc.

Printed in the United States of America

Berrett-Koehler books are printed on long-lasting acid-free paper. When it is available, we
choose paper that has been manufactured by environmentally responsible processes.
These may include using trees grown in sustainable forests, incorporating recycled paper,
minimizing chlorine in bleaching, or recycling the energy produced at the paper mill.

Library of Congress Cataloging-in-Publication Data

Sashkin, Marshall, 1944–
    Leadership that matters: the critical factors for making a difference in people's lives
and organizations' success/by Marshall Sashkin and Molly G. Sashkin.
        p. cm
    Includes bibliographical references and index.
    ISBN 1-57675-193-7
    1. Leadership. I. Sashkin, Molly G. II. Title.
HD57.7.S27 2002
658.4'092—dc21   2002028154

Project management, composition, and interior design: Shepherd Incorporated
Copyediting: Sharon Kraus

FIRST EDITION
08 07 06 05 04 03   10 9 8 7 6 5 4 3 2 1

Leadership
That
Matters

For Bill

and

For Ern

Mizpah, Gen. 31–(49)

Contents

Acknowledgments

We are grateful to the many researchers and scholars whose work we have used to develop our approach to defining and understanding *Leadership That Matters*.We have drawn freely from the ideas of classical writers such as Max Weber as well as the theory and research of more recent scholars such as Albert Bandura and Martin E. P. Seligman. Their contributions form the foundation on which our own approach is grounded.

We are especially indebted to friends and colleagues who have shared with us their particular expertise in the field of leadership. We wish to thank particularly our collaborator William E. Rosenbach. We also deeply appreciate the helpful ideas and suggestions of Warren Bennis, Robert M. Fulmer, Paul Green, Robert J. House, J. G. (Jerry) Hunt, Elliott Jaques, Harry Levinson, David McClelland, and Abraham Zaleznik. We are also grateful to several individuals who read and gave helpful comments on early drafts of our manuscript, including Frank Basler, Chet Delaney, Karen Manz, and Ann Matranga.

All of these friends and colleagues have contributed important ideas, good advice, and useful comments on our own views. We have drawn liberally from their work, their ideas, and their very helpful feedback. However, neither they nor any of the many others whose work we've benefited from are in any way responsible for (or even necessarily in agreement with) the views presented here.

The good and useful concepts we offer are, for the most part, attributable to those who have worked hard to develop and apply knowledge about leadership. Whatever problems or limitations there are with our concepts and arguments can only be blamed on us!

Marshall Sashkin   **Seabrook, Maryland**
Molly G. Sashkin   **December 2002**

Introduction

The ancient Roman writer Horace said that what you write should be kept private for nine years before being shown to others. Perhaps that gives an author enough time to reflect and decide whether to share it at all! This book has been in the making for over a decade now, so it's clearly time to share our thoughts with others.

Since 1980 we have worked on an approach to understanding leadership. We called our approach "visionary leadership" because we felt that at heart our approach is about seeing the big picture. To us, this means having a broad scope of understanding people and how they behave in organizations. Even more, the term "visionary" implies a long-term view, a strategic perspective that extends over time.

We haven't stopped using the term "visionary leadership." However, we now feel even more comfortable with the description we use as the title of this book: *Leadership That Matters.* We adopted this new term for several reasons. First, we realized that our concept of leadership is not limited to those at the top of the organization, such as CEOs and senior executives. Visionary leadership matters to people throughout an organization, and not just because they are all affected by it. We believe everyone has the potential, at least to some degree, to have an effect as a visionary leader.

Another reason for putting less emphasis on the term "visionary leadership" is that it has been so often misused. That is, to some visionary leadership is purely a personal trait, while to others it implies that the central role of a leader is to come up with a detailed vision, a future ideal, and then "sell" that vision to followers. We don't believe that either of these views is correct.

In this book we will show that while leadership that matters does depend on certain characteristics of the leader, it involves much more than the leader's personality. We will also debunk the notion that leaders come up with ideal visions of what the future will be. To us visionary leadership is about *creating* the future, not *predicting* it.

When our friend Steve Piersanti observed that our book seemed to be about the sort of leadership that makes a difference, that really matters to people, we realized that he had found the focus of our approach. We decided to use his term—leadership that matters—as the primary description of our approach to understanding leadership in organizations.

What Is Leadership That Matters?

Leadership that matters does so because it makes a difference. This difference occurs in the lives of followers, in a group or organization. There's also a difference in group or organizational performance. And there is an important difference in the organization itself as a result of leadership that matters. In this book we explain, in detail, just what this means and how it happens.

What Makes This Book Different?

Questions people often ask about a book are "What is it about?" and "What's so special about it?" Obviously, this book is about leadership. What makes it special is more difficult to address. After all, there are thousands of books about leadership. Certainly some of them are good books that address important leadership issues. Why, then, is still another book needed about leadership? Three things in particular make this book uniquely useful. First, we use a very wide range of research-based information sources. Most books on leadership rely solely on the author's own opinions and experiences. Second, we focus on leadership behavior, leadership characteristics, and the social context of leadership. Most other approaches incorporate just one or two of these factors. And third, our view of the purpose of leadership is quite different from other authors' perspectives. We see leadership as more than motivating followers to achieve goals or defining and then "selling" them on certain goals.

Sources of Information

Most books about leadership present the author's own personal conclusions based on his or her experiences and the meaning that authors have found in those experiences. Like others, we have personal experiences with leadership that we want to share. However, the most important experiences we will deal with come out of theory and research, not just from our own limited experience or that of a few individuals.

The theory and research we will refer to in this book are the results of work by social scientists. These are people who have been involved in the formal study of leadership. Such research has been going on for more than a hundred years. In that time a substantial amount of verified knowledge about leadership has been accumulated. It makes sense, to us, to rely on and build on that body of research knowledge.

A Comprehensive Approach

Most leadership theories focus on a certain set of behaviors or skills, on particular personal characteristics of leaders, or on the organizational context of leadership. A few approaches incorporate two of these three elements. No other approach, in our view, includes all three. All three are, however, necessary components of any meaningful approach to understanding leadership.

The Purpose of Leadership

The final, and perhaps the most important way our approach to leadership differs from others, is in our view of the purpose of leadership. The English author and essayist Samuel Johnson said, "The only aim of writing is to enable the readers better to enjoy life or better to endure it."[1] This happens, we think, because great authors lead readers to find or make meaning in their own lives. The same can be said of good leaders in general.

Most leadership scholars and researchers assert that leadership is about motivating followers to accomplish goals defined by the leader. We believe that is the work of managers, not leaders. Other writers on leadership, including many popular authors, do, however, argue that the role of leaders is to make meaning for followers.

What they mean is that leaders develop a "vision," an ideal image of some future state. Leaders then present followers with this vision in such a compelling way that followers "sign on" to help attain the leader's vision. We see some truth to this notion of leadership, but we believe that there's much more to it. That is, leaders create the conditions that enable others—followers—to make their own meaning. While that meaning always has a uniquely personal element, it will also contain certain common themes. These are elements that are shared by all those who are part of the leader's organization.

To do this, leaders must have certain skills as well as specific characteristics, including "vision." The full explanation of our own vision of leadership is the central focus of this book.

Where Do Our Ideas About Leadership Come From?

Most of our concepts about leadership that matters come from the research and practice of a number of people, many of whom have helped us on this journey of understanding. What we have contributed to an understanding of leadership is a clear description of how these various concepts all fit together. In this book we show how the various elements and aspects of leadership come together to provide a more complete, as well as a practically useful, understanding of the nature of leadership in organizations.

We took the concepts of transactional and transformational leadership from James McGregor Burns. The research and mentoring of Warren Bennis and Bert Nanus guided our own development of measures of transformational leadership behavior. Our own identification of these behaviors is confirmed in the work of Jim Kouzes and Barry Posner. Even so, we concluded that a set of behaviors, no matter how well defined and documented, could not account for the sort of transformations in people and organizations described by Burns.

We finally realized that our friend Robert House was correct in identifying a personality aspect of transformational leadership. His own ideas were based in good part on the earlier work of David McClelland. With advice from both House and McClelland, we incorporated certain personality aspects into our approach.

The first personality element we added to our model of leadership was the power need. More than a quarter-century ago McClelland found that the need for power is essential to what he termed the "leadership motive pattern." The need for power is the basis of "charisma," the aspect of personality that House identified as central to leadership.

House's associate, Boaz Shamir, extended House's approach by incorporating a second important element. This second crucial aspect of leadership has been studied by many psychologists, including Albert Bandura, Julian Rotter, and Martin Seligman. It has been given a variety of names, including "internal/external control," "agency," "self-efficacy," and "learned optimism." We call this personality element "self-confidence." It is the basis for the ability to take action, which has been shown by researchers at the Center for Creative Leadership to be important for leadership success.[2]

The personality factor involving the need for power is emotionally based. It is grounded in our feelings—including fears—about personal security and survival, what Abraham Maslow saw as the most basic and fundamental human motives. Self-confidence drives behavioral action. What about cognitive ability? That is the third personality element of special importance for leadership.

Effective leaders are not dumb. Raw intelligence or "IQ" is not, however, the personality factor we refer to. Rather, this third, cognitive element concerns a person's ability to understand cause-and-effect relationships, especially as they play out in complex ways and over time. We credit two psychologists, Elliott Jaques and Sigfried Streufert, as the primary sources of our ideas about this third important personal attribute. We drew heavily, in particular, on the theory and research of Elliott Jaques, our friend of many years.

To understand how leaders transform organizations in the ways implied by Burns, that is by constructing culture, we drew on the classical work of the German sociologist Max Weber as well as the later work of American sociologist Talcott Parsons. Our ideas were further informed by the important work of Edgar Schein.

Summary

Our comprehensive approach incorporates behavioral elements, personality aspects of leadership, and the social structure or culture of organizations created by transformational leaders. We draw on diverse sources and synthesize key ideas into a new approach. We believe that the result is a more complete understanding and explanation of the nature and purpose of *Leadership That Matters.*

Chapter
ONE

What Is Leadership?

Good leadership consists of doing less and being more.

Lao Tzu[1]

To those who really understand leadership, Lao Tzu's assertion is no surprise. The classic *Tao Te Ching,* from which we took the above and other quotations in this book, was written by Lao Tzu more than two thousand years ago. The *Tao* is the source of many common sayings, such as "A journey of a thousand miles begins with a single step."

One reason the *Tao* was written was to help enlighten the warlords who then ruled various parts of China. One of Lao Tzu's main aims was to show these rulers how to be better leaders. The essence of his eighty-one lessons can be found in Chapter 17 of the *Tao.* Our version goes like this:

❖ **Some leaders accomplish a great deal and are loved and praised by followers.**

❖ **Lesser leaders use threat and fear to get results.**

❖ **The worst leaders use force and lie; they are despised.**

❖ **But of the best leaders, when the work is done and the goal attained, the people say, "We did it ourselves!"**

We think that this is a wonderful illustration of how leadership matters. Leadership based on the leader's engaging personality and style is not leadership that matters, in the long run. Cults fade and their leaders are forgotten, except to historians. And how often has a leader who was once loved and praised later turned to fear and threat of punishment to get results?

A person may achieve great things through his or her efforts, but not necessarily through effective *leadership,* leadership that matters. Nor does leadership matter just because the leader is powerful. Anyone who can use a gun can make people follow orders, but it's not leadership that matters, it's the gun.

This book is about *leadership that matters,* leadership that counts, that makes a difference in people's lives. In a time of increased uncertainty, perhaps even apparent chaos, it is tempting to listen to those who believe that leaders are little more than creations of their times, reflections of larger social forces over which they and we have no real control. Even some leadership scholars have argued that our attribution of positive outcomes to the efforts of leaders may be little more than a romantic illusion.[2] Such logic suggests that what we believe to be the effect of good leadership—or even the result of bad or evil leadership—may really be the outcome of social forces that we don't understand.

For example, hardly anyone would deny that Mohandas (Mahatma) Gandhi had some influence on India's struggle for independence from Great Britain. However, the above argument would emphasize the post-World War II economic issues that made it desirable for England to eliminate the costs of maintaining its far-flung colonial empire.

Looking to the darker side of leadership, some scholars argue that Adolph Hitler's rise to power in post-World War I Germany was not due primarily to his charismatic leadership and appeal to the masses. Rather, Hitler's rise was, in this view, mostly the result of desperate economic conditions. These included a worldwide depression on top of punitive economic conditions imposed on Germany after the war.

Our premise, that leadership matters, runs counter to the arguments illustrated above. We don't deny that social circumstances have important effects. However, we strongly disagree that the effects of leadership are mostly romantic illusion or an explanation for societal dynamics that we can't otherwise understand.

There is clear evidence today that leadership does matter. Leaders help reduce ambiguity and uncertainty in our lives. They do so by constructive acts that use complex social forces to achieve concrete, long-term aims and goals. But they do more: leaders *make meaning.* That is, they provide clear and positive *reasons* for their aims, actions, and accomplishments. One reason, then, that leadership matters is because leaders add clarity and direction to life and make life more meaningful.

Even more important, leaders help us learn to make our own meaning in our lives. That is, leaders teach us that we can control our own lives and that we are capable of creating meaning ourselves, through our own actions. This may sound a bit vague; that's because it is complicated and difficult to explain, as well as to do. The central aim of this book is to show just how leaders do these things, how we can all learn to do them better, and in the process become more self-directed leaders ourselves.

Instead of beginning with a long and detailed explanation of leadership, we propose to start by asking you to examine your own experiences of leadership. Have you ever personally known or worked for or with someone you consider a truly exceptional leader? Think not of some famous person or politician but of a real individual you knew or know now, someone with whom you had significant interaction. This need not be someone you know or work with today; a leader from any time in your life will do, even if you knew this person twenty or more years ago.

Now go a step further. Think of a specific time and place, a real interaction that you had with this person you've identified as an exceptional leader. When you have that specific occasion clearly in mind, close your eyes and play it back in your mind's eye, as though you were watching the leader and you on video. Take just a minute, right now, to do this.

After you have visualized and reviewed this memory, take a piece of paper and write down some things that come to your mind as descriptive of the leader. Or use the box provided below. You might just list words or brief phrases, or you might write a line or two.

Describe the person you thought of as an exceptional leader:

We've conducted an exercise based on what we just asked you to do with a great many groups. Afterwards we ask participants to share some of what they've written down. Their responses always fall into three categories, which we describe below. Look back at your own responses and see where they fit.

The first category consists of terms like

- intelligent
- creative
- honest
- friendly

- confident
- persistent
- patient
- forceful

Some of your comments and descriptions may fit into this group. When we ask people why these items are grouped together, almost everyone says quickly, "They're all *traits*, personality characteristics."

The second category of terms usually includes

- listens well
- coaches
- acts consistently
- gives feedback

- shares feelings
- supports us
- gives others credit
- delegates

Again, it would be surprising if none of the descriptive terms you came up with fit in this category. What is the category? It's not hard to see that all of these terms describe actions or behaviors. Most involve other people, too, but the central common feature is that they are leadership *behaviors*.

Finally, look at the third category, which often includes terms like

- involves the team
- sees the "big picture"
- is politically astute
- looks for information

- has a vision
- grabs my attention
- is committed to aims
- understands our environment

This third group of descriptions is more difficult to label. Sometimes there are very few terms that fit in this group. That's because while the first two groups of terms are relatively simple to characterize, this one has more complicated content. Is "has a vision" a trait? Perhaps, but it is clearly more than a trait like "patience." Is "involves the team" a behavior? Yes, but it goes beyond a simple behavior; it has to do with "the team."

What links the terms in this last category? They all relate, in some way, to a broader context or situation in which leadership is expressed. We call this last category *situational context*.

You may think that we constructed this three-part categorization to try to sort out and identify a set of common traits, actions, and contexts. That's not at all the case. Our point is that these same three categories emerged in each of the hundreds of groups with which we've worked using this exercise. The first two categories are always obvious, while the third is harder to see at first but, once recognized, is just as clear.

Why should the three categories be so important? These three categories—leadership traits, leadership behaviors, and the situational context of leadership—represent the three primary approaches that have historically been used to understand leadership.

Personality, Behavior, and Situational Context

The personality of leaders has been a subject of commentary for thousands of years. For example, the classical work of the Roman writer Plutarch, who lived in the first century A.D. and wrote a history of the lives of great men, is still read today. Leadership as personality and biography is surely the earliest approach to understanding leadership.

The study of great leaders' personalities has continued to the present day. Who has not thought of Franklin Roosevelt or, more recently, John Kennedy, as leaders who stood out by virtue of their personality and character? Successful business leaders have also been the focus of special study. Books have been written, for example, about Bill Gates, founder of the incredibly successful and important Microsoft Corporation. Various biographers have speculated about the aspects of Gates' personality that enabled his entrepreneurial success as leader of that organization.

Recent studies of leadership have also focused on leaders' behaviors. Many have, for example, examined the actions of Gandhi, whose personal behavior led India to independence.[3] The great humanitarian physician Albert Schweitzer said that with respect to leadership, "personal example is not the most important thing—it is the *only* thing."

Nor has history ignored the context of leadership, such as the strategy used by Ulysses S. Grant that led the Union to victory in the Civil War. Especially interesting is the contrast between Grant as a great military leader and Grant as president. Many historians consider Grant to be one of the least effective of all U.S. presidents. In a military context Grant could not be defeated. As a political leader he was a disaster.

The three categories of personality, behavior, and context are also important because they replicate the results of almost a hundred years of formal leadership research. As we will see in Chapter Two, social scientists from the early part of the twentieth century to its recent end started with personality as the explanation for leadership. They moved on to look for explanatory behaviors when traits proved inconclusive. Finally, they searched the complexities of the situational context in an effort to understand leadership scientifically.

Leadership That Matters: A New Synthesis

No one of the three approaches to understanding leadership comes close to providing a comprehensive understanding of what leadership is and how it works. As Warren Bennis and Bert Nanus have pointedly said,

> Multiple interpretations of leadership exist, each providing a sliver of insight but each remaining an incomplete and wholly inadequate explanation.[4]

To see how leadership works, how it really matters, you can't just look at traits, or at behavior alone, or simply at the situational context. A person's underlying character is surely relevant for leadership. Personality traits alone, however, are inadequate to explain or understand the nature of leadership. The behaviors required for effective leadership are not just simple skills; they are complex and often subtle. They are, moreover, determined both by the leader's character and by the situational context. To understand the nature of leadership we must examine all three of these areas together.

It's not easy to build a comprehensive leadership approach. Psychologists who focus on the individual tend to see most leadership behavior as related to one's personality. Social psychologists concentrate on interpersonal and group factors in leadership. Those who take a more organizational viewpoint center their study on how the organizational context determines leaders' actions. In reality, all three viewpoints are important. One must attend to them all without leaving out one or another.

Unfortunately, most leadership theories and approaches focus on just one or, in some cases, two of the three elements. In contrast, our approach, *Leadership That Matters,* explicitly incorporates all three of the key aspects of leadership: personality, behavior, and the organizational context. The sort of integration and synthesis we offer is complicated. We identified key factors that, when taken together in context, provide a more complete and comprehensive understanding of leadership than can be had by studying any one of them in isolation.

In preparing our synthesis we drew on a large number of important contributions to an understanding of leadership, made by various scholars and practitioners over the past hundred years. We will build this new synthesis step by step, over the next several chapters.

To arrive at this synthesis we must first see where we have been. That means examining the key research findings of the past hundred years in each of the three areas. That is the subject of Chapter Two. In that chapter we review the accumulated research knowledge relevant to leadership traits, leadership behavior, and the situational context of leadership. We found that while each focus provides a "sliver of insight," none offers an explanation that goes far beyond its focal sliver.

Perhaps it was the failure of leadership research to adequately explain what makes leadership matter that led to a whole new way to look at leadership. We define this new perspective as *transformational* leadership, in our conclusion to Chapter Two.

In Chapter Three we examine in detail this new way of understanding leadership behavior. Leadership researchers and scholars such as Warren Bennis, Bernard Bass, and James Kouzes and Barry Posner were the first to explore this "new paradigm," looking for a new set of behaviors that might be the basis for leadership that matters.

The behaviors we describe in Chapter Three are quite different from those studied by "classical" leadership researchers of the 1950s, '60s, and '70s. These new considerations include such behaviors as caring, empowering, and sharing a vision. Like others, we were convinced that the new transformational leadership approach added a different and important behavioral perspective to our understanding of how leadership matters. Even so, we concluded that a focus on leadership behavior alone—new or old—could not adequately and fully explain how leadership matters.

We realized that a complete and, hopefully, comprehensive leadership approach would have to include "slivers of truth" from each of the three areas of leadership research. This would include leadership traits and the situational context of leadership as well as leaders' behavior.

Chapters Four, Five, Six, and Seven present the results of our study of the personal characteristics of leaders, in the framework of the transformational leadership approach. We searched for a new way to understand leadership, not in terms of fixed traits but through leaders' *character*. We found some answers in the work of a number of eminent psychologists. Their contributions, and our interpretations of them, are detailed in Chapters Four through Seven. In these chapters we explore leaders' confidence, their orientations to power, and their capacity to think through complex action plans over time.

The third research area described in Chapter Two centers on the situational context of leadership. Chapter Eight offers a new and far more sophisticated way to look at the *organizational context* of leadership. We draw on the work of organizational psychologists and sociologists whose aim was to understand the nature of organizational culture. What we found is that transformational leadership, leadership that matters, is essentially about creating the sort of cultures that enable organizations—and the people in them—to achieve exceptional performance results. This sort of leadership is about changing, that is, transforming organizations. Chapter Nine shows how such leaders transform the social context.

Such transformation is not simply a matter of changing organizational structures and processes. It is not enough to eliminate levels of management and "flatten" the hierarchy, or to design new ways to hire, reward, and promote people. In Chapter Ten we see how leaders transform and develop *people*. Leadership that matters does so because it changes individuals, including leaders, for the better.

In Chapter Eleven we review key research studies conducted to test our formulation of the new leadership approach. We report real-world studies that support our concept of leadership that matters with hard evidence of performance and results.

We present several issues and challenges regarding leadership in Chapter Twelve. These include the question of men's and women's leadership (are they different?), the nature of empowerment, the uncertainty and ambiguity we must live with, and the effects of globalization.

Finally, in our Conclusion we present a synthesis of all that we have discussed in the book. Rather than simply summarizing or repeating our conclusions, we link them to the work of other major leadership approaches. All are grounded in a new, transformational leadership concept. Our aim is to identify essential common elements and show how our approach, *Leadership That Matters*, addresses and incorporates them.

Summary

We began this chapter by inviting you to consider with us the nature of leadership. We then identified three basic elements of a definition: the leader's personality, his or her behavior, and the situational context of leadership. Finally, we sketched out how we will, in the chapters that follow, use these elements to create a new synthesis. We called this new approach *Leadership That Matters*.

Our aim in this book is not only to better understand leadership, but to consider how one can become better at practicing it. We will present a new way to understand and practice leadership that speaks to those who are, or aspire to be, in positions of leadership. That's why we have tried to incorporate personally relevant self-assessment materials in most of the chapters. In this way we hope to show how leadership can matter to you.

The first step of our journey is, in Chapter Two, an overview of the many thousands of steps taken before us, by leadership scholars and researchers of the past hundred years.

Chapter
TWO

What Have We Learned About Leadership?

A journey of a thousand miles begins with a single step.
                    Tao Te Ching, **Chapter 64**

To begin to understand leadership that matters, we start with the beginning of leadership research. We will review some results of the past hundred years of formal research on leadership. But, before we can look at these research results, we must consider the definition of leadership and the difference between leadership and management.

Leaders and Managers

Historically, researchers made little distinction between the terms "leadership" and "management." In contrast, today there appears to be considerable agreement that management and leadership are not at all the same. Much of the research on leadership, however—even recent research—uses the two terms interchangeably.

Most of the research from 1900 to the early 1980s was limited to the study of supervisors and lower-level managers. Even through the 1950s you could count the number of research studies involving senior executives and CEOs on the fingers of one hand. It was not until 1977 that Abraham Zaleznik, an internationally recognized leadership scholar at Harvard University,

17

published a classic essay outlining what he asserted were key differences between managers and leaders.[1]

So, in looking over the history of leadership research we have to keep in mind that the "leaders" studied were generally first-line supervisors and lower-level managers, not middle managers, executives, or CEOs. For now, just remember that the studies we are looking at didn't make such distinctions. Later, we'll consider again the difference this made in research results, as we look more closely at the difference between leaders and managers.

Leadership Research

Traits Are Great! Research From 1900 to 1945

More than fifty years ago, the dominant approach to leadership was called the "great man" theory. (We would, today, call it the "great person" approach to leadership.) This approach assumes that great leaders are born that way. Therefore, if we can identify those personal characteristics or traits that make them effective we can understand the secret of leadership. Fifty years ago, this approach didn't seem unreasonable. After all, the new science of psychology had, by the turn of the century, proven that measuring individuals' intelligence—or "IQ"—was possible. What's more, this measure was a good predictor of general success at work.

In the first decade of the twentieth century, as the world edged its way toward war, the U.S. Army applied the idea of testing and selection to help identify potential leaders. Army psychologists went to work to develop what came to be called the "Army Alpha" test. They used this simple general mental aptitude test to select potential officers during World War I.[2] This early leadership test is still, at least in remnants, part of what is now called the "ASVAB," or Armed Services Vocational Aptitude Battery.

Does this approach really work, though? In the 1920s, researchers began working to identify and measure predictors of effective leadership. By 1945, there were literally hundreds of studies. Ralph Stogdill, then a young scholar at Ohio State University, reviewed more than one hundred of the best research reports. His aim was to see if he could find some common themes or reach some definite conclusions about leadership traits and characteristics.[3]

Stogdill found that leaders were, in fact, generally a bit more intelligent on average than people overall. However, the difference was not significant; it did not serve as an adequate predictor of leadership. Leaders were also more outgoing and personable than the average person. But, again, this difference was not significant and could be of no real value for identifying leaders or predicting leadership effectiveness. Leaders were also more creative, more assertive, and more responsible than the average person; they were even taller and heavier! However, none of these differences proved useful for identifying leaders, because none of them was statistically significant. It seemed that leadership traits simply did not matter.

Many people believe, even today, that Stogdill demonstrated that leadership is not a matter of traits or characteristics. Actually, his findings and conclusions were more complicated than that; we'll explain how later. Nevertheless, a result of Ralph Stogdill's classic research review was to close off most personality-based leadership research. One consequence was the beginning of a new leadership research focus. Stogdill and his Ohio State colleagues (like researchers at other universities) embarked on an ambitious research program to identify the *behaviors* associated with effective leadership.

Behavior to Savor! Research From 1945 to 1965

If it's not *who they are*, Stogdill's logic went, maybe it's *what they do*. Of course, Stogdill and his associates were not the only ones who picked up the challenge of identifying the behaviors used by effective leaders. Two other groups of researchers were particularly active, at the University of Michigan and at Harvard.

Researchers at the University of Michigan's Institute for Social Research made several studies of supervisory leadership. They were focused on the behavioral strategies related to effective performance.[4] One major study focused on "gandy dancers," a label well known to railroad workers. Gandy dancers are the laborers who lay down and straighten track. They work in crews and swing large sledge hammers in a rhythm that reminds one of dancing. ("Gandy," it is said, refers to the maker of the sledges, Gandy Co. of Chicago, whose name was stamped on the handles.)

The Michigan researchers observed supervisors' actions and then surveyed their subordinates. The researchers concluded that they could rate supervisors' behavior on a single dimension, with one end labeled "employee-centered" and the other called "task-centered." An employee-centered supervisor might, for example, observe a crew that was making slow progress. The supervisor might ask the employees what he could do to help them. Or, he could tell them how much he appreciated their efforts while exploring whether there were any problems.

In contrast, a task-centered supervisor who observed a productivity problem would act quite differently. He might, for example, tell employees that they were not working fast enough. Or, he might exhort them to work harder, or stand over them giving detailed directions. The results of these studies, published in the mid-1950s, appeared to show that the employee-centered supervisors got better performance than the task-centered bosses.

About the same time, in the early 1950s, Stogdill and his associates were busy observing factory work crews at the International Harvester plant near Columbus.[5] They, too, found some supervisors who were employee-centered, who focused on giving support and encouragement and providing assistance when employees seemed to need help. But the Michigan researchers had already used that label. So, the group at Ohio State, observing that these behaviors were considerate of employees, called this whole category of behavior "consideration." The Ohio State researchers also found supervisors who were clear taskmasters, giving orders and riding herd on subordinate employees. Since the Michigan group had already taken the term "task-centered leadership," they coined a new term: "initiating structure." That is, by providing directions to employees, these supervisors were *initiating* a more *structured* way to do the work.

Despite some obvious similarities in the findings of the Michigan and Ohio State researchers, there was one very big difference: the Ohio State researchers discovered that a supervisor could be both considerate *and* directive (or initiate structure). These were not the opposite ends of a single dimension; instead, they were two separate dimensions.

Of course, some supervisors were primarily considerate. The behavior of some others consisted mostly of initiating structure, that is, giving directions. But there were also some who appeared to engage in a lot of *both* forms of behavior, while some others exhibited little of either. It seemed natural to ask if perhaps those supervisors who did both got the best performance. Those who concentrated on just one or the other type of leadership might, then, obtain less positive results, while those who did neither would achieve little.

Some scholars, most notably Robert Blake (then a professor at the University of Texas) and his associate Jane Mouton, saw little need for additional research. They were convinced they had the secret to effective leadership. Blake and Mouton proposed to teach leaders to be both considerate (they called this expressing "high concern for people") *and* structuring (their term here was showing "high concern for performance"). This would, they insisted, result in the best possible performance results.

By the early 1960s, Blake and Mouton had devised a simple assessment to measure the extent to which a person expressed one or the other concern (or both, or neither). They also designed a training program to teach people how to be "high" on both concern for task and concern for people. The organization they established to deliver this training (Scientific Methods, Incorporated) is, to this day, a successful international leadership training and development consulting firm.[6]

The third group of researchers, led by R. Freed Bales and his associates at Harvard University, was also interested in group leadership. Recall that at the University of Michigan, researchers studied railroad work crews (gandy dancers). At Ohio State, the research population consisted of factory workers. Who do you suppose that Bales studied at Harvard, in the late 1940s and early '50s? Why, Harvard undergraduates, of course! Because every student had to serve three hours as a subject in a social psychology experiment, collecting a lot of data was relatively easy.[7]

Bales and his associates designed a simple experiment. They formed small groups of three or four students at random. Each group was assigned a topic for discussion, such as "What will postwar economic development look like?" No one student was assigned to be discussion leader, so Bales had to come up with a way to identify the emergent leader. He invented the one-way observation window. Groups met in a small room with a large mirror. However, observers in the next room could see through the other side of the mirror. They watched and recorded the discussion (listening through a hidden microphone). After the discussion, the researchers debriefed the students by interview and a short questionnaire.

Like the Michigan and Ohio State researchers, Bales identified two types of leadership behavior. He created yet another label for what had been called "employee-centered" (appropriately, since these Harvard undergraduates were not employees), or "considerate" leaders. Instead of using either of these terms, Bales coined the term "socio-emotional" leadership. His label for the other dimension was, however, more simple: task-centered leadership behavior.

It's interesting to note that Bales identified a *third* category of behavior, which was neither task- nor relationship-focused. That is, some students seemed to just want attention or to push the discussion in some odd, personal direction. Bales called this "self-centered" behavior. However, because such behavior was always dysfunctional for the group, Bales dropped it from his general scheme, which ultimately consisted of the two basic categories of task and socio-emotional behavior.

One additional finding of interest came out of the Harvard research. Because no leaders were designated, in each discussion group a leader emerged "organically." Since the discussion topics varied, this is not a surprising result. That is, one might expect that who took on the role of the group's task leader would vary from session to session, depending mostly on who was interested in or knowledgeable about the topic. That was just what the researchers found. While that person was usually the one identified as "the leader," though, another group member often served in the role of a socio-emotional leader. This "informal" leader made sure that everyone got some airtime and that the discussion stayed friendly. The group members were typically aware of this role (as were the researchers). But there was more to it.

The students had to fulfill three hours of experiment credit. Since the discussions were usually just a half-hour, the researchers put each student through several discussions. That's why, as we mentioned earlier, these researchers were able to accumulate quite a lot of data.

The researchers found that the same person took on both roles, of task and of social leader, in only a very a small number of cases— about 5 percent. However, when this did happen it generally happened in *all* of the group discussions in which that person participated. In other words, those who emerged repeatedly as both task-centered and socio-emotional leaders exhibited a lot of what the Ohio State researchers called consideration and initiation. That finding may have given added credibility to the sort of leadership training developed by Blake and Mouton (and by others). That is, it seemed reasonable to argue that such training could improve leadership and the subsequent performance of the leader's subordinates. Perhaps this was the sort of leadership that makes a difference.

Did supervisors who had been trained to exhibit both task- and employee-centered leadership behaviors actually get better results? Those who had moved quickly to develop programs for training leaders in task- and relationship-centered leadership behaviors were less quick to design and conduct research studies to see if such training actually improved leadership effectiveness. However, the Ohio State researchers carried out such research.[8] They developed their own training program for the International Harvester factory supervisors, showing them how to be considerate while initiating structure. The results were clear.

First, most of the trainees promptly went back to whatever they had done before the training course. This "washout" effect is well-known in training and development. Participants often see workshops and seminars as a respite from "real work," a short vacation of sorts. Afterwards, the participants go right back to their old ways of doing things. This is not necessarily a matter of laziness; often they go back to the same situation in which the same people have the same expectations of them. Significant change is not always welcomed!

Of course, some trainees do change; the idea of developing or improving leadership skills is not just a hopeless wish. But, when there is a change in leadership behavior, what is the effect? Fleishman and Harris, two of the Ohio State researchers, found that the trained supervisors who practiced what they had learned did get results. They had work groups with lower rates of absenteeism, tardiness, and accidents as compared with those who had not been trained. What's more, they had fewer employee grievances.

However, what the trained supervisors did *not* have were higher-performing work crews. By the end of the 1960s, the conclusions were clear to anyone willing to examine the evidence. While exhibiting a lot of task- and employee-centered behavior has some clear benefits, those benefits are limited and most certainly do not include dramatic improvements in productivity. Yes, exhibiting a lot of skilled task-centered and relationship-focused leadership behaviors, at the same time, does matter. Such leadership makes *some* difference. But it's clearly not *the* difference these researchers (or we) were searching for.

Embracin' the Situation! Research From 1969 to 1978

If leadership is not simply who one is, and is not just a matter of engaging in the correct behaviors, perhaps the secret is in doing the right thing at the right time. That is the simple logic of several leadership approaches commonly called "situational" or "contingency" theories. These approaches propose that the right thing to do depends on—that is, is contingent on—the situation. Sometimes it is best to focus on the task. At other times, the leader should concentrate on "consideration." In still other cases, the leader must do both. Finally, in some circumstances it might be best for the leader to be neither considerate nor directive. In those cases, the leader should delegate or, perhaps, just let the employees alone.

Two theoretical approaches, still used today, were developed at about the same time in the late 1960s and early '70s. Robert House, now a senior professor at Wharton, was instrumental in defining the "path-goal" theory of leadership in 1971.[9] The logic was as sensible as it was simple: When the task is clear and an employee pretty much knows how to do it, only a very foolish leader gives a lot of directions. The effective leader says, "Look, I know you see how to do this and I recognize your competence. If you need help, call me." That leader then leaves the employee alone.

In the case of an unclear, complex task and a relatively unskilled, inexperienced employee, the effective supervisor provides clear and detailed step-by-step directions. When the task is complex but the employee is skilled, the leader may offer some directive advice and be sure to be available for questions. When a task is simple but the employee is inexperienced, the leader will give directions as needed but mostly give encouragement. In later years, path-goal theory was expanded and extended, first to add more leadership "styles" (participative and achievement-oriented)[10] and, more recently, to incorporate other contextual factors.[11]

Still another (and better known) situational approach was first presented in a 1969 article in a popular training magazine.[12] It was developed by Paul Hersey, then a professor at Ohio University (not affiliated with Ohio State University), and his associate, Ken Blanchard. The first version of their approach was called the "Life Cycle Theory of Leadership." They defined the situational context as a combination of (a) the skill and (b) the motivation of the employee. Employee task skill (or knowledge) and employee motivation were combined into a single dimension initially called "maturity" but later revised to the less loaded term "readiness" (to do the job effectively).

When an employee is not at all ready, that is, has inadequate skill and lacks motivation to get the job done, the appropriate leadership strategy, according to the Hersey-Blanchard theory, is to be very directive. The supervisor tells the employee what to do, how to do it, and supervises closely to make sure it gets done. If there is some readiness, evidenced by willingness (motivation) but inadequate skill, the supervisor becomes a coach, guiding the employee through the details of the task while providing encouragement. With still greater readiness, the employee is skilled and knowledgeable but lacks confidence. In that case, the leadership approach is based on giving support, that is, consideration, while refraining from giving directions or instructions. Finally, some employees are fully ready to take on a job challenge, both willing and able. In that case, the effective leader delegates and gets out of the way.

By the late 1970s, the theory was formally known as "situational leadership."[13] Hersey and Blanchard's approach, with its sensible analytic rules and straightforward prescriptions for action, was by 1980 one of the most widely used and recognized leadership applications in organizations. It remains in widespread use more than twenty years later.[14]

Just as we asked whether research studies found the behavioral leadership approaches to be effective, we must ask whether research evidence supports either of the situational approaches we have described. There have been many studies of path-goal theory. The research findings have, however, been mixed; some findings support while others contradict the predictions of the path-goal approach.

Relatively few research studies have been conducted to test Hersey and Blanchard's approach, but the outcomes of these reports have also been mixed, with some supporting the theory and others not. In fact, neither of these situational contingency theories—nor any other such approach—has strong research support to back it up.[15] In terms of research, it's simply not clear how much of a difference situational leadership makes, or whether it does matter at all.

The success of the contingency concept and, in particular, its application in the Hersey-Blanchard situational leadership model, may not be so surprising. The truth is that the prescriptions made by these situational approaches boil down to applied common sense.

Do most supervisors and low-level managers (that's what they really are, even though both researchers and trainers may call them "leaders") really need path-goal theory to tell them that if the task is complex and the employee is unskilled, they had better show the employee, with careful and detailed directions, how to do it? There is even research that shows that delegation works best when an employee is capable and shares management's values, expressed by the employee's commitment to the job.[16] In Hersey and Blanchard's model, that employee is completely "ready" and the leader is best advised to delegate in this situation. Is it really surprising that the research confirms that in such situations delegation works well?

But do these situational leadership approaches work better than the behavioral models that preceded them? It's hard to tell, because research that compares the effects and effectiveness of alternative leadership models is all but nonexistent. Our best answer, based on our reading of the research, is that the effectiveness of situational approaches is probably somewhat less than that of behavioral approaches. Certainly the broad guidelines offered by either House's path-goal or Hersey–Blanchard's situational leadership theory make sense. Either can probably be of some help to leaders, especially inexperienced leaders in lower-level positions. Despite the commonsense appeal of situational models, research suggests that the results they produce when applied are not especially impressive.

A Real Deal! Research From the 1970s Onward

None of the three basic approaches we have reviewed—trait, behavioral, or situational—provided a convincing or significantly useful answer to the puzzle of how to achieve leadership that matters. It's not surprising, then, that research has continued, at least to some degree, in each of these areas during the last quarter of the twentieth century.

Personality or trait measures of leadership largely disappeared fifty years ago, when the behavioral approach became dominant. Even so, there have been efforts to assess leadership using personality measures such as the Myers-Briggs Type Indicator (MBTI).[17] Leadership research involving the MBTI has, however, concentrated on describing the proportion of executives that fit each of the sixteen MBTI types.[18] We have not found any research that tries to connect MBTI type with leadership effectiveness. While Myers-Briggs type does matter, there is no evidence that it matters with regard to leadership.

Although the MBTI is the most popular approach for understanding personality differences, it is not widely recognized in academic circles. However, over the past twenty years an unusual degree of agreement has developed among academic personality psychologists about the basic dimensions of human personality.[19] These "big five" dimensions are shown in Table 2-1.

As with MBTI leadership research, there appears to have been no effort to link the big five personality factors to leadership performance. It is, nonetheless, interesting that the factors described by Center for Creative Leadership researchers as those most likely to "derail" executives seem to involve problems with one or another of the big five, as shown in the right-hand column of Table 2-1.[20] The obvious parallels suggest that while leadership may not be the result of having and applying certain traits, *failure*

TABLE 2-1	Parallel Comparison of the "Big Five" Personality Factors and McCall and Lombardo's "Derailing Factors"

Big 5 Personality Factors	Derailing Factors
Introversion/Extroversion	Inability to act
Openness to Experience	Fails to learn from experience
Conscientiousness	Cannot be trusted
Agreeableness	Cannot get along with people
Emotional Stability	Narcissism

in leadership may well be attributable at least partly to the *lack* of key traits.

Early in this chapter we mentioned that Stogdill's conclusions about the trait approach, based on his 1948 review of more than a hundred studies of leadership traits, were more complex than most people realize. Although his report virtually ended the substantial amount of research on leadership traits, Stogdill himself said to one of us, years ago, that although he was trying to push for more behavioral research he never intended to stop research on traits.

In fact, a close reading of his review shows that Stogdill actually suggested that, rather than specific individual traits being associated with leadership, *groups* of traits were so related. In fact, he identified five such groups of traits, shown in Table 2-2. It is also worth noting that there is considerable and obvious overlap between Stogdill's categories and both the big five and the derailing factors shown in Table 2-1.

Although the dominant behavioral approach of the 1950s and '60s, which centered on the two factors of task and relationship orientation, has waned, it—like the trait approach—is not extinct. Fifty years after the Ohio State studies, graduate students doing doctoral research still use the questionnaire developed to measure Consideration and Initiating Structure, the LBDQ ("Leader Behavior Description Questionnaire").[21] After fifty years of research there would seem to be little left to learn by using this questionnaire. That the LBDQ continues to be the mainstay of graduate student research may be because it is read-

TABLE 2-2	Stogdill's Five Trait Clusters
Capacity	• Intelligence • Judgment
Achievement	• Scholarship • Knowledge
Responsibility	• Dependability • Aggressiveness • Self-confidence • Desire to excel
Participation	• Activity • Sociability • Cooperation • Adaptability
Status	• Position • Popularity

ily available and no one seems very concerned about copyright. (Professional versions of the LBDQ are also still used to select low-level supervisors.[22])

The most current version of a situational contingency approach has been going strong since the mid-1970s. Originally labeled the "vertical dyad linkage theory," this approach is now generally referred to as leader-member exchange, or "LMX." It is based on the straightforward idea that leadership is a two-person ("dyadic") relationship. The relationship is effective when the leader exchanges some reward (something the follower wants) for work that the follower agrees to perform.[23] The original idea was that every leader-follower pair cuts a unique "deal." Of course, this gets very complicated when there are more than a few followers. Added complexities arise when teams are involved.

At first glance it seems reasonable that leaders and followers must work out an acceptable exchange, a reward or payment for the follower's performing certain duties as directed by the leader. However, the theory is not at all clear about exactly what leaders do in defining the exchange relationship. In fact, LMX researchers have used many specific behavior measures—including consideration and initiating structure—to assess the leader-member exchange relationship. Overall, the LMX approach fails to specify what actions a leader must take under which contingencies.

One way that LMX returns to the concept of generally applicable behaviors is by addressing the *quality* of the "relationship-based exchange."[24] In recent research, quality has been defined and assessed in terms of three factors: respect, trust, and obligation. However, developing and carrying out a good quality exchange relationship, one which involves mutual feelings of respect, trust and obligation, might involve a wide range of specific behaviors, depending on the parties and their circumstances.

To make it possible to use LMX without getting unreasonably complex, some researchers modified the approach to focus on just two general types of exchange relationships. Leaders develop a "high-exchange" relationship with members of an "in group," who are close to them and serve as informal lieutenants. This high-exchange relationship includes intangible rewards, that is, feelings such as friendship and loyalty, along with more concrete rewards. A "low-exchange" relationship is reserved for all others, members of the "out group." This relationship is limited to the bare essentials, often a paycheck and a cursory nod on the part of the leader.

By narrowing the focus to the two basic types of high- and low-exchange the LMX approach certainly becomes more manageable. However, it also loses much of its appeal. That is, a central feature of the early LMX approach was that it dealt with the unique character of every leader-follower exchange relationship.

Because of the complexity of the LMX approach, as well as the many ways researchers have tried to apply it, it is difficult to state any clear or strong research findings with respect to the effect of LMX leadership on performance. There is some research showing that when leaders and followers give positive reports about the quality of their "exchange relationship," followers express satisfaction and their performance is high.[25] This is hardly surprising, and is limited by serious measurement problems as well as issues about how to define a positive exchange relationship.

It is also unsurprising that this approach is almost unheard of in organizations, despite being the focus of much current research. That is, the concrete and economic aspects of the leader–member exchange are essentially obvious as the basis of the employment contract. And, while few would deny that there are intangible aspects of exchange, most people don't like to think about exchange in this sense. A classic example is the relationship between a person who gets a ride to work and the other person, the driver. We don't really want to recognize that the person who gets the "free ride" may actually be paying with friendship. We doubt that either leaders or followers would respond well to a proposal to bring this aspect of exchange explicitly into the organizational work setting.

Nonetheless, the LMX approach and research have contributed to our understanding of leadership. The approach explicitly addresses the fact that in organizations the relationship between leaders and followers or, more accurately, between managers and those who report to them, is based on the concept of *exchange*, that is, an economic or partly economic transaction between leader and follower. LMX assumes that this economic exchange is the explicit and central feature of the leader-follower relationship and of leadership in general.

Our reason for spending so much time on LMX and this exchange focus is that it contrasts with a different, and in some ways contradictory, sort of leader–follower relationship. This shift in thinking about leadership is the most important aspect of leadership theory and research of the past twenty-five years.

A New Leadership Paradigm

By the mid-1970s it was clear that seventy-five years of research and application had yielded little definitive or practically useful knowledge about leadership. Indeed, we (the authors, not researchers in general) nearly gave up on leadership research—until we heard of the new work by House and the work of another scholar, James McGregor Burns. In fact, many agree that it was Burns who inspired what has come to be called a new leadership paradigm.[26]

Thomas Kuhn earned his doctorate in physics and began his career as a physicist. He became, however, the twentieth century's leading philosopher of science.[27] He did so by pointing out that major scientific advances typically occur when a new way of looking at, and understanding, a major issue challenges the "old way." This is what happened when Galileo challenged classical (Ptolemaic) astronomy by asserting that the planets, the Earth included, circle the sun rather than the sun (and other planets) circling Earth (assumed to be the center of the universe). Kuhn called this a "paradigm shift."

A paradigm shift makes the old way of thinking obsolete. This new way of thinking explains better what the old paradigm was supposed to. The new paradigm also incorporates what was good about the old paradigm, even while directly contradicting the old paradigm in other, important ways.

The central purpose of this book is to provide an introduction to this new leadership paradigm, with two particular emphases. First, we want to emphasize how the new paradigm relates to you, personally, in terms of your own leadership activities. Second, we hope that you will, at the end, conclude that our presentation gives a convincing and sound basis for both understanding and applying the new paradigm.

To begin to explore this new paradigm in a personal way, complete the short questionnaire appearing in the box that follows on the next page. Read over the instructions below. Then read each statement and circle the letter that represents the extent to which you agree with each of the ten statements in the box that follows.

Leadership Beliefs Inventory

Instructions: Following are ten statements about one's beliefs and actions as a leader. Please respond to each statement by indicating the extent of your own personal agreement (or disagreement) with the statement. Circle the number in the column that represents your response, using the following column key:

> **SD** = strongly disagree
> **D** = disagree
> **N** = neutral, neither agree nor disagree
> **A** = agree
> **SA** = strongly agree

There are no "right" or "wrong" answers, nor is there any intended implication that agreement or disagreement with a particular statement is "good" or "bad." Your responses should be based only on your own personal views, the way you see yourself as a leader, and your own philosophy about leadership.

	SD	D	N	A	SA
1. I typically ask more of followers than they expected.	1	2	3	4	5
2. My primary mission as a leader is to maintain stability.	1	2	3	4	5
3. I believe that leadership is a process of changing the conditions of people's lives.	1	2	3	4	5
4. As a leader I enjoy rewarding followers for jobs well done.	1	2	3	4	5
5. When I give assignments I am able to generate enthusiasm.	1	2	3	4	5
6. I believe that leadership is a process of exchange between leader and follower.	1	2	3	4	5
7. Regarding my work as a leader, I have a strong sense of mission.	1	2	3	4	5
8. The most important aspect of my role as a leader is to provide job and task clarity for followers.	1	2	3	4	5
9. My destiny as a leader is essentially within my control.	1	2	3	4	5
10. As a leader my role is to facilitate activities and events so that the organization operates smoothly.	1	2	3	4	5

Scoring

Put the numbers you circled in the spaces provided beside the item number.

Item	Score A		Item	Score B
1			2	
3			4	
5			6	
7			8	
9			10	

Total A: ☐   **Total B:** ☐

Add up the numbers in each of the two "score" columns, Score A and Score B. Put the sums in the boxes. These are your two LBI scores.

Interpretation

The Leadership Beliefs Inventory is a measure of your attitude toward the two dimensions of the new paradigm of transformational leadership. The scoring instructions directed you to add up your scores for the five odd-numbered items, in the left-hand column, and, similarly, to add up your scores for the other five even-numbered statements, in the right-hand column.

The first score, "A," represents your attitude toward the new paradigm of leadership, commonly called "transformational leadership." The second score, "B," is an assessment of your attitude toward traditional concepts of leadership based on equitable transactions, what we would call "good management."

Look, in particular, at the contrast between statements three and ten. The new leadership paradigm is about making meaningful changes in people's lives, while traditional management is all about maintaining the status quo.

Your scores should not be considered to be measures of your own leadership. The LBI assesses only your *attitudes,* that is, how you generally think about leadership. This may or may not indicate how you actually behave as a leader.

Note: The Leadership Beliefs Inventory is a short version of a questionnaire designed by Marshall Sashkin in working with Warren Bennis, jointly conducting advanced leadership seminars as part of the summer Cape Cod Institute in 1994 and 1995.

Exploring the New Paradigm

It is especially interesting that the inspiration for the new paradigm came not from a psychological researcher or a business school scholar. Burns is a political historian, best known in his field for a Pulitzer Prize-winning biography of Franklin Delano Roosevelt. (Burns served as a junior staff member in the last Roosevelt administration during the 1940s.) His success with FDR's biography led Burns to wonder about leadership more generally.

Burns spent several years preparing a book, simply titled *Leadership.* Still in print after almost twenty-five years, his book examined a number of exceptional national and social leaders. In it Burns included unsavory leaders, such as Stalin and Hitler. He focused most, however, on leaders like Gandhi, who Burns considered the best example of transformational leadership. Other leaders illustrated the new paradigm, too: leaders from the past, such as Abraham Lincoln, as well as modern leaders such as Martin Luther King, Jr., and, of course, Franklin Delano Roosevelt.

Burns asserted that such leaders transform followers into more capable, self-directed leaders. Moreover, by transforming followers, leaders could transform an entire society. In the process, said Burns, leaders and followers raise one another to new heights of achievement and moral development. To quote Burns, a leader

> looks for potential motives in followers, seeks to satisfy higher needs, and engages the full person of the follower. The result . . . is a relationship of mutual stimulation and elevation that converts followers into leaders and may convert leaders into moral agents.[28]

Burns contrasted what he called "transformative" leadership with the old ways of thinking about leadership. As we have seen in this chapter, these old ways, the old paradigm, defined leadership as a *transaction*, an exchange between a leader—that is, a "boss"—and a follower, or "subordinate." The most typical such exchange is pay for doing a job, which pretty well describes all of the leadership views we have reviewed in this chapter. Even the most current academic approaches (such as LMX, which includes other, noneconomic exchanges) still center on this basic exchange paradigm.

Burns called these old approaches "transactional" leadership. He saw this type of leadership at the opposite end of a transformative-transactional dimension of leadership. As we noted earlier, transactions don't always involve money or material goods. There is even a field of social psychology called "social exchange theory," based on the premise that we exchange not merely money for goods or services but feelings, such as friendship, for favors, such as a ride to work. Some social exchange theorists—and some leadership scholars, too—argue that there is no such thing as transformational leadership. These scholars assert that everything is, at bottom, transactional.[29]

We, and many others who study transformational leadership disagree. Transformational leadership is different in nature from transactional leadership. Trying to pin the difference down, one leadership scholar, Tom Sergiovanni, observed that managers—transactional leaders—base relationships with followers on a process of "barter," while for transformational leaders, the process is better described as "bonding."[30] We think of good transactional leaders as effective managers who, as Warren Bennis said, "Do

things right." That is, they make sure that the organization oper-
ates smoothly. In contrast, said Bennis, transformational leaders
are concerned not just with doing things right but with "doing the
right things."[31]

The historical research on which Burns based his argument is
quite different from the quantitative and experimental social science research on leadership reviewed in this chapter. Thus,
research to explore Burns' concepts and this new paradigm came
from sources other than Burns himself.

We have already mentioned the work of House, who left
behind traditional leadership theories (including his own) to
focus on the psychological motives behind transformational leadership.[32] Soon afterward, Bernard Bass elaborated Burns'
approach by looking for behaviors characteristic of transformative leaders. Bass took a quantitative research approach, developing questionnaire assessments to identify and study the underlying dimensions of transformational leadership behavior.[33]

Bass' strongest finding was that Burns was wrong in asserting
that transactional and transformational leadership are opposite
ends of a single dimension. Bass showed that they are actually two
different dimensions, just as task-focused behavior and consideration are separate scales. Bass' questionnaire also identified certain behaviors used by transformational leaders.

Warren Bennis had the same aim as Bass but used a very different method. Bennis used qualitative information, conducting long
interviews with 90 exceptional leaders in a wide range of organizational contexts. For example, along with business and government leaders, Bennis interviewed the internationally renowned
orchestra leader Zubin Mehta and the then-head of the Girl
Scouts, Frances Hesselbein. The analysis of these interviews was
published in the book *Leaders* by Bennis and Bert Nanus.[34]

Bennis and Nanus, too, identified a set of several specific actions
used by transformational leaders. So did two other researchers, Jim
Kouzes and Barry Posner.[35] What are these leadership behaviors?
A detailed discussion of the behaviors that characterize transfor-
mational (in contrast to transactional) leadership is the focus of
Chapter Three.

Summary

In this chapter we began to address questions about the nature of leadership and why it matters. Leadership is not really what scholars studied for most of the twentieth century. For more than seventy-five years, formal social science research labeled "leadership" actually concentrated on supervision and management: defining a job goal clearly, making sure it gets done, and fulfilling a fair contract. Almost all the theory and research of the twentieth century focused on the exchange relationship between managers and employees.

Leadership, in contrast to management, involves not just defining the job but explaining why the job is being done. Leading means not just overseeing followers' activities and making sure that followers have what they need, in skills as well as resources, to do the job. Leaders don't just fulfill a contract between themselves and their employees, they develop a compact between themselves and their followers. Leadership matters because it means something to followers—and to leaders. Good management is important for good performance, as are consequences (such as pay and other rewards). But leadership that matters does so because it is more than good management and it means more than a paycheck alone. The actions that make for this kind of leadership are the focus of the next chapter.

THREE

Leadership Skills and Behaviors

The effective leader is aware of the importance of small actions.
Tao Te Ching, **Chapter 63**

In Chapter One we identified the three major themes of research on leadership: traits, behavior, and the situational context. In Chapter Two we saw that none of these themes produced a leadership approach, model, or theory that gave a convincing or especially useful answer to the questions, "What is leadership?" and "How can leaders be more effective?" It was the political historian James McGregor Burns who addressed these issues in a new way. He argued that leadership is about transforming people and social organizations, not about motivating employees to exchange work efforts for pay.

Burns didn't explain just how leaders actually go about this transformational leadership process. Obviously, leaders must engage in actions—behaviors—that have this effect, but what are these behaviors? What dimensions underlie them? In this chapter we will explain how we identified the dimensions of transformational leadership behavior. This was a crucial first step in understanding the nature of transformational leadership.

Research to Identify Transformational Leadership Behaviors

In the early 1980s, Warren Bennis, a professor at the University of Southern California, conducted an extensive study of exceptional leaders. He interviewed 90 CEOs, in private and public organizations of all sorts.[1] Included, for example, were Frances Hesselbein, then head of the Girl Scouts of America, and Zubin Mehta, an internationally recognized orchestra conductor. These individuals were all nominated as exceptional leaders. Bennis interviewed each subject personally. The interviews lasted from two hours to two days.

When all was done, Bennis reviewed notes and records of the interviews. He looked for common threads connecting these exceptional leaders. Bennis identified several patterns of action, which he variously called "strategies," "competencies," "skills," and similar labels. The best known report of this research is his book *Leaders,* coauthored with Bert Nanus. In that book, Bennis and Nanus identified five behavior patterns, or strategies, characteristic of these outstanding leaders. They suggested that, by their actions, leaders manage five issues central to the leader-follower relationship. These issues are *attention, communication, trust, respect,* and *risk.*

The leadership researchers Jim Kouzes and Barry Posner (at the University of Santa Clara, California) addressed the same issue as Bennis and Nanus. They, too, wanted to identify crucial transformational leadership behaviors.[2] To do so, they asked managers to write detailed memoirs of their own best, most positive leadership experiences. Kouzes and Posner analyzed these "personal best" cases (some of which were quite lengthy) and identified specific characteristics of each case. Then the researchers constructed statements describing leadership behavior, based on the many specifics identified in the cases.

Kouzes and Posner developed a long list of statements describing leadership. They asked hundreds more managers to rate exceptional leaders they had known personally, using these descriptions. Finally, they examined the results using factor analysis, a statistical procedure that helps identify a set of categories into which the descriptive statements sort out. They identified five clear factors. Each factor contained two specific behaviors. The factors and behaviors are:

Challenging the Process: ❖ *searching for opportunities* **to do things better**

                              ❖ *experimenting and taking sensible risks* **to improve the organization**

Inspiring a Shared Vision:	❖ *constructing a future vision*
	❖ *building follower support* **for the vision**
Enabling Others to Act:	❖ *fostering collaboration* **(as opposed to competition) among followers**
	❖ *supporting followers in their personal development*
Modeling the Way:	❖ *setting an example* **by one's own behavior**
	❖ *focusing on step-by-step accomplishments* **by followers, so that large-scale goals seem more realistic and attainable through a process of many "small wins"**
Encouraging the Heart:	❖ *recognizing followers' contributions*
	❖ *finding ways to celebrate followers' achievements*

The strategies identified by Bennis and Nanus and the practices uncovered by Kouzes and Posner are quite similar. You can see this easily in Table 3-1.

The differences between the two sets of behaviors are small. A reading of the researchers' books, in which they describe the behaviors in detail, shows this clearly.[3]

Thus, two independent research teams, using very different research approaches, came to essentially the same conclusions. Both identified the same set of leadership behaviors as crucially important for transformational leadership. It seems reasonable that this is more than mere coincidence.

We used the leadership strategies identified by Bennis and Nanus as our primary guide. Based on these five strategies, we developed a short questionnaire to measure the extent to which a leader uses each. We published the first version of The Leader Behavior Questionnaire in 1984.[4] It measured the

TABLE 3-1	Comparison of Kouzes and Posner's Leadership Practices With Bennis and Nanus' Leadership Strategies
Challenging the Process Search for opportunities Experiment and take risks	**Management of Risk**
Inspiring a Shared Vision Envision the future Enlist the support of others	**Management of Attention**
Enabling Others to Act Foster collaboration Strengthen others	**Management of Communication**
Modeling the Way Set the example Plan small wins	**Management of Trust**
Encouraging the Heart Recognize contributions Celebrate accomplishments	**Management of Respect**

extent to which a leader engages in each of five transformational behaviors:

Focused Leadership: Actions that seem to literally grab people's attention, to focus them on the important issues in a discussion.

Communication Leadership: Use of effective communication skills—active listening, appropriate use of feedback, etc.—to get complicated ideas across clearly.

Trust Leadership: Behaviors that develop trust are consistency of action (dependability) and follow-through on promises.

Respectful Leadership: Actions that show that the leader cares about followers, such as expressing congratulations to individual followers for achievements.

Risk Leadership: Actions designed to get individuals fully committed to new ideas and projects, often by involving them and giving them key responsibilities.

After almost twenty years of research and refinement, the latest version of our questionnaire, The Leadership Profile,[5] centers on four specific transformational leadership behaviors. We combined the first two, focused leadership and communication leadership, into a single measure of communication leadership. The other three dimensions are quite similar to those on the LBQ. We'll briefly review each of our four final dimensions of transformational leadership behavior.

Communication Leadership

Bennis and Nanus listed general communication skills as one of their five leadership strategies. We believe that both transactional and transformational leaders need good communication skills. What's unique to transformational behavior is the skill of focusing attention and making complex ideas clear by using metaphors.

For example, the late Admiral Grace Hopper was on the team that planned and built the first computer. In fact, it was she who labeled computer problems "bugs." The first computer was huge; it filled a large room. This computer didn't use transistors; they hadn't been invented yet. It ran on old-fashioned vacuum tubes. The filaments glowed and attracted moths in the summer. The moths would sometimes hit live wires and short out a circuit. That's what led Admiral Hopper to call problems "bugs" in the computer. We now apply this metaphor to all computer-related problems. Although it has become very common, most people don't know its origin.

Soon after the end of World War II, Sir Winston Churchill gave a speech at an American college. Describing the Russian takeover of eastern Europe after the war, he used a striking metaphor. He said, "An iron curtain has descended across the Continent." Since the fall of the Soviet Union we don't hear the term "Iron Curtain" very often. However, from the 1940s through the early 1990s, it was part of everyday speech.

Hopper and Churchill were, like most transformational leaders, skilled in creating and using metaphors. They used metaphor to make complex ideas concrete and to get followers excited by their messages.

Credible Leadership

We renamed this behavior category because the nature of trust is often confusing. In our view, trust involves being more certain about a person's actions, now and in the future. In other words, trust reduces ambiguity and uncertainty. Trust enables us to feel more comfortable and secure in our relationship with a person we trust.

How does a person "behave" trust? Trust in a person, by others, is a consequence of one's actions, not an action by itself. Our research shows that there are two types of actions that underlie the development of trust in a person. These are consistency and credibility.[6]

Actions that are *consistent* lead to the development of trust. For example, consistency between what you say and what you do reduces other people's uncertainty. This leads them to trust you, because they can see that your actions match your words. Developing trust calls for consistency between word and deed. In contrast, when a person tells you to "do as I say, not as I do," you are not likely to trust that individual. Transformational leaders treat people consistently, too. For example, they show respect toward others, whether friends or strangers. Consistency calls for acting the same way, over time, and giving a constant message.

Credibility requires that one do what one says one will do. This means keeping promises and fulfilling commitments. In other words, leaders build credibility by telling the truth. With consistent behavior, credible actions by leaders increase certainty still further. Most people experience anxiety in uncertain, ambiguous situations. Transformational leaders, by their consistent and credible actions, reduce that anxiety through trust.

Among recent U.S. presidents, Ronald Reagan stands out as an exemplar of both consistency and credibility. Reagan gave the same message, day after day and year after year. A person might like or dislike that message, but one was never uncertain about Reagan's position. Moreover, Reagan demonstrated credibility in action. He said he would fire any federal employee who tried to strike. When the air traffic controllers did just that, he fired them all. It took years to rebuild the system, but Reagan showed by his action that he would do exactly what he said he would. He was a credible, a consistent, and a trusted leader.

Contrast this with Bill Clinton's actions. Clinton's policy positions often shifted with the winds of popular opinion; the only consistency was his inconsistency. On top of that, he lied about his past actions regarding a particularly unsavory scandal, displaying a clear lack of credibility. This, along with a lack of consistency, meant few people put trust in Clinton as a leader.

Trust has consequences. That people generally trusted Ronald Reagan probably helped his vice president and chosen successor,

George H.W. Bush, get elected. In contrast, Bill Clinton's lack of trustworthiness may have cost his vice president and hoped-for successor, Al Gore, the few votes he needed—in Florida or another close state—to secure the electoral college votes he needed in order to be elected president.

Caring Leadership

Transformational leaders show that they care about people. This involves respect but goes even further. Caring means valuing individuals' special skills and abilities. Caring leaders also make sure that people feel included, part of the group or organization. And, of course, such leaders show respect for individuals' differences.

Several years ago we consulted with a three-star general in Europe. We helped design and run a "command conference," involving about 150 senior officers. Having taken an overnight flight, we got off the plane quite early in the morning and more than a little sleepy. However, the general wanted to give us a tour of the base. In fact, he insisted, and we weren't about to decline, since we were there at his request. We became more alert when we noticed something interesting: As we walked around the base, the general greeted each person by name.

Now, on an army base almost everyone wears a name tag, so that may not seem especially surprising. What surprised us was that the general did not greet his subordinates by their last names (which were on their name tags). Rather, he greeted each person by his or her first name. The general had apparently memorized the names of everyone on the base, in the three months since he had taken command. Such behavior conveys a deeply felt sense of caring and does not go unnoticed.

Caring is, of course, more than remembering names. Not too long ago, we were on a Southwest Airlines flight, sitting next to a passenger wearing jeans and a windbreaker. Noticing that the jacket had a Southwest logo, we asked if he worked for the airline. "No," he replied, "my wife does. She's a senior agent. I'm just heading home from a visit to her while she works on opening a new station."

We took this opportunity to ask if he had met Herb Kelleher, the recently retired CEO of Southwest. Kelleher had founded the airline and led it to increasing profitability with every year. Even when every other airline in the industry was losing millions or billions of dollars, Southwest made a profit. We asked our seatmate if he had met Kelleher at the house party Kelleher holds every year for all Southwest employees. "Yes," our new friend said, "but it was when my wife was sick that I really got to know Herb."

We asked him to tell us more. He went on, "Five years ago, they diagnosed my wife with a brain tumor. She went down to M.D. Anderson [a nationally known cancer treatment center in Houston] where they were doing a new kind of surgery, using this 'electronic scalpel' that cuts with a focused beam of radiation. It was the only way to get the whole tumor. The operation took several hours; the part of the tumor they finally removed was as big as an orange. That was five years ago, so we think she's okay now."

"What did Herb have to do with this?" we asked. "Are you referring to the company's medical benefits?" "No," he replied, "it's just that Herb was with me there, holding my hand through the entire operation."

Still another example of caring that goes beyond the expected is that of Aaron Feuerstein, owner and CEO of New Malden Mills. Feuerstein's firm manufactures Polartec, an artificial fabric that's an exceptional insulator used in top-quality winter clothing. We interviewed Feuerstein about a crucial event in his organization's history. Several years ago, in early December, his factory in the small town of Lawrence, Massachusetts, burned down.

Some advised Feuerstein to just take the insurance money—a couple of hundred million dollars—and retire to Florida. He was determined, he said, to rebuild. He felt an obligation to the community, because his company was a key employer in the city of Lawrence. So, rather than lay off hundreds of employees just before Christmas, Feuerstein (himself an Orthodox Jew), kept every employee on the payroll, even though there was no factory.

Caring encompasses the simple respect shown by recognizing individuals by name. And it goes all the way to a concern for others that is so deep and abiding that the only word to really describe it is "love."

Creating Opportunities

Bennis and Nanus called this strategy "risk leadership" and "deployment of self." They saw that it involved a willingness to empower others in ways that some observers might see as dangerous to the leader. They used a negative example to illustrate their point, concerning the highwire walker Karl Wallenda and his troupe, "The Flying Wallendas." For some reason Wallenda became unable to "risk" letting any member of the troupe but himself set up and test the equipment. Before long, he insisted on doing it all, the setup and the checks and double checks. He simply couldn't trust anyone else; the risk was too great. However, it was also too much for one person. Eventually he failed to secure one last wire; he fell to his death.

The "risks" that Bennis and Nanus referred to may be seen as risks by outside observers (and by Karl Wallenda). Transformational leaders, however, don't see their actions as risky. That's because they don't simply put followers in charge of difficult or dangerous tasks and hope that the followers will succeed. Rather, they design opportunities for others to take charge and be in control of their own work. A key term is the word "design."

That is, a transformational leader makes sure that followers have the knowledge, skills, and resources to do the job and do it right. If followers need help, the leader is available. However, the leader never makes followers look bad or feel ignorant if they ask for assistance. An outside observer may still think there is risk involved. The leader, however, knows that there is no real risk—because the followers have been prepared to succeed. Creating opportunities for success is especially important because it produces empowered followers who become self-assured and confident of their own capabilities.

Returning to presidential leadership for examples, we again nominate Ronald Reagan. President Reagan was known for his willingness to define and assign a job. He would then step back and let who he had put in charge do the job without interference. Some criticized this as "hands-off" management. Reagan, however, was quoted as saying, "Surround yourself with the best people you can find, delegate authority, and don't interfere!"[7]

Contrast this with Jimmy Carter, Reagan's predecessor. Carter was known for "micromanagement," that is, being unable to let go of control over even the most trivial decisions. For example, he insisted on personally keeping the schedule of use of the White House tennis court.

Rather than leaving you thinking that we must be favoring Republicans, consider another example of a president who created opportunities, John F. Kennedy. By establishing the Peace Corps, Kennedy ensured that generations of followers would have the chance to develop into effective leaders. The Peace Corps prepares volunteers to take on difficult challenges. The volunteers' successes, for which they have been prepared in advance by good training, build in them the resources for effective leadership. Follow-up research shows that Peace Corps graduates go home to take on leadership roles at the local level. They are commonly found in business and civic activities of all kinds.

Leadership Behavior and Performance

We designed the LBQ questionnaire to be filled out by followers, as well as by leaders. Followers can report more objectively on the extent to which a leader actually engages in the behaviors we want to measure. By 1988, we had developed a modest base of research evidence. Our results showed that followers rate the performance of leaders who score high on the five behaviors as exceptional.

During this time, we worked with various students and colleagues to refine and test a behavioral model of transformational leadership. Karl Major, for example, compared high school principals who scored high on the transformational behaviors with principals who scored low.[8] He found that the schools with the more transformational leaders had significantly higher student scores on standardized achievement tests, as compared to schools with less transformational leaders.

Judy Endeman[9] extended the study of school leadership to the school district level. She formed two groups of districts. In one group, the superintendents scored high on the transformational behaviors. In the other group of districts, superintendents scored low. Those who scored high had district cultures that were achievement-oriented and teamwork-centered, as measured by a validated questionnaire that assesses organizational culture.[10] In contrast, the districts led by superintendents with lower transformational behavior scores had cultures that were less achievement- and teamwork-focused.

Similar results have been found in business organizations. National Australia Bank is one of the largest in that nation, with assets greater than A$100 billion.[11] District managers with higher transformational leadership behavior scores had districts scoring higher on the four dimensions of culture measured by our culture questionnaire, as compared with district managers who displayed low levels of transformational leadership behavior. These more transformational leaders also had higher performance ratings and better records of goal achievement.

Sheryl Colyer studied leadership in a large retail organization. She found that those store managers who scored higher on the leadership behaviors also had the more profitable stores. Their stores had significantly greater profit in terms of sales per square foot of store space, as compared to stores of managers with lower scores.[12]

Overall, these results encouraged us. Leaders who exhibited transformational behaviors achieved substantially better results, compared to leaders who did not use these behaviors. What's more, we could measure these results in terms of hard performance outcomes. They also showed up as linked to indicators of organizational health, such as culture. But we were not convinced that we had all of the solution to the leadership puzzle.

Summary

Three sets of independent researchers—Bennis and Nanus, Kouzes and Posner, and ourselves—came up with evidence to support a set of common concepts. These concepts center on a set of key leadership behaviors. It seems only reasonable to conclude that such agreement is based on more than chance. Has, then, the puzzle of leadership been solved? Not really. Despite the consistency that is clear in Table 3-1, and despite our research findings, we saw little evidence other than anecdotal that tells how leaders apply these skills to get exceptional results.

What's more, it seemed to us that if leadership were simply a matter of applying behavioral skills, then the old research of the 1950s and '60s should have been more productive. That is, teaching people leadership skills is a relatively straightforward matter. Why then didn't it work better?

The behavioral skills of transformational leaders that we studied may be better defined and more clearly focused than the transactional skills (task and relationship focus) we described in Chapter Two. Still, there are some clear similarities. We had some doubts that teaching leaders these new, transformational behaviors would produce results much better than did training factory supervisors to emphasize both task- and employee-centered behaviors.

Finally, we had the feeling that there was more to effective leadership at top organizational levels than just applying certain skills. Human behavior is certainly based in part on learned skills, but it also depends on one's intent or willingness to use them. Behavior depends, too, on our feelings, that is, emotions, or what psychologists call "affect." Furthermore, people base their actions, at least in part, on conscious decisions, determined by thought or cognition.

All these concerns led us to look for some other aspects of leadership that might explain how transformational leaders obtain exceptional performance outcomes. This is the focus of Chapter Four.

FOUR

Charisma and Character

Power comes through cooperation, independence through service, and a greater self through selflessness.

Tao Te Ching, **Chapter 39[1]**

In Chapter Three, we described how various researchers, including ourselves, adopted Burns' ideas about transformational leadership. The aim was to identify the behaviors associated with this new concept of leadership—an approach that raises leaders and followers to new levels of achievement and new heights of moral development.

We had some success in identifying such behaviors. However, we became concerned about this exclusive focus on leadership behaviors or, as training jargon now has it, "skillsets." We remembered that researchers of the 1950s and '60s who studied leadership behaviors came to some false conclusions. Many believed, incorrectly, that by learning to use certain behavioral skills, one would become an effective leader.

The focus on behavioral skills proved to be quite limited in terms of producing strong effects on performance. We therefore became convinced that teaching leaders a new skillset could not account for the effects of transformational leadership. We felt that we had to look for something else, something more than behavioral skills, to really understand transformational leadership.

Our search was first stimulated by a colleague, Robert House, now a professor at the Wharton School of Business. As we mentioned in Chapter Two, in the early 1970s Robert House developed one of the first situational/contingency approaches to leadership, the path-goal theory. But by the mid-'70s, House had concluded (as we did later) that effective leadership involves more than just using certain behavior skills in the appropriate situation. Despite the apparent death blow Ralph Stogdill had dealt to trait theories of leadership a quarter-century earlier, House believed (as we came to believe) that leadership had something to do with the character of the leader.

In developing his new approach, which he called "charismatic leadership," House drew on the work of an early sociologist, Max Weber. He also grounded his ideas in the more current work of Harvard University motivational psychologist David McClelland.[2] We believe that House identified a new and important aspect of leadership.

To understand the role that character plays in leadership, we begin where House did, with the work of Weber. We then link that work to McClelland's contribution regarding leader motivation, which, according to McClelland, centers on the need for power. That need can be expressed in two very different ways, which we will describe. Finally, we will share some ideas about how the need for power develops. This chapter builds the foundation for our discussion in Chapter Five on the nature of the leader-follower relationship.

Max Weber: Bureaucracy and Charisma

The term *charisma* has historically been used in the study of religion as well as in religious worship. However, it was the German social scientist Max Weber who introduced it to scholarly and, ultimately, popular use.[3] Weber was also the first to clearly describe the nature of bureaucracy.[4] In fact, he coined the term, and social scientists generally recognize his contribution.

You may not think that being recognized as the "father of bureaucracy" is much of a tribute, but Max Weber would. That's because he believed that bureaucracy would not only be the basis for more effective and humane organizations but would ultimately lead to mass democracy. And to a degree, he was right. Weber's ideas become more understandable if we see them in the context of his own life experience.

Max Weber: A Brief Biography[5]

One must keep in mind that Weber lived in an era of great turbulence. The rise and fall of Napoleon, though before Weber's birth in 1864, was recent, and weighty, history. In Weber's own time, there were frequent European wars, often started by hereditary rulers. Germany only became a unified nation when Weber was a child. Moreover, these political conflicts occurred against a background of rapid industrialization. Desperate peasants migrated to cities, where they were exploited by factory owners. The French sociologist Emile Durkheim observed that one result of this trend was a large increase in the suicide rate. Durkheim proposed that the suicide rate increased because these new industrial workers lost their social support networks and became alienated from society.[6]

In this time of great social and industrial change, Max Weber was brought up in a traditional Prussian family, in which the father was the absolute ruler. This was a time when all authority was typically based either on hereditary right or on paternal "ownership." It's not hard to understand why, on both a personal and a social level, Weber's interests turned to understanding the nature of authority and leadership.

After a brilliant study of the Catholic church,[7] one of the world's oldest and most successful organizations, Weber applied his analysis to organizations of all kinds. As already noted, Weber lived in a time when people saw authority in organizations as the natural and absolute "right" of owners. Similarly, most people assumed that absolute authority in the family belonged to the father as family head. Thus, paternalism applied to the factory as well as to the family. But Weber felt that paternalism was not a solid foundation on which to build organizational structures.

Within his own family, Weber had observed tyranny at the hand of his own father. He was distressed at what he felt was his father's abusive behavior toward his mother. Perhaps, then, it's not surprising that he disdained patriarchal authority. When, as a student of the social structure of organizations, he observed similar patterns of tyrannical control by managers and owners, he may have found that equally distasteful. Clearly, Weber was critical of the traditional authority of the father as head of the family and of its parallel in the private sector.

For example, a factory owner might require workers to live in and pay for company-owned housing. The owner could even demand that employees carry out orders unrelated to their work. Today we call it an unethical conflict of interest when the owner of a hotel chain, such as Leona Helmsley, forces employees to work on her personal home.[8] During the nineteenth and even into the twentieth century, however, such actions would be taken for granted, not seen as inappropriate.

In the larger social context, Weber had experienced the effects of the actions of hereditary rulers on Europe in the wars of the nineteenth century and the "Great War," which we now call World War I. At the time, in 1915, they called it "the war to end all wars." It started when a member of a ruling family, the Archduke Ferdinand of Austria-Hungary, was asassinated. The war snowballed as a result of the reactions of the German leader, Kaiser Wilhelm II, and the consequent responses of other rulers, including Czar Nikolas of Russia and King George V of England.

As a loyal German, Weber was a strong supporter of the Kaiser's government during the war. Nonetheless, he believed that hereditary kingship—the "divine right" to rule that was supposedly granted by God—was a poor basis for authority in society. In sum, Weber was highly critical of traditional concepts of authority (including some we've not discussed, such as feudalism).

Weber and Bureaucracy

On what sort of authority structure should social systems be based, then? Weber came up with a new approach, a new basis for the authority of leaders. He called it *legal-rational* authority because it was based on a legal contract between the parties involved. This contract spelled out what one party could ask of and expect from the other, and what the other might receive in return for obedience. In other word, the contract was based on a rational negotiation between the parties.

What was really new about this approach was that legal-rational authority put clear limits on what leaders might ask of followers. No longer would factory owners be able to order employees to do whatever bidding they wished. No longer could the boss, for example, order the employee to attend a particular church. Perhaps more important, owners could no longer force workers to labor whenever and for as long as the boss demanded. The contract limited what bosses could require. It also defined what workers would receive in exchange for their labors.

Weber called this new system "bureaucracy."[9] Today we often disparage bureaucracy; the very term brings to mind inefficiency and abuses by officials. However, historically, it's easy to see why Weber thought bureaucracy was a great social innovation. In fact, he believed that bureaucracy would, in his words, "inevitably lead to mass democracy." In a technical sense, Weber pointed out, this would happen because of the strict rules and regulations that must be followed under bureaucracy. Bureaucracy relies, fundamentally, on the rule of law and equality before the law. As bureaucracy pervades a society—its government, business, and social institutions—a stronger and stronger framework is built for the rule of law, under which all persons are equal before the law. Such a framework is the basis for mass democracy.

Weber also may well have believed that the legal-rational employment contract would free workers from unjust and unreasonable demands made by their employers. Thus, workers would be increasingly able to—and expect that they had a right to—control their own lives. That climate, in turn, would result in the strengthening of democratic institutions.

If we look closely at what Weber defined as his rational-legal system, we see that it is much the same as what Burns called "transactional leadership." Thus, transactional leadership is not really new. What's more, the practice—if not the concept—of bureaucracy goes back long before Weber, to the ancient Chinese system of government instituted at least four thousand years ago. But are the three systems of authoritative leadership that we have discussed—divinely granted hereditary rights of rulers, traditional authority of the head of a family, and legal-rational (or contractual) authority—a complete list of the options? Not really.

Weber and Charismatic Authority

Weber also observed that some leaders arose without paternal or divine authority and certainly without the legal-rational authority of bureaucracy. Some, such as Napoleon, appeared from nowhere yet came to play great leadership roles, nationally and internationally. From where did their leadership authority derive? Weber went back to a concept he had come across in his historical analysis of the Catholic church; he labeled such leaders "charismatic."

The concept of charisma is, itself, very old. Charisma is an ancient word. While the source is often cited as the ancient Greek word "kairismos," this term goes back even further, to ancient Persian (Farsi). To the Persians, and to the Greeks, charisma meant a gift bestowed on a person by the gods.

Weber was saying, in effect, that charismatic leadership referred to one who derived leadership authority through some unknown, god-given gift to that specific individual. One difference between the authority of the hereditary ruler and the charismatic is that the divine right and power to rule is granted only to the charismatic, not to his or her descendants. Moreover, charismatic leaders are easily recognized as such, while hereditary rulers are often quite uncharismatic. That is, the hereditary ruler may appear dull and incapable of inspiring or exciting followers.

Weber argued that hereditary kingship often was the long-term result of charismatic leadership. That is, the exciting charismatic leader, with an obvious divine gift, establishes a dynasty. That leader's successors then inherit that gift, at least in theory. But, whatever the source and however it might be institutionalized, Weber seemed less concerned with where charisma comes from than with its consequences and effects.

Although Weber was the first modern social scientist to apply the term "charisma" to explain certain examples of leadership, his label really explains very little. Nevertheless, the larger scope of Weber's work did provide the basis for understanding the leadership Burns called "transactional." And, ultimately, it led scholars to reconsider the nature of charismatic leadership, in the hope that it might shed light on what Burns called "transforming" leadership.

A Modern Approach to Charismatic Leadership

More than a half-century after Max Weber's death, Robert House, whom we mentioned at the beginning of this discussion, began a new exploration of charisma.[10] He looked not only at behavioral skills associated with charismatic leadership but at certain aspects of the character or personality of the leader, as well. He based his ideas on the work of a renowned Harvard University social psychologist, David McClelland.[11] Over a long career, McClelland concentrated on understanding human motivation.

McClelland first studied the need for friendship and social contact, which he called the need for "affiliation." His findings were, however, unexciting. It was clear that almost everyone had at least a moderate need for social relationships. After all, how many hermits do you personally know? So McClelland went on to study other, potentially more interesting, needs.

McClelland's research during the 1960s led him to believe that a crucial motive for success as an entrepreneur was the need to achieve.[12] Experiments McClelland conducted in India, training small-business entrepreneurs, suggested that seminars that focused on increasing entrepreneurs' achievement need could enhance their success.[13] He then tried to identify this need in managers and executives of a large U.S. company. But he discovered that their dominant need was not for achievement, like the entrepreneurs.

To McClelland's surprise, he found that these managers and executives were characterized by a strong need for power. To be sure, they were achievement-oriented and certainly had an above-average concern for achievement. But that was not their strongest motivational need. Their strongest need by far was the need for power, which McClelland defined as "having an impact, control, or influence over another person, group, or the world at large."[14]

If you think about it, this makes a great deal of sense. For the most part, entrepreneurs succeed (or fail) because of their own efforts. It's only reasonable that their strong need for achievement has something to do with their success. In large organizations, however, a manager or executive who tries to succeed through personal effort, that is, by doing things him- or herself, is more likely to "burn out" than to achieve the desired results.

In a large, complex organization, most work is done and most work-relevant goals are attained through the coordinated contributions of many people, not through one person's efforts. It is more than just a cliché that in large organizations managers get things done with and through people. Gaining such cooperation is not a simple matter. It means that managers must use power and influence, if they expect to get things done. Thus, McClelland titled his classic *Harvard Business Review* article "Power Is the Great Motivator!"[15]

Two Kinds of Power: Type I—Prosocial Power

There was, however, an interesting twist to McClelland's findings. That is, while the managers and executives generally had a strong need for power, this need could be expressed in two very different ways. Some used power and influence to attain organizational performance goals. To achieve such goals, they typically shared power; not only did they try to influence others, they were themselves open to being influenced. They didn't see power as a "zero-sum game," where the more others have, the less you have. Instead they believed that everyone could have more influence.

Organizational research studies conducted at the University of Michigan showed that this was possible.[16] These studies demonstrated that in organizations where power was concentrated in top management roles, most people felt they had little influence. Hardly surprising! In other organizations, where power was distributed across organizational levels, everyone seemed to feel influential; again, not very surprising. The interesting results appeared when influence was added up, across levels, to get a measure of the *total* influence in an organization. In the organizations where power was concentrated at the top there was, overall, less influence than in organizations with a broader distribution of influence.

Even more interesting was the finding that the organizations with a more broad distribution of influence had significantly higher performance and productivity, compared to the organizations in which power was concentrated at the top. The researchers pointed out that this was because things get done through influence processes; when more people have influence, more work gets done. Power used this way is "prosocial," because it has a positive benefit for the whole organization.

Two Kinds of Power: Type II—Personalized Power

What about the other type of manager and executive, whose strong need for power is shown in ways different from what we've just described? You've probably known someone like this yourself.

This type of manager expresses the need for power by obtaining special privileges, such as a corner office, a company car, a private reserved parking space, and a personal assistant who delivers coffee promptly every morning at 9 a.m., preferably with a bit of servile groveling.

These managers see power as something personal. They exercise power in order to differentiate themselves from everyone else and prove their special status. Moreover, they appear to desire and even enjoy dominating others. Clearly, these managers use their power primarily for personal benefit, which is why McClelland labeled this form of power "personalized" power.

Managers who covet and use personalized power often have little concern for performance. They are also, understandably, usually not well-liked. They are, however, often feared, because they will quite literally do anything to obtain, maintain, and exert power. Although they do not get exceptional performance, they generally are able to move on to other and often higher-level positions before the department or division that they controlled falls apart as a result of their ill-treatment.

Most interesting of all is that these managers, whose need for power is expressed in personalized ways, are typically rather unsuccessful—except for attaining their powerful position. McClelland's research found that they were frequently depressive, often alcoholic, typically divorced, and had few, if any, friends. These are, generally, very unhappy people.

Changing Needs and Motives

We often think of motives and needs as being based in personality, like a "trait," which is relatively fixed. But motives and motive patterns—in particular the need to achieve and the need for power—though based in personality, are not fixed attributes. They can be learned and unlearned, changed and developed. This may not always be easy to do, but in a number of well-designed experiments McClelland showed that it is possible.

Earlier, we noted that by encouraging the need to achieve among entrepreneurs in a business seminar, McClelland was able to raise their level of achievement, compared to other entrepreneurs.[17] To see whether he could similarly change the power need toward the more socially beneficial type (prosocial power),

McClelland designed a program for alcoholics, who, like some managers, are characterized by a personalized power need.[18]

His program, included as part of a standard alcoholism treatment program, aimed to help individuals gain better control over their impulses, delay gratification of needs, and learn how to use influence to attain positive (prosocial) aims with others rather than trying to control others. His measures of power confirmed that those who went through his program developed more pro-social power needs. More important, McClelland found those who completed his program were more likely to stay sober, as compared to a similar group of alcoholics who attended a similar program without the elements designed by McClelland.

McClelland's identification of personalized power and pro-social power is made more clear by his model of how the need for power develops. That is, everyone needs power: This need represents the need for control over one's world that is basic for survival. But this need for control develops as we mature and is expressed in very different ways at different stages of development.

The Development of the Power Need

Stage I: Depending for Power on One's Relationship With Others

In this first stage of development of the power need, typical of infancy, a person gets control of the outside world through another person. In the case of infants, that person is normally the mother. As children mature, though, most recognize that they can gain more control over their world through their own actions. In that case, the individual goes on to the next stage of development. But some continue to depend on others for a sense of control. Those who do may focus their lives on being liked by and, in this way, depending on others. These *dependers* have a very strong need for "affiliation," that is, for friendship and close relationships with others. Remember, almost everyone maintains at least a moderate desire for social relationships throughout life—we're not hermits. But dependers focus on this need to an unusually great extent, and often to the exclusion of other important needs.

Stage II: Achieving Power
Through One's Own Actions

In this stage individuals develop—indeed revel in—their ability to control their personal world through their own actions and achievements. These *independent achievers* are sometimes called on to become managers, as a result of their successful performance. Although in certain situations achievers may be successful as managers, more often they fail, unless they move on to the next stage in the development of the power need. A classic example is the exceptional salesperson who is promoted to sales manager. Often such an individual is unable to see personal managerial success in terms of the success of others. Instead, the sales manager keeps selling while simultaneously trying to satisfy the managerial requirements of the job. Some burn out trying to do it all themselves.

Stage III: Managing Power
Through One's Effects on or With Others

Those who progress to this third stage of development may at first simply continue their efforts at personal achievement. What's different is that achievement now occurs in a social context. Stage IIIa characterizes competitors, whose achievements are individual and personal but who want the sort of recognition that comes from "winning" in comparison to others. Many people go on to a second aspect of this stage, which McClelland labeled IIIb. That is, they come to recognize that in social settings, particularly work organizations, the most organizationally significant outcomes aren't due to their own, individual effort. They realize that important organizational achievements come from the coordinated actions and achievements of many people. As effective *managers*, then, they look for and use others' need for achievement.

Robert Crandall, former CEO of AMR (parent company of American Airlines), is a good example of an effective and successful manager. Transactional leaders or managers like Bob Crandall rely on the compliance of followers in response to assurances of rewards (or sanctions). This often takes the form of an explicit contract. With honest contracting and hard negotiating, Crandall made American Airlines one of the most successful in the business. He was the first in the industry to succeed in gaining pilots' agreement to a two-tier salary structure. Pilots hated the agreement, but they accepted it.

Contracts can, of course, be misused. To the end of his career Crandall was still trying to live down his well-known attempt to cut an illegal price-fixing deal with other airline CEOs. This leads us to examine some ways that this stage of development—and expression—of the power need can go wrong.

As we have already noted, some individuals see the social context of power and control but cannot give up their drive for personal achievement as the source of power. These people are, in a sense, "stuck" halfway through this development stage. They turn personal achievement, and the power and control it gives them, into a competition with others and become *social achievers*. They seek out situations in which they can win over others, measuring their own control in terms of winning over the competition. This behavior is not necessarily a bad thing. Competition among exceptional athletes, for example, is usually exciting and interesting. In organizations, many effective managers see their work as winning a competition with other firms for customers.

The drive for power and the need to win over competitors can become so great that competition gets out of hand. It can become so strong that it damages or even, in some cases, destroys the organization. While CEO of Continental Airlines, Frank Lorenzo "led" the airline into bankruptcy not once but twice. Continental survived in part by getting rid of its CEO. Lorenzo went on to head Eastern Airlines, through a bitter struggle with its unions. He ultimately "won"—although he destroyed the airline in the process. It is in such cases that we may see the operation and effects of charisma and how charismatic leadership differs from transformational leadership. Some scholars point out that charisma is merely a follower's-eye view of a transformational leader.[19] We agree that charisma is in the mind of the follower and not some special "gift of the gods" given to the leader. But we also believe that charismatic and transformational leadership are very different.

A person at this third stage in the development of the power need wants to have an impact. Such an individual may also see the social context of power and realize that making an impact is not simply a matter of one's own personal effort and achievement. But instead of trying to compete personally with others, as social achievers, or becoming effective managers, some individuals use their strong power need to learn to act in ways that followers see as charismatic. Followers are then likely to do as these leaders wish. They may even permit the leader to control and dominate them far more than is reasonable. In this way they translate their striving for power into what McClelland called personalized power, the direct control and even domination of others. Later in this chapter we will explain in more detail how *charismatic leaders* do this.

Stage IV: Leading Institutions—Using Power to Transform People and Organizations

At this final stage, managers become transformational leaders. Managers understand the social context of power and influence and know how to share influence. This use of power in a positive, prosocial way benefits everyone. In this final stage in the development of the power need, good managers move beyond that managerial role to an understanding of how to construct the social context. This is what Edgar Schein speaks of when he describes the way that leaders create organizational cultures. In Chapter Eight, we will discuss how this happens. For the moment, we just want to point out that it is at this highest level of power need development that we see transformational leadership.

The Four Stages of Power Need Development

Table 4-1 (on the next page) shows how power is expressed at each of the four stages. We also indicate how that expression can be done in either a personalized or a prosocial manner. Thus, we see in Table 4-1 the connection between the two types of power need expression and the four stages of development of the power need. Table 4-1 also shows how the three types of leadership—transactional, transformational, and charismatic—appear in the context of the stages of power need development.

Summary

In this chapter, we showed how the twentieth-century concepts of legal-rational and charismatic leadership first appeared in the work of Max Weber. The modern versions of these concepts began

	TABLE 4-1	The Four Stages of Development of the Power Need[20]

Stage	Personalized Expression	Prosocial Expression
I. Dependers	Depending on parent or other authority figures	Friendship and social interaction
II. Independent Achievers	Acquiring things; getting and owning objects	Achieving goals
IIIa. Social Achievers	Winning over others	Achieving in ways that result in social benefits and corresponding recognition
IIIb. Managers (Transactional Leaders)	Getting the job done by doing it oneself if necessary	Empowering others to achieve goals; control *with* others
Charismatic Leaders	Dominating and attaining control *over* others	
IV. Transformational Leaders	Inculcating one's own values in others	Identifying shared values; helping achievers become good managers and managers become transformational leaders

to appear in the research of David McClelland during the third quarter of the twentieth century. By defining the two types of power need expression, prosocial and personalized, McClelland helps us to understand more clearly the difference between legal-rational authority, which we now see as transactional leadership, and charismatic leadership. His analysis of the development of the power need takes us a step further by showing how the three types of leadership are used in different developmental stages.

We have examined the power need as it applies to transactional and transformational leaders, but we have only touched on power as it relates to charismatic leadership. Equally important is the nature of the power need as it applies to followers. In Chapter Five, we examine these concerns by looking at leader-follower power relationships in the context of the leader-member relationship.

Chapter

FIVE

Leaders, Followers, and Power

*Good leaders serve followers, just as good followers serve.
A relationship of service goes both ways and benefits both. But
to truly be of service is even more difficult for the leader than
for the follower.*

Tao Te Ching, **Chapter 61**

We concluded Chapter Three by mentioning the start of a
search for some elusive factor that might explain the success of
transformational leaders. Some call this factor "charisma."[1] However, using charisma to explain leaders' success is merely another
way of saying that we don't know why they succeed. That is, we saw
in Chapter Two that research of the early twentieth century failed
to identify any clear leadership traits. And in Chapter Three we
concluded that behavioral skills alone didn't seem to define effective leadership, either. Simply labeling charisma as its source is not
a satisfactory explanation for transformational leadership.

In Chapter Four, we proposed that one very important factor
is the need for power. We traced the concept of charisma, to better understand two crucial issues in leadership. The first concerns
the differences among transactional leadership, transformational
leadership, and charismatic leadership. We showed that we could
understand these differences in terms of the exercise of power.
We examined how leaders develop a need for power. Finally, we
looked at how leaders use power in positive and negative ways.

In this chapter, we continue to examine the differences among
the three types of leadership. As we do this, we will also explore

the relationship between leaders and followers. In particular, we will look at how leaders use power in that relationship.

We define three basic ways that power and influence work in terms of the three types of leadership. This analysis is based on the work of Harvard social psychologist Herbert Kelman. It will help us to explain and understand in greater depth just what separates transformational leaders from transactional and charismatic leaders. Next, we examine the patterns of relationship between leaders and followers. Finally, we look more closely at the true nature of charismatic leadership. We will show why charisma is more often a warning sign than an indicator of leadership excellence.

Three Basic Influence Processes

Kelman identified three different ways—strategies—by which people are influenced.[2] We've summarized his argument in Table 5-1. In the discussion that follows, we describe each of the three basic ways that leaders can influence followers.

Getting a Reward or Avoiding Punishment

The first strategy involves rewards or, sometimes, punishments. That is, one person might influence another to do something— say, sweep a walkway or build a product—by offering to give that other person a reward, such as a cash payment. Punishment is the other side of the reward coin. That is, there are often specific penalties for failure to perform a job. For instance, the person might not be paid or might even be fired. One can avoid these penalties by achieving the stated goal (sweeping the walk or com-

TABLE 5-1 Three Influence Processes		
Charismatic Leadership	**Transactional Leadership**	**Transformational Leadership**
Obedience through identification, in expectation of becoming powerful like the leader	*Compliance* in expectation of reward (or to avoid punishment)	*Internalization* of shared values that guide actions

pleting the assignment). Compliance in light of potential reward or punishment is the basis both for Burns' transactional leadership and Weber's legal-rational authority model.

Internalizing Shared Values

Another approach is to base one's request on shared values and beliefs. These are strongly held views that serve as guides to doing what is right. For example, assume that you own an apartment building in which I live. I might sweep a walkway not because you pay me to, but because I use it, as do you. Underlying this is our shared viewpoint and value that a clean walkway will be safer and more pleasant to use. Even deeper, beneath this simple view, might be a more basic shared value. That is, both parties may share a strong sense of respect and concern for maintaining property that benefits them.

The above example is, of course, trivial. Think about a more serious case. Consider an executive in a manufacturing firm and a division manager who reports to this executive. Both accept the importance of the mission of their organization. Suppose that the division manager contributes an idea for improving a work process. The manager might do so not to get a reward but because a shared value, the importance of the firm's mission, has been "internalized." Generally, this happens as a result of what a transformational leader says and does. This is consistent with the description of transformational leadership.

Identifying With the Leader

The third influence process is key to understanding charismatic leadership. Such a leader convinces followers that by doing as he or she orders, that is, acting like the leader says he or she would act, the follower will become like the leader. Charismatic leaders imply that through a magical process of identification the follower will actually come to possess the leader's power. Identification is the process that is the basis for much advertising. That's why celebrities are so often hired to promote particular products. Ads that don't involve celebrities often show positive outcomes affecting product purshasers. In that case the target consumer is expected to identify with the purchaser—and with that person's good fortune.

This third influence process is characteristic of charismatic leaders. Charismatic leaders promise followers that they will literally become as powerful as the leader. This is not, however, a true contract, as is the case with transactional leadership. Charismatic leaders do not intend to—nor could they—deliver on that promise.

Leaders and Followers: Power Relations

We now see how leadership differs at different stages of development of the power need. We've also described the three ways that leaders influence followers. We can now look at leader-follower relations for each of three forms of leadership: transactional, transformational, and charismatic. That is, we are interested in what type of leader attracts what type of follower.

Transactional Leadership Pattern

We labeled as *managers* some of those at the third stage of power need development (Stage IIIa; see Chapter Four). These individuals express their need for power, that is, their need for control over their lives, by directing their power need in a prosocial manner. They use power and influence productively by sharing power and extending influence to followers. These individuals are *transactional* leaders, that is, good managers.

Transactional leaders can often manage very well. They get things done right by defining clear task responsibilities and expectations of followers. They provide followers with the authority needed to fulfill their responsibilities. They contract with followers regarding the consequences of achieving defined expectations—usually, the rewards for successful task accomplishment. Effective transactional leaders design systems of rewards (and sanctions) that are fair. Leaders and followers may then enter into clear contracts. They can engage in transactions that both find equitable and advantageous.

Transactional leaders use power and influence to achieve organizational goals through the efforts of others. It should not be surprising that the followers of these effective transactional leaders are likely to be *independent achievers,* at the second stage of power need development (see Table 4-1). Independent achievers aim to control their world by means of their own actions. Such individuals follow naturally the lead of good managers, *transactional leaders,* as we have just described them.

Effective transactional leaders get positive results by using power prosocially. They act to benefit not just themselves but other employees and the larger organization, as well. However, although their effective management approach gets things done right, it does not always ensure that the right things get done. What's more, while fair transactions benefit all those involved, they do not transform followers or organizations.

Charismatic Leadership Pattern

We began the discussion of leader-follower relationship patterns by talking about independent achievers (at the second stage of power need development; see Table 4-1) and managers (at the third stage of development). But we seem to have skipped over *dependers* (who are at the first stage of development of the power need).

Dependers are neither transactional nor transformational leaders. While some are followers, they are not mature followers. Rather, their followership is based on desire for a dependent relationship with the leader. By identifying with the leader, they aim to incorporate the leader's power within themselves. These followers are accurately described as "subordinates." That is, in all things, they subordinate themselves to the wishes of the leader.

What of leaders who seek out such followers? Although they are typically at the third stage of power need development, they are neither social achievers nor effective managers. And they certainly are not transformational leaders. Rather, they are driven by a power need that is expressed in personalized ways. That is, they seek control by controlling other people, directly and indirectly. They engage in interpersonal relationships designed to make others dependent upon them. They are the charismatic leaders. As such, they need followers who are dependent and obedient, the chief characteristics of dependers.

Of course, such relationships are not the sort we normally think of as "interdependent"—or even as healthy. Because of the dependent follower's immaturity, it's usually the leader who initiates the relationship. Moreover, a sort of seduction occurs in such a situation. That is, as we observed earlier, this sort of leader makes false promises. The charismatic leader claims that if the follower does as the leader wishes, the follower will become just like the leader: all-powerful.

Charismatic leaders strive to create charismatic feelings among followers by imitating the key behaviors used by transformational leaders. They don't really have a vision to communicate. They don't engage in consistent, credible actions—but they do try to give the appearance of trustworthiness. Neither do they have real respect for followers; they may express respect in words, but not in actions. They certainly don't empower followers with real authority and responsibility. But they are able to give the impression of some, if not all, of the behaviors characteristic of transformational leaders. That is often enough to produce the feelings in followers that we call "charisma."[3]

The charismatic leader provides precisely what dependers look for: a powerful other to depend on, whose power can be magically incorporated into the follower. *Charismatic leaders* recognize these followers' strong need for a close relationship. They use that need, asking only for followers' obedience. There is, then, a seductive reciprocity between charismatic leaders and dependent followers, with leaders and followers appearing to meet one another's needs.

The problem, of course, is that charismatic leaders cannot fulfill the promises they make. The dependent infant is successful, in a sense, in incorporating the mother's power and thus controlling the world. But it is *only* "in a sense" that this occurs. That is, control and power are not really incorporated into the person of the infant. It is, perhaps, realization of this fact that spurs most of us to further development of the power need. Most of us move on, at an early age, to Stage II of development, independent achievement.

Independent achievers are unlikely to become followers of charismatic leaders. Instead, they seek out situations in which the leader is an effective manager, a transactional leader who will make good on a realistic contract.

In contrast, dependent followers wish to depend on someone with whom they can identify. These followers aspire to incorporate within themselves the leader's apparent power. And in turn, charismatic leaders look for dependent followers who can be encouraged to identify with them. This process of identification is crucial if the charismatic leader is to convince dependers to obey him or her.

Charismatic leaders are sometimes characterized as having narcissistic personality disorders.[4] While narcissism is an essential aspect of charismatic leadership, it is not always unhealthy, at least in small amounts. In fact, some degree of narcissism may be necessary for all leaders. We all are—and should be—at least a little bit self-centered. What's more, all followers *must* identify with the leader, at least to some degree. After all, why would you want to follow someone you did not admire?

Charismatic leaders, however, are far more narcissistic than is healthy. They put their dysfunctions to use to benefit themselves, by seeking out and appealing to persons with complementary problems. At the extreme, we see individuals like Osama bin Laden, who the political psychologist Jerrold Post characterizes as "malignant narcissists."[5] It is no understatement to say that such individuals—other examples include Jim Jones and David Koresh—can be very dangerous.

McClelland suggested that, in psychoanalytic terms, the dependent followers of charismatic leaders are fixed at an oral stage of development. This is a stage in the normal development process at which the infant depends on the mother's breast for sustenance. It is interesting that at least one charismatic leader who was a malignant narcissist, Jim Jones, imposed his final will upon dependent followers by having them drink poison.

In organizations, most charismatic leaders are not as dangerously destructive as Jim Jones. Even so, they don't advance organizational goals especially well. Their real concern is not for followers or the organization; their only concern is self-concern. That's why we call them "narcissistic." In Greek mythology, Narcissus fell in love with himself. When he saw his reflection in a pool, he became so enthralled that he starved to death rather than leave his own image. While some charismatic organizational leaders do "self-destruct," most simply make life difficult for those who have to deal with them.

Transformational Leadership Pattern

The four-stage power need development model helps to understand how transformational leaders and managers complement one another. As followers, managers understand how the achievement and power motives operate. They often know how to help others to develop and direct these motives. In this sense, they are prepared to act as effective managers. They are also ready to begin the transformation into leaders. In fact, one important aspect of the work of transformational leaders is transforming managers into leaders.

Transformational leaders identify, articulate, and help others internalize shared values and beliefs. Such leaders define control as deriving from a "higher" source: the community. Transformational organizational leaders are not concerned with inculcating the values and beliefs of the past. Neither do such leaders aim to inculcate their own values and beliefs in the members of the community. Rather, the transformational leader's work is to first derive a set of values and beliefs from the current community of organization members (including the leader). Transformational leaders then act to make these values and beliefs explicit so that they can be shared consciously.

Managers' need for power is expressed prosocially, by sharing power and influence with others to achieve organizational goals. As followers, managers are well-positioned to work with transformational leaders, with the aim of becoming transformational leaders themselves. At the same time, they can become more effective managers by using transformational leadership behavior to further transformative aims. That is, they learn how to empower others, primarily those who report to them, but often peers as well. This can encourage those others to empower their own colleagues and lower-level employees. Managers who learn to model such transformational behaviors may eventually become transformational leaders. As such, they develop and transform their own followers—independent achievers—into effective managers.

Not every independent achiever wants to be a manager of others. We can all, however, become better managers of ourselves. Our development of transformational leadership skills makes it more likely that individuals' achievements will have positive organizational impacts.

Summary: Three Leader–Follower Interaction Patterns

We have seen that McClelland's model of the four stages of power need development is especially useful if we link the developmental stage of the leader to that of the follower. We also saw that Kelman's three basic influence processes can help us understand how different types of leaders, at various development stages, engage followers at different stages of development. Table 5-2 summarizes these patterns of relationship.

So far, our discussion shows how skilled charismatic leaders might lead individuals astray. How is it that such leaders develop mass followings? Surely the large numbers of followers enlisted by demonic charismatics like Hitler are not all enticed because they are dependers, at Stage I of power need development. Jerrold Post, a psychoanalyst who studies the character of political leaders, suggests that charismatic leaders first develop a base of dependers (Stage I followers.) Once the charismatic leader has formed this core group of dependers, he or she can use them to convert independent achievers, social achievers, and managers into obedient followers. The charismatic leader's message would not usually attract these individuals at Stages II and III of power need development. The personal appeal of dependers can, however, win over many.[6]

Even under normal conditions, groups often fall into what the group psychiatrist Wilfred Bion[7] called "basic assumptions." These

TABLE 5-2	Patterns of Leader-Follower Relations		
Leadership Type	**Charismatic Leadership**	**Transactional Leadership**	**Transformational Leadership**
Leadership Outcomes	Obedience	Performance	Interdependent action
	Attained through identification with the leader	Achieved through reward and/or punishment	Guided by internalized shared values
Leader's Power Motive	Control *over* others	Control *with* others (Stage IIIb)	Empowered leaders and followers are guided by a shared vision (Stage IV)
Followers' Power Motive	Dependent followers	Independent achievers (Stage II)	Interdependent, empowered followers-as-partners (Stage III)

are irrational beliefs that prevent the group from engaging in productive work. One such basic assumption diverts group members' efforts into actions that follow the directives of a leader who will (supposedly) be their salvation.

By identifying with and obeying the leader, followers—individually and in groups—are promised and come to believe that they will become like the leader. That is, they will be powerful and in control over their world. Much advertising is based on this sort of promise: drink Pepsi and you, too, will be a superstar like Michael Jordan. Drink Diet Coke and you, too, will be the subject of female office workers' fantasies. But the promise and outcome can be deadly rather than trite. "Drink this," said Jim Jones, "and you, too, will become all-powerful." But the only thing Jim Jones delivered was death. Whether morbid or mundane, charismatic leadership is typically a process of exploitation based on false promises.

Is Charisma Always Bad?

Charismatic leadership can, obviously, be dangerous. At the extreme, malignant narcissists lead followers to death and destruction. Examples of such outcomes are not limited to the twentieth century. In his recent book, Dash chronicles the horrific story of the Dutch East India Company ship *Batavia* (see box), almost 400 years ago. But less extreme charismatics can also be dangerous in organizations. One reason is simply because they may not have the capacity to lead large, complex organizations effectively. The charismatic leader's aim is to maximize personal control, not to achieve organizational goals.

Batavia's Graveyard

In 1628, the Batavia, owned by the Dutch East India Company, sailed for Java with more than 300 people on board. Ship operations were under Captain Jocobsz, a skilled officer but also an alcoholic whose womanizing could cross the line into rape. The ship's operations were directed by Francisco Pelsaert, a competent merchant who was also a thief, stealing from his employer.

As happened in those times, the Batavia went off-course and washed up on a reef off the west coast of Australia. There were some barren islands close enough for the crew and passengers to reach. The islands had neither food nor water.

It was not long before the captain and his merchant counterpart set off in a small boat to seek rescue, abandoning their 300+ charges. This was, however, the perfect opportunity for the ship's second-in-command, a young man named Jeronimus Cornelisz. Despite having gone bankrupt as a pharmacist, Cornelisz had managed to obtain a position with the Dutch East India Company. He found that he could disappear into this large bureaucratic firm. This didn't really surprise him, as Cornelisz believed that his every personal action was divinely directed.

Jeronimus Cornelisz was also a charismatic leader. He could persuade intelligent men that he had their interests at heart and that by following his advice they would profit greatly. That probably had something to do with how he obtained his position to begin with. In this situation, he convinced a small group of former crewmen and passengers to accept him as their leader, now that the captain and chief merchant had abandoned them.

First, he split up the party, sending groups of passengers to nearby small islands. Then, to consolidate control, he ordered his followers to deal with those left—by killing them. Cornelisz and his followers butchered men, women, and children, ultimately slaughtering more than 200 of them in a frenzy of murder.

Mike Dash, author of the book *Batavia's Graveyard* (New York: Crown, 2002) calls Cornelisz a "psychopath . . . devoid of conscience and remorse . . ." We would simply call him a charismatic leader, a malignant narcissist of the most dangerous type.

In sum, the presence of exceptionally strong charismatic feelings among the followers of a leader should be a cause for concern. Cynthia Ozick, considered by many to be one of today's best American writers, has commented on the importance of hope for great leadership, but notes that

> there is a difference between wanting significant leadership and wanting a leader. The craving for a hero is very dangerous, both for the putative hero and for his followers.[8]

Can Transformational Leaders Be Charismatic?

Several years ago we asked David McClelland for advice regarding our view of charismatic leadership. He asked why we believe that charismatic leaders can't also be transformational. He commented that in a study of leaders of religious orders, he had "found several who could only be described as charismatic, yet their effect was transformational and 'good,' in their impact on the organization."[9] How can this be, if the two forms of leadership are so dramatically different? Must charismatic leaders always have negative effects? McClelland didn't seem to think so.

One reason that transformational and charismatic leadership are so often confused is that both transformational and charismatic leaders often seem to act alike. Both types communicate what appears to be a clear vision. Both types appear to demonstrate consistency in their actions, so that followers develop a sense of trust in them. Both types seem to show respect toward followers. Both types tell followers they are part of a larger long-term plan.

The difference, however, is that charismatics do these things only superficially. Transformational leaders are concerned with substance, not impressions. The ultimate aim of transformational leaders is to empower followers; that of charismatic leaders is to disempower them and create dependency.

When followers feel that a leader has a lot of charisma, it may mean nothing more than that the leader uses many charisma-producing behaviors as he or she carries out transformational leadership activities. Alternatively, it may mean that the leader has no vision and followers run the risk of running like lemmings into the sea. Worst of all, the presence of exceptional levels of charismatic feelings may signal that the leader has a vision so destructive that it can only be attained by getting followers to do whatever the leader orders, no matter how crazy it may seem. This can happen because the followers identify with the leader, who appeals to their desire to be powerful like her or him. The charismatic leader promises followers, implicitly or explicitly, that they will become just as powerful if they will simply do whatever the leader says.

In and of itself, charisma may be nothing more than the side effect of sound leadership actions. But when a leader becomes known as much for his or her charisma as for achievements, it may be time to look closely at what the leader is trying to achieve. There may be no real vision, which can result in poor organizational performance. Or, the leader's true vision may be dangerously destructive.

Max Weber recognized that he was oversimplifying the analysis of leadership by defining three "ideal types"—traditional, legal-rational, and charismatic. Similarly, we realize that our own "ideal types" analysis oversimplifies the true complexity of interaction between transformational and charismatic leadership and, in particular, between the processes of identification and internalization.[10]

Effective transformational leadership is based primarily on the internalization of shared values held by leaders and followers. Even so, there must be some degree of identification with the leader by followers. After all, without some desire to identify with and "be like" the leader, why would followers become interested in finding shared values? Why would followers want to work with leaders to achieve common goals based on those values and beliefs?

If Some Narcissism Is Good, Isn't a Little More Even Better?

In a recent *Harvard Business Review* article, Michael Maccoby, a social scientist and psychoanalyst, examined the nature of narcissism in organizational leaders such as GE's Jack Welch and Apple's Steve Jobs.[11] Such leaders, argued Maccoby, don't just get followers to identify with them. They aim to "get the *organization* to identify with them" (italics added). Maccoby explained that he is not describing "the extreme pathology of borderline conditions and psychosis." However, the examples he gave raise questions.

For instance, Maccoby considered Steve Jobs a "productive narcissist," and observed that Jobs "publicly humiliates subordinates." He then noted that these productive narcissists are typically very sensitive to criticism, are poor listeners, lack empathy, don't like to mentor, and "are relentless and ruthless in their pursuit of victory."

We agree that a touch of narcissism—and charisma—in leaders may be quite productive and beneficial for the organization. As we have discussed, followers must, at least to a degree, be able to identify with the leader. But the details of Maccoby's argument serve also to reinforce our caution regarding such narcissistic charismatic leaders. We do not believe that humiliating subordinates can possibly be healthy for the individuals involved or productive for the organization. Leaders who are poor listeners, lack empathy, and don't like to mentor are neither transformational nor effective.

Must a Leader Be Either Charismatic or Transformational?

We have purposely emphasized the differences between transformational and charismatic leadership. In reality, transformational leaders surely employ, at least to a degree, followers' desires to be like and to identify with them. This is hardly surprising. The leader's motivating force is the need for power, whether the leader is transformational or charismatic.[12]

Some potential for charismatic as well as for transformational leadership is within us all. Even a charismatic tyrant such as Chile's former dictator August Pinochet did ultimately give up control to a democratically elected government. Even a transformational leader like Franklin Roosevelt tried to use his formidable charismatic abilities to force the Supreme Court to uphold certain of his policies, by "packing" the Court with appointees.

It is understandable, then, that a leader might express, in his or her actions, both personalized power, as control over others, *and* prosocial power, by empowering and transforming others. This may account for the confusion between transformational and charismatic leadership. The confusion is not simply due to people using different terms to mean the same thing. In fact, the two forms of leadership are essentially different in nature and consequences, even though they both arise from the same basic source: leaders' needs for power and control. The confusion in understanding the nature of and the terms used to describe transformational and charismatic leadership, which is widespread, often obscures the fact that these two types of leaders apply their skills to very different ends. That is why we have tried so hard to clearly distinguish these two very different forms of leadership.

Summary

In this chapter, we have seen how leaders' power need is expressed in different ways, by analyzing the three types of leadership. One aim was to explore and explode the myth of charismatic leadership, the notion that the effects of transformational leadership are due to the leader's charisma.

Our second aim in this chapter was to examine in depth and in detail the nature of the leader-follower relationship in each of the three forms of leadership. We saw that the power need—its level of development and how it is expressed—is crucial not just for leaders, but for followers, too.

Power has much to do with feelings about leadership, followership, and a basic sense of control over one's life. Power may well be, as McClelland called it, "the great motivator" of leaders, as well as of followers. It is not, however, the sole factor behind transformational leaders' success or the only important aspect of transformational leaders' character. In Chapters Six and Seven we will explore two other aspects of leadership character that are important for understanding transformational leadership, as well as for its practice.

SIX

Leaders With the Confidence to Act

Everyone must decide whether or not to act. Understanding how things happen will help make clear the right decision.
Tao Te Ching, **Chapter 73**

In Chapters Four and Five we described a crucial aspect of transformational leadership, the need for power. It is neither a skill nor an aspect of the situation or context in which leadership occurs. It is part of the character of the leader.

A leader might, however, be more likely to act successfully on the basis of the power need in certain situations and contexts. For example, Adolph Hitler might not have been able to use his psychotic power need so effectively, had the economic situation in 1930s Germany been different. It might even have made a difference had Hitler received critical appreciation for his work as a painter.

Regardless of the situation, and irrespective of skills, the need for power is part of everyone's personality. This need is an aspect of what we call "character," the relatively stable dimensions of an individual's personality. The power need is about feelings, what psychologists call "affect." It concerns, in essence, the need we all feel for a degree of control over our lives and the world we live in. In Chapters Four and Five, we explored how this need develops and how it is directed.

How leaders use power is central to understanding leadership, whether transactional, transformational, or charismatic. But the need for power is not the only important aspect of the leader's character. We found that there are personal characteristics besides the need for power that influence how leaders act.

In this chapter, we will examine another key personal characteristic. Before we do, you may wish to read and respond to the two brief stories that follow (see boxes). Your responses will help you to understand where you stand on this transformational leadership characteristic. Imagine yourself in the position of the central character in each story. Decide what you would do in that situation, and check the box for the option you would select.

Story One: The Heart Operation

You are forty-two years old and have just been told by your doctor that you have a serious heart ailment. Your condition is severe enough that you have been ordered to radically alter your lifestyle. Your work has been the central focus of your life, but you must now drastically reduce your workload. You must also completely change your diet and give up most of your favorite leisure activities. Only if you adhere rigorously to these major changes is there any possibility that you will have a normal life span; otherwise, chances are that your disorder will get worse over the next few years, possibly even to the point of completely incapacitating you. A consulting cardiologist has informed you that a recently developed surgical procedure might correct the situation and restore your health. However, despite the success of such procedures in recent years, there is still risk involved, especially given the nature of your disorder; there is a possibility that you might not even survive the operation.

Listed below are several probabilities, or odds, that the operation will prove successful. **Check the *lowest* probability of success that you would consider acceptable for the operation to be performed.**

I would have the operation if the chances that it would be a success were

❏ 9 in 10
❏ 7 in 10
❏ 5 in 10
❏ 3 in 10
❏ 1 in 10
❏ I would not have the operation no matter what the odds.

Story Two: The Hostage

You are a regional manager with an international manufacturing firm that has high visibility around the world. Because of this, you have been taken hostage by a terrorist organization engaged in a long-term "liberation" struggle. You have been held prisoner for several months, and conditions have been quite bad. Your diet is inadequate, the bare room in which you are isolated is cold and infested with vermin, and you have only the clothing you were wearing when you were kidnapped. Despite this, you are hopeful, because you have heard the terrorists discussing communications with your firm regarding ransom demands. You believe that the company will pay for your release.

With nothing else to do, you have spent the past three months closely observing the activities and routines of your captors. You have developed a plan that might allow you to escape, by disabling the sole guard who is left to watch you for a short time each week (while the others attend a meeting in another part of the city). Of course, there is no guarantee you could pull it off, and if they stopped you or caught you before you got to safety, they would probably kill you on the spot.

Listed below are several probabilities, or odds, of a successful escape. **Check the *lowest* probability of success that you would consider acceptable before you would attempt to escape.**

I would attempt to escape if the chances of success were

❑ 1 in 10
❑ 3 in 10
❑ 5 in 10
❑ 7 in 10
❑ 9 in 10
❑ I would not try to escape no matter what the odds.

What's Luck Got to Do With It?

The two stories concern attitudes and actions with regard to fate and the control we assume we have over our fate. Our attitudes about luck, or fate, are not simply a matter of the disposition we were born with. Our experiences, and what we learn from them, play a large part in defining these attitudes. To explain just how this happens, we will examine the results of some fascinating, if cruel, experiments done in the 1960s.

These research studies were done with animals, mostly dogs and white rats. For simplicity, we'll refer to the latter, the rats.[1] You've probably heard of a "Skinner box." It's a small cage, invented by the famous behavioral psychologist B.F. Skinner.[2] He believed that he could explain all behavior by understanding how certain stimuli in the environment become associated with reflex-like responses. What separates such responses from actual reflexes is that they are learned.

In his classic studies, Skinner put white rats in small cages. If they pushed a lever, they would get a food pellet. Most rats learn this pretty fast. But a Skinner box has another feature: a wire grid on the floor. That grid can be electrified; in that case, rats learn even faster to hit the switch to turn off the current. Unless, of course, the switch is disconnected. Then, the rat just huddles in a corner, shaking, until the electricity is off. (This sort of experiment would not be permitted today, but it was permissible then.)

You may wonder why the researchers would disconnect the switch if their aim was to train the rats to turn off the electricity. Well, that was just one part of the research. The researchers really wanted to study the difference between the rats that had an opportunity to learn to switch off the current and those that were not allowed to learn to do so (because the switch was disconnected).

The key test was to drop the rats into a large tub of water. The rats that learned to hit the switch and turn off the current swam like crazy to the edge of the tub and climbed out. But the rats whose switches were disconnected had learned a different lesson: No matter what they did, they could not control what happened to them. So when they were dumped into the tub, they gave a few perfunctory paddles . . . and then drowned. They had learned that they were helpless to control their fate and, therefore, hardly bothered trying.

It was a cruel experiment. But think how much more cruel it is to teach such a lesson to children—or to adults, for that matter. Yet it happens all the time. In many organizations—schools, factories, and even white-collar jobs—the "employees" learn that they can't control what happens to them. Each time that happens, a person dies a little bit. That individual has learned to expect to have less and less control over his or her life. People who have learned this tend to stop trying.

In contrast, some people are fortunate enough to learn, like the rats with the switches that worked, that they can do something about what happens to them. The actor Will Smith tells a story from his childhood. His father ran a small installation and repair shop for the freezers used in supermarkets. Business was good and Will's father decided to enlarge his shop. He tore out a wall, to extend the shop. Then he had Will (who was about ten years old) and his younger brother work every day after school on building the new wall. First they put in the extension of a foundation. Then they built the wall, brick by brick. They even worked during the summer. It took them more than a year to finish the job. Will said he thought it would never be done. Then, when the work was finally complete, Will's father stood with his sons in front of the finished wall and, looking at them, said "Never believe that there's *anything* you can't do!"[3]

This lesson is so important that some social scientists call it a "self-fulfilling prophecy."[4] That's because the belief that you can do something is often enough to encourage you to try. Trying to do something, when you believe you can, may lead to success. Not trying, in contrast, will surely not.

Harvard psychologist Robert Rosenthal put a slightly different spin on the same idea.[5] He called it the "Pygmalion effect," after the play by George Bernard Shaw, which became the musical (and movie) *My Fair Lady*. Shaw's play, titled *Pygmalion*, was inspired by the Greek myth of a sculptor, Pygmalion, who created a statue of the most beautiful woman imaginable. Similarly, Henry Higgins wanted to "create" a perfect English lady out of the basest "clay." He selected Eliza Doolittle, who had an extreme cockney accent, and attempted to teach her to speak the perfect English of an upper-class lady. But Eliza couldn't do it, until she came to *believe* that she could. It's not that wishing makes something happen. However, believing that you can do something, whether achieving a goal or learning a skill, is often the crucial first step in deciding to act, to make it happen.

These are hardly the only viewpoints on this theme. Stanford University social psychologist Albert Bandura calls this phenomenon "self-efficacy," the sense that one has that one can be effective.[6] Bandura has also used different terms for this same concept, including "efficaciousness" and, simply, "agency." The last term is related to the concept of being the agent of one's own destiny. Henry Ford may have said it best by using a few simple words:

> *"If you think you can . . .*
> *or think you can't . . .*
> *you're probably right!"*

We have yet another label for the concept behind all this: *self-confidence.* Transformational leaders have a strong sense of self-confidence. Sometimes this seems like a willingness to take risks, but transformational leaders are not really "high rollers" in terms of risky behavior. This leads us back to consider in detail the two stories presented at the beginning of this chapter, and your responses.

Earlier, we noted that the stories concern one's attitudes toward fate. To put this simply, there are two opposing views, illustrated clearly in classical literature. On the one hand, Shakespeare has Hamlet state that "it is not in the stars to hold our destiny but in ourselves."

In another of Shakespeare's plays, Julius Caesar observes that "the fault . . . is not in our stars but in ourselves."

In contrast, Goethe asserts, "Man supposes that he diverts his life and governs his actions, when his existence is irretrievably under the control of destiny." Which of these views one takes often affects one's reponses to the two stories.

When Is Taking Risks Risky?

The two stories you read are part of a longer test designed to measure a person's tendency to take risks. With the permission of the original authors, we modified and updated the stories, which they wrote in the 1950s.[7] We also wrote some new ones, like "The Hostage," which seemed more current. We published the revised assessment for use as a measure of managers' tendency to take or avoid risks.[8]

Your score is simply the odds you picked. For example, if you said that you would have the operation if the odds of success were at least 5 in 10, then your score is 5 for story one. (If you said you would not have the operation, or try to escape, no matter what the odds, your score is 10 for that story.) The higher the score, the lower the risk you are willing to accept; lower scores show a willingness to engage in riskier action. We're interested not so much in getting a total score as in comparing scores for the two stories.

In reviewing data we had collected using our assessment, we saw something not noticed by the researchers who wrote the original stories: The stories could be sorted, roughly, into two groups. The first group consisted of those stories in which what happens is pretty much in the hands of the central character. The second group contained stories in which the outcome was outside the control of the central character.

What is surprising is the choices of people who have a strong sense of control over their own fate. It's that they tend to score *lower* on story two than story one. That is, they are willing to take a greater risk (accept lower odds of success) in dealing with the hostage situation than with undergoing heart surgery. On the face of it, that seems incredible, but there is an explanation that makes sense.

In story one, you have no control over what happens. Oh, you can try to pick a good surgeon, but success or failure is up to the surgeon, not you. In contrast, in the hostage escape, it is *all* up to you, whether you succeed or are caught (and, perhaps, shot). People who feel a strong sense of self-control, of confidence in their own capability to decide their fate, are willing to take what appears to be a greater risk when they are, objectively, in control. When they are clearly not in control, they become more cautious, more conservative in risk-taking. Their apparent willingness to take a greater risk in a very dangerous situation (like the hostage story) than in a relatively safe situation (the operation) makes sense when you look at it this way.[9]

What's Leadership Got to Do With It?

In Chapter Two we mentioned the early work of Bennis and Nanus.[10] They identified one of transformational leaders' strategies as "management of risk." What they meant was that transformational leaders are willing to let others have important roles in carrying out crucial tasks. They "empower" others, rather than controlling everything themselves. Bennis and Nanus also observed that a leader who can no longer do this is, oddly enough, self-defeating. By refusing to empower others, a leader may think that any risk is removed or reduced, because the leader maintains control. But this is a false security.

Bennis and Nanus used the example of Karl Wallenda, leader of a troupe of circus highwire performers. In the act, everyone had a performance role as well as a specific responsibility for setting up and testing the apparatus, the highwire. For unknown reasons, Wallenda became unable to trust anyone but himself to check every detail of the high-wire setup; he couldn't even trust his own family members. He had to check every detail himself. Eventually Karl Wallenda lost control and fell to his death. He had overlooked some detail; the result was disaster. By trying to maintain total control, Wallenda, paradoxically, created the circumstances that led him to lose control and fail.

The paradox is, however, more apparent than real. Leaders who are capable of empowering others, of sharing control, make sure that those they empower are actually capable of carrying out their charge. Effective leaders make sure that empowered followers have the knowledge, skills, and resources to accomplish the tasks for which they are responsible. To an outside observer, it may appear as though the leader is giving up control. In reality, the leader has first taken action to ensure that followers will succeed.

Effective leaders don't take chances; they are not "risk takers," in the sense of gambling. Their self-confidence enables them to design situations in which they have minimized risk. Empowered followers can then act without the leader feeling that she or he is "taking a chance." In contrast, leaders who cannot share power and empower others, who cannot trust others with a degree of control, actually feel that they cannot trust themselves. What they have lost is their own sense of self-control, of self-confidence. This almost guarantees their failure.

Effective leaders are neither micromanagers who maintain control nor gamblers trying to beat the odds. Rather, their strong sense of control enables them to share power and control—*after* they have designed the situation for success.

Confident Leaders Build Confidence

The sense of control required for effective leadership permits leaders to design situations in which followers develop their own internal sense of control, their own self-confidence. Some people, including some scholars, think that the way to increase confidence in others is to "build self-esteem." They do this by praising followers and telling them they can succeed. This never works.[11] The way we learn confidence is by acting and succeeding. That is, we see the evidence of our own success. Transformational leaders build followers' self-confidence by putting them in situations in which they can succeed through their own efforts. Only then do effective leaders praise followers and observe that they can, in fact, succeed. To do this, leaders must first have self-confidence themselves.

Self-confidence is a key personal characteristic of leaders who help followers *transform* into self-confident leaders. This process is an important part of what transformational leadership is all about. It's why it is called transformative. Without self-confidence, leaders would not be capable of transforming others. Self-confidence, then, is a crucial foundation of transformational leadership.

This is where we come full circle in our argument. Self-confidence is all about being willing to act as a transformational leader. Without this characteristic, one would be unlikely to act, to engage in leadership behavior. Even more important, without the confidence to act, a leader's actions would probably be ineffective and aimed at preserving the leader's sense of control. But our discussion of the nature of "risk" in leadership makes clear that transformational leadership is about sharing power and influence with others, not controlling others.

Summary

We have now examined two important personal characteristics of transformational leaders. In Chapters Four and Five, we identified and explored how leaders' need for power—control over one's life—is expressed and developed.

This chapter examined self-confidence, the aspect of character that enables leaders to act. Putting together these two elements, control and confidence, we see that leaders' sense of self-confidence allows them to feel in control, instead of at risk, when empowering followers. Transformational leaders don't handle risk by trying to maintain personal control. Instead, they reduce risk by making sure that the followers they have empowered can achieve the goal.

We have now defined and explored two of three important transformational leadership characteristics. The third characteristic concerns the way leaders think. It is this third and final aspect of transformational leaders' character that we address in Chapter Seven.

Chapter
SEVEN

Vision—How Leaders Think

Some leaders look but don't see how things happen . . .
Understanding how things happen makes the right actions
obvious . . . Effective leaders understand the consequences
of actions.

Tao Te Ching, **Chapters 35, 73, and 74**

Chapter Three concluded with our recognition that there must be more to transformational leadership than learning a set of skills. Specifically, we came to believe that certain aspects of the leader's character play a crucial role in guiding leadership action. Our notion of character is more than the old idea of fixed "traits." We see key elements of the leader's *character* as attributes that leaders can develop. The elements of leadership character parallel three basic aspects of human personality: emotion, cognition, and action.

In Chapter Four we began to explore the emotional nature of transformational leaders' character. In that chapter we examined a central element of leadership character: the sense of power, or control, over one's own life. Everyone needs such a sense of personal control, but this need is especially important for leaders. In Chapter Five we continued our examination of leaders' need for power. Our focus there was on how leaders express power in their relationships with followers. Transformational leaders can empower followers because they are comfortably secure in their own sense of power. They *want* to empower followers because they understand that this is how work is done and goals attained in organizations.

Chapter Six focused on the second aspect of transformational leaders' character, the orientation to action. The key characteristic here is self-confidence. Such confidence is the basis of leaders' capacity to act. We showed how such self-confidence is learned, rather than innate. Moreover, when transformational leaders' actions empower followers, one result is that followers become more confident themselves.

In this chapter we will examine the third aspect of transformational character, which concerns the leader's cognitive capability. We call this *vision*. Our concept of vision is different from that commonly put forth as an element of leadership. We will, first, define vision and explain where we got our notions about vision. Then we'll show how transformational leaders practice it. Finally, we will put together the three elements of transformational leadership character.

What Is Vision?

Leaders are often spoken of as "visionary" or as "having a vision." Some say that a leader's most important work is constructing a vision. This is commonly understood to mean that a leader comes up with an image of an ideal future condition. The leader then explains this vision to followers and convinces followers to do what is necessary to attain the vision. This is *not* our view of vision.

Our notion of vision is summarized well by University of California political philosopher John Schaar:

> The future is not a result of choices among alternative paths offered by the present but a place that is created. Created first in mind and will, created next in activity. The future is not some place we are going to but one we are creating. The paths to it are not found but made, and the activity of making them changes both the maker and the destination.

Transformational leaders don't simply think up a vision and sell it to followers. If it's more than just a slick sales pitch, the long-term vision that a leader develops will always derive, at least in part, from followers' needs, ideas, and ideals.

In fact, the "vision" is less important than the act of "visioning," that is, the process of constructing a vision. The process of developing a vision doesn't mean dreaming. Many years ago there was a TV show called *Criswell Predicts*. Every week Mr. Criswell, an elegant, white-haired gentleman dressed in a tux, would stand before a camera and, in a deep and impressive voice, intone "I predict . . ." He predicted, for example, that in the year 2000 we would all be flying around in personal mini-planes. Another prediction was that we would communicate using videophones. Some of Criswell's predictions were pretty wild; others were simply projections of existing trends. Whether wild fantasies or extensions of current realities, few—if any—of Criswell's predictions ever came true.

Predicting the future is notoriously difficult. But visioning is not about *predicting* the future we will someday see. It is a step in *constructing* the future we want. This requires *thinking*, and thinking hard. Extensive psychological research tells us more about what this means.

Cause and Effect

Sigfried Streufert, a professor in the school of medicine at Pennsylvania State University, has conducted considerable research in cognitive psychology, the way we think.[1] Cognitive ability involves being able to think clearly about cause and effect. Imagine a pool table. You take the cue stick and hit the white cue ball into one of the numbered balls near another that's just in front of a pocket. Your cue ball hits the first numbered ball and it gently strikes the other ball, which rolls into the pocket. It's not hard to see that you planned a series of cause and effect actions. You moved the stick to hit the cue ball, which you planned would hit the first numbered ball, which you had envisioned hitting the second ball, which you then could see falling into the pocket. What's more, just about anyone watching you could have seen and described this chain of cause and effect actions.

Similarly, leaders also make plans based on a vision of a goal, and then take action to carry out their plans and attain their goals. Two things separate our example from what leaders actually do; both are matters of degree, rather than basic differences.

First, the plan of action that a transformational leader envisions consists of cause and effect chains, just as in our pool table example. But the actions taken by leaders are *more complicated.* For example, the leader may develop an action plan—based on and involving followers' ideas and not just the leader's—for entering a new market with a new product. The plan involves a complex series of actions, and the consequences of some of these actions will then determine subsequent actions. This can quickly get complicated.

Of course, championship pool can also be complicated. With some physical skill, most people can successfully complete the sort of simple pool shot described above. But it takes an expert player to plot out a really complicated shot. Such a shot might involve several balls being hit in sequence as a result of the player's shot at the first. The final result would be the last ball hit going into a pocket, while leaving the cue ball in position for another shot.

This suggests the second important distinction between a simple pool shot and the planning and action of a leader—or of a great pool player. Maybe you recall the classic movie, *The Hustler.* Jackie Gleason played the real-life pool expert, Minnesota Fats. The "hustle" was convincing a potential player, the "mark", to agree to a high-stakes game, thinking that he might be able to beat the "shark." However, Minnesota Fats needed just one shot. Every shot that followed was perfectly set up so that he could win the game without giving the mark a single chance.

Championship pool players like Minnesota Fats plan and carry out a sequence of shots so that they can set up and hit one ball after another into a pocket and win the game, without allowing the other player to take a shot. This sequence can involve more than a dozen balls. The player must plan where each ball ends up after each shot. Players with great vision incorporate into each pool shot actions that will set up the next and subsequent shots. All this calls for complex thinking. It also calls for complex thinking over time. Before we discuss the second important distinction between a simple pool shot and the planning and action taken by a leader, we would like you to participate in a short activity. Read the material in the box below and follow the instructions.

Vision at Work

Think for a moment about the most important work projects you are currently involved in. You might want to make a short list:

_____

_____

_____

_____

Now identify the work project that extends over the longest time period, from start to expected completion. How long is the time span over which that project extends? Check off the option below that most accurately matches your longest project's time span:

a ❏ three months or less
b ❏ more than three months, up to one year
c ❏ more than one year, up to two years
d ❏ more than two years, up to five years
e ❏ more than five years, up to ten years
f ❏ more than ten years, up to twenty years
g ❏ more than twenty years

Your choice is coordinated with Table 7-1 on page 98.

It's About Time!

The second important distinction between leadership and pool involves _time_. For example, the process and plan for entering a new market with a new product is likely to extend over a year or more, far longer than the longest pool game. The actions leaders design and take to reach organizational goals typically occur over a period of months or years. Action plans change often. Sometimes this is the result of new and more accurate information. Even more frequently, leaders must redesign such plans due to the consequences of prior actions, consequences that they did not foresee.

Fifty years ago the greater Los Angeles area had a good light-rail mass transit system. But in the 1960s that system—electric and diesel—was dismantled, to promote automobile use. One consequence was massive increase in air pollution, so severe that major new systems had to be designed to clean auto exhaust fumes. Ultimately, construction began on a new subway system, which is still only partly completed. Extensive new plans and programs resulted from an apparently simple vision of automobiles as primary transportation. Yet no one, it seems, had been able to foresee these consequences. What an incredible mess might have resulted had Criswell's prediction of individual mini-aircraft been accurate!

Our ideas about vision are based in part on the work of Elliott Jaques, an M.D. and psychoanalyst who also has a Ph.D. in social psychology.[2] In working with both private and public organizations, Jaques observed that those at higher organizational levels were typically paid more—hardly a new insight. But he also noted two things that had not been observed by others.

First, Jaques saw that as you go up a hierarchy, the jobs become more complex. Managing larger numbers of individuals and groups is one important factor that makes a higher-level job more complex. Even more important is the degree of complexity in the job itself, that is, the number of different projects and responsibilities and the way they interconnect.

Second, Jaques noticed that higher-level jobs, for which people were paid more, typically involved activities and responsibilities extending over longer time periods. Over years of research, he developed a theory of organizations and leadership.[3]

According to Jaques, at each level of an organizational hierarchy, leaders are needed who can think through chains of cause and effect to understand the effects of actions. These leaders are able to figure out what to do to achieve desired outcomes. At lower levels—supervisors and first-level managers, for instance—leaders must think through actions and outcomes that will occur over a period of weeks or months. Middle managers must do this with somewhat more complicated chains of cause and effect action over time periods of up to a few years. At higher organizational levels executives and CEOs must determine how increasingly complicated chains of events will affect one another over several years. In the largest and most complex organizations some CEOs have to be able to think about actions and their consequences over time spans of ten years or more.

This doesn't mean having a detailed plan of action that will lead to outcomes years down the road. Nor does it mean having a strategy for attaining some desired end state. Rather, thinking through cause and effect chains that involve long time spans and complex interactions involves thinking and acting now, in the present moment. However, effective transformational leaders also have the intended future effects and outcomes clearly in mind. Of course, circumstances and conditions change over time. The leader who can think about actions and outcomes over relatively long time spans and in relatively complex ways frequently rethinks actions, taking into account changes as they occur.

The ability to engage in this sort of visioning involves what we call "cognitive capability."[4] Those with greater cognitive capability are able to think in more complex ways over longer periods of time. Cognitive capability isn't the same thing as intelligence, nor is it a fixed unchangeable trait. Like confidence, the aspect of leadership that permits one to act, cognitive capability is developed partly on the basis of our experience. And, like the need for power (the emotional aspect of transformational leadership character), cognitive capability develops in stages, over one's entire life.

It is quite possible for a leader with less cognitive capability to be more effective than one with greater cognitive capability. The former individual might be in a position that calls for just the degree of cognitive capability he or she possesses, while the latter might be in a position calling for more cognitive capability than the person has. Jaques argues that leaders are most effective when they are in positions that require the degree of cognitive capability they possess. Successful leadership depends on having the cognitive capability that the job requires and developing more cognitive capability as one moves up the hierarchy.[5]

Table 7-1 gives typical ranges of cognitive capability, in terms of time perspective, for different leadership positions in a typical organizational hierarchy.[6] Table 7-1 also provides a key to help interpret the result of the *Vision at Work* activity we asked you to engage in earlier, identifying your longest-term work project. The letter of the option you checked off, shown in the left hand column of Table 7-1, gives a rough idea of the degree of cognitive capability required by your current work. Of course, this gives, at best, only a very crude indication of one's actual cognitive capability. You might, for example, be in a job that requires much less of you than you could give. And some people are asked to carry out work of a greater complexity and over a longer time span than they may be comfortable, or even capable of, dealing with.

TABLE 7-1	Time Span, Organizational Level, and Task Activities at Different Levels of Cognitive Power	

Time Line	Level	Task Activities
A. Three months or less	Supervisor	Uses practical judgment to solve problems as they occur
B. Three months to one year	Team Leader	Directs the performance of work by a group; anticipates and avoids problems by reflecting on experience
C. One year to two years	Department Manager	Develops and implements plans relating to department/unit goals; able to develop clear plans for following a path to a goal
D. Two years to five years	General Manager	Plans and coordinates the work of several interdependent departments or units; considers alternatives and how actions affect one another
E. Five years to ten years	Division Head	Directs complex systems composed of groups of units or departments; designs the organization of interactive systems
F. Ten years to twenty years	Senior Executive	Oversees the operation of complex, interdependent systems; constructs and manages networks of relationships
G. Over twenty years	Chief Executive	Designs and shapes systems, both technically and socially

Jaques' research showed that employees are more satisfied with their jobs when the job responsibilities, in terms of time perspective required, match their cognitive capability.[7] When people are asked to do work that forces them to think beyond their capabilities they generally perform poorly and often leave (or are fired). When they stay in such positions they are dissatisfied. So are employees who are given work that calls for less cognitive capability than they have. They often feel overpaid, too.

It is difficult to accurately assess an individual's stage of development of cognitive capability. However, your response to the *Vision at Work* activity can tell you something about the time spans you're comfortable with and the cognitive capability level associated with them.

The complexity of visioning over long time periods is more apparent if we examine four specific thinking skills that are involved in visioning.

Four Steps in the Visioning Process[8]

Whether one is involved in creating a 10-year or 10-week vision, four distinct actions are required, each calling on a particular thinking skill. The four steps are described in order of difficulty. The difficulty of using each of these thinking skills becomes greater as a vision becomes more complex and extends over longer time spans.

Step 1: Expressing a vision.   The first skill is expressing the vision, that is, taking action to carry out the vision and behaving in a way that advances the goal of the vision. Consider the case of a mid-level manager responsible for several engineering product development teams. Imagine that this manager has determined that self-managed teams with greater independence of action are more effective. The manager has a vision, a mental plan, of teams that operate this way and has decided to take leadership action to develop such teams. To express this vision the manager might meet with one of the teams and give the team an assignment for which the team would be fully responsible, without the manager's intervention.

Consider how this might work at a higher level of the organization. Imagine that the CEO of an auto-parts manufacturing company wants to create a program to involve all employees in managing the firm. The CEO sees this as a plant-level program. To make this vision real, the CEO must be able to plan and carry out the following actions:

- design and write a set of policy actions to create a plant-level worker involvement program;
- meet with relevant parties (plant-level managers as well as workers) to develop a document detailing the new policy and program;

- meet with, and arrange meetings of, all plant-level managers and all employees to review and revise the program, and to plan for its implementation;
- work with relevant managers to identify ways to track the program's effects and effectiveness; and
- oversee the monitoring of the program, working with relevant parties on any further modifications needed.

Notice, then, that the CEO's vision is far more complex in plan and action than the vision of the mid-level manager. Even so, both must be able to express their vision in action, to think through what specific actions they must take and to carry them out. Expressing a vision requires that the leader understand and perform the sequence of cause-and-effect actions required to make the vision real.

Step 2: Explaining a vision. The second skill is explaining the vision to others—clarifying the nature of the vision in terms of its required action steps and aims. Again, consider our example of the mid-level manager who has given a team an assignment that defines that team as self-managed and specifies the team's boundaries of authority and autonomy. The manager must now explain the plan to the members of the team, making clear what team members need to do to effectively operate as a self-managed team, and why.

Now think again of the CEO who envisions worker involvement at the plant level. The CEO who can express this vision still may not succeed in implementing it. Our CEO must be able to explain the steps in carrying out the vision to others. Unless the CEO can explain the vision to the program manager, constant uncertainty will arise as to steps and handling of problems and issues. Unless the CEO can explain the program to plant managers, their support for the vision will fade as the CEO loses touch with the day-to-day program details (as is inevitable for any chief executive). Explaining involves more than merely restating the vision's nature or aim. Transformational leaders must be able to explain how the actions required for the vision link together, in cause-and-effect chains, to attain the goal.

Step 3: Extending a vision. The third required thinking skill is extending the vision—applying the sequence of activities to a variety of situations so that the vision can be implemented in several ways and places. To continue with our examples, the mid-level manager will probably want to extend the vision to other teams (remember that several teams report to this manager). This will mean meeting with the other team members or, at least, key individuals in each team. The manager might ask members of the first self-managed team to coach the other teams, with the manager's guidance. Of course, this also means that the manager would have to explain the action steps to the new coaches. Thus, the manager's work is becoming more and more like leadership rather than management. And the complexity of the task is also beginning to appear.

In the CEO's case, she or he will probably, at some point, want to extend the vision to other parts of the organization. This might mean working with the program manager to revise the worker involvement plan and apply it to headquarters staff departments, as well as to the plant. Doing so will call for changes in how the program is implemented and may even require alterations in the worker involvement program itself. The expressed vision is an important frame of reference, but the leader must be able to adapt it to varied circumstances. Again, the leader must be able to both implement these changes and explain them to others.

At this point in our examples we can still see that the CEO's work as transformational leader is more complex than that of the manager. Even so, both face more complex challenges in extending than in expressing or explaining their visions.

Step 4: Expanding a vision. The fourth thinking skill involves expanding the vision—applying it not just in one limited way, and not even in a variety of similar ways, but in many different ways in a wide range of circumstances.

The mid-level manager might seek to expand self-managed team operations to other departments and divisions. One might do this through contacts with peers. This manager might, for example, set up an informal "team self-management group" consisting of managers of teams throughout the organization. That group might then meet to consider new applications of self-managed teamwork. The group could also consider a variety of new ways to develop self-managed teams.

The CEO who has a vision of worker involvement at the plant level, and tries to implement it as outlined above, still may not be as effective a transformational leader as possible. Full success would involve more than extending the program to another part of the organization. It would mean thinking through the spread of the worker involvement vision throughout the organization. The leader must consider different ways the program might be spread, for example, unit by unit, or by divisions. Next, the leader must determine what organizational changes are necessary for consistency with the new employee involvement process.

This fourth cognitive skill is more complex than the others. And, it is clear that the leadership work of the manager is less complex than that of the CEO. The CEO must now engage in myriad sets of interrelated cause-and-effect actions to expand the vision. Although the manager must also create a set of new cause-and-effect actions to expand that vision, those actions are more clear-cut, less numerous, and less complex than the actions required of the CEO.

Summary: The cognitive skills of visioning. Just about anyone can carry out the four skills of visioning—expressing, explaining, extending, and expanding—for short-range visions. That would involve plans and actions that extend over as little as a day or as long as a year. Fewer people have the cognitive power to engage in the four skills of visioning over periods of one to three years. Fewer still can do this over periods of five to ten years. The person who can think through a vision over a time span of ten to twenty years is rare.

Jack Welch, recently retired CEO of General Electric, provides us with a good example of cognitive power at the top of a very large and complex organization. In a little more than twenty years he guided the organization through dramatic changes. Who would have expected to see GE leave the small-appliance business and become one of the world's largest financial services firms?

It would be ridiculous to think that Jack Welch had these changes explicitly planned when he took over, more than twenty years ago. But he was able to apply a very high level of cognitive power to take advantage of opportunities—and to avoid pitfalls. The result is the corporation we know as GE today. It's an organization quite different from the one Welch started out with more than a generation ago.

Welch did have a broad vision for GE over the twenty-year time span during which he was CEO. He certainly thought in terms of growth, profit, and market dominance. An example is his "rule" that if GE could not be either number one or number two, the company would get out of that business. However, he developed much of the detail of his action plans along the way. This is exactly how transformational leaders transform organizations. They don't start with a grand, step-by-step plan designed to attain a specifically defined outcome. Instead, they have a basic design that they work on over time, filling in details and making needed changes and modifications as they go.

Leaders and Followers: Cognitive Capability

Leaders use their cognitive capability to understand complex causal chains. They then act to attain outcomes that will benefit the organization and advance a vision, a relatively long-term plan of action. Any top-level leader needs a substantial degree of cognitive power to be effective. But transformational leadership needs more than cognitive power. A leader's effectiveness results as much from helping to develop followers' cognitive abilities as from exercising his or her own.

A transformational leader with the degree of cognitive capability required for a top-level position makes important long-term strategic decisions. Still, how much do these decisions affect what goes on in the organization on a daily, weekly, monthly, and yearly basis? It is the thought and action of managers and lower-level employees that have the most effect on current and short-term future operations.

The finest long-term plan and the wisest long-range proposals will surely fail if those who must act today and tomorrow cannot do so. An executive leader with great cognitive capability may be tempted to simply exercise his or her own vision. However, it is much more important that such leaders help followers expand and improve their vision and develop their own transformational leadership character. Later, we will discuss in more detail how leaders transform followers into more self-directed leaders.

The ABCs of Transformational Leadership Character

We began our search for the characteristics of transformational leaders where transactional leadership ends (and is still stuck). That is, transactional leadership research came to focus on what behaviors to use in what situations in order to get effective results. We realized, though, that this was like trying to understand canine behavior by studying tail-wagging. Leadership behavior is the tail, the means, not the head, or cause.

In Chapters Four and Five we saw that some scholars and practitioners seemed to be aware of this research flaw. McClelland and House focused on the leader's character in terms of the need for power—the emotional foundation of transformational leadership.

Based on the work of Rotter, Rosenthal, Seligman, and Bandura, we identified self-confidence (or efficacy), in Chapter Six, as a second important transformational leadership characteristic. Self-confidence is the personal characteristic that enables leaders to plan and take action.

Finally, in this chapter we drew on the research and applications of Jaques, Streufert, and their associates. This body of work enabled us to identify cognitive capability—the ability to think over the long term and to do so in terms of complex cause-and-effect chains—as the third personal characteristic of transformational leaders.

We see these elements as the ABCs of transformational leadership character. The formula is more than just a simple way to remember the three key personal characteristics of transformational leaders. These letters represent the three central aspects of human nature:

❖ **A is for** *affect* **or, in other words, emotion and feelings.**

❖ **B is for** *behavioral intent,* **that is, the confidence to act.**

❖ **C is for** *cognition,* **or thought, the basis for vision.**

These three elements are, of course, intimately connected. Our thoughts reflect our feelings, and our actions may develop out of logical thought or nonrational emotion. Sometimes these connections are not what people assume. For example, one of the founders of scientific psychology in the United States, William

James, observed that we do not run (from some danger) because we are afraid but are, rather, afraid because we run.[9] James believed that the feeling of fear was a *product*, a result, of the behavior of flight rather than its *cause*. Physiological research, some twenty-five years later, provided some evidence that James was right.

The most basic element, in our view, is *affect*—that is, emotion. The word "emotion" derives from the ancient Greek "motive" which concerns movement and has evolved, in another derivation, into the concept "motivation." Emotion is processed in the oldest structures of the brain. This makes sense because emotion (not to mention movement) is central to the fundamental issue of survival. Abraham Maslow identified this motive—safety and security for survival—as the most basic human need in his hierarchy of needs.[10]

The need for control over one's world—McClelland's "power need"—is, similarly and logically, the first and most important aspect of transformational leadership character. That's why we examined it first, in Chapters Four and Five, as a key aspect of our approach to transformational leadership.

Another basic aspect of human personality is one's *behavioral intention,* or orientation toward action. Some leadership approaches deal only with behavior;[11] we find that to be inadequate for understanding or developing transformational leadership. In Chapter Six, we dealt with the leader's behavioral orientation in terms of efficacy, or agency, that is, having the self-confidence to take action. Its absence, the inability to act, has been identified as one of the most important factors that "derail" otherwise promising leadership careers.[12]

Other transformational leadership approaches,[13] like ours, see the power need as a central issue. Typically, however, these others neglect the other side of affect, or feeling: *thinking*. Cognitive capability, as described in this chapter, is crucial for leaders who must understand complicated cause-and-effect relationships.

Summary

We believe that our approach to understanding transformational leadership, leadership that matters, is solidly grounded in a sound model of human psychology. In Chapter Three we identified the areas of behavior that are of greatest importance. However, these behaviors are only applied effectively when a leader possesses the personal characteristics—affect, behavioral orientation, and cognitive capability—that enable him or her to determine what to do and how to do it. But knowledge of leadership behavior and character is not enough to fully understand transformational leadership.

What Else?

The model of transformational leadership we have presented may seem complicated. Even so, it's not the whole story. That's because we've left out a final key element. We started with an understanding of transformational leadership behavior, in Chapter Three. In Chapters Four, Five, Six, and Seven we identified the essential aspects of transformational leadership character, which directs behavior. But the psychologist Kurt Lewin was famous for (among other things) the following simple statement:

> An individual's behavior is determined by personal factors and by the situation in which that person finds him or herself.[14]

We started with the behaviors of transformational leaders and saw how they are determined by the leader's character, the personal factors. But the situational leadership researchers and practitioners we mentioned in Chapter Two had a point when they looked for different characteristics and alternative behaviors that would be more effective for different situations. What about the situational or contextual factors important for transformational leadership? That is where we must look next, in Chapter Eight, to complete our basic model of transformational leadership.

EIGHT

Leadership in Context

Change: What is flexible survives, what is unchanging dies.
                    Tao Te Ching, **Chapter 76**

Goals: A journey of a thousand miles begins with a single step.
                    Tao Te Ching, **Chapter 64**

Teamwork: Leaders and followers are part of a single whole;
strength comes from this unity.
                    Tao Te Ching, **Chapter 39**

Culture: Leaders instill three values—compassion, sharing,
and equality.
                    Tao Te Ching, **Chapter 67**

In Chapter Three we examined research designed to identify and measure the behaviors and skills used by transformational leaders. We identified several transformational leadership behaviors that came up consistently, across research studies. This led us to define and present our own versions of four especially important behaviors. These behaviors are skilled communication, trust-building, expression of care and respect for others, and creating empowerment opportunities. We realized, however, that this could not be the whole answer to the puzzle and practice of transformational leadership. These skilled behaviors express and illustrate transformational leadership in action. They do not, however, address the nature of transformational leadership and how it works. These actions are the result of transformational leadership, not its cause or source.

In Chapters Four, Five, Six, and Seven we described a set of personal characteristics common to transformational leaders:

❖ *a sense of power and control over one's own life* **that enables leaders to share power and influence with others;**

❖ *the confidence to act,* **which permits leaders to use the key behaviors we identified earlier; and**

❖ *the cognitive capability needed to understand complex cause-and-effect relationships* **and use them to develop plans that will achieve desired goals.**

These transformational leadership characteristics are not necessarily inborn traits. Some leaders are endowed with them naturally, but others develop the characteristics over time. Our discussion showed how these characteristics develop and how to foster their development.

Logically, then, it might seem that we have found the key to transformational leadership: develop the personal characteristics needed to effectively use the behavioral skills of transformational leadership. If you don't have the skills, learn and practice them. If that sounds too simple, that's because it is.

In Chapter Seven we observed that behavior is a result of the interaction between a person and the situation that person is in.[1] So far we've discussed the behaviors of transformational leadership and the personal character of such leaders. But we've not considered the *situation.* This is the third and final major aspect of transformational leadership we must examine to understand this new way of thinking about leadership.

Behavior Is a Function of the Person and . . . What Situation?

The old situational leadership approaches we discussed in Chapter Two identified certain key aspects of situations. For House the key aspects were the task structure and the employee's experience; for Hersey and Blanchard employee motivation and employee skill were key.[2] These leadership approaches guided leaders to choose one or another leadership style or use one or another specific type of behavior. How to put the various situational factors together, to decide which style or behavior to use, can get quite complicated. This is especially true if one includes enough aspects of the situation to approximate a realistic context.

Regardless of which specific situational factors are the focus, or how they are combined to determine how to lead, the research (as we noted in Chapter Two) is clear about what happens when managers try to apply these approaches. While all of the situational approaches seem to work to a degree, none of them enables leaders to dramatically improve their effectiveness. In fact, none seems to work better than the older "one best way to manage" theories. Those behavioral approaches simply told leaders to show a lot of concern for people (followers) and to express a high concern for production (the task).

Looking at the situational context in terms of transformational leadership calls for a very different perspective from that of the situational leadership approaches. Those approaches were designed for managers, transactional leaders. The situation was assumed to be "fixed." That is, leadership was defined as determining what actions to take or which "style" to use, to get the best results in a particular situation.

The issue addressed by transformational leaders is much more complicated. That's because transformational leaders don't merely try to work within a situational context. Instead, they construct the situational context. To understand what this means we must first examine the nature of the situational context, that is, just what transformational leaders are trying to construct. Then we will look at how they do it.

The Context: The Nature of the Situation

Fortunately, we do have some guidance to help understand the nature of organizational situations. This guidance comes not from psychology or management, but from the two greatest sociological thinkers of the last century. It shouldn't surprise you that one of these individuals is our old friend Max Weber. The other is an American, Talcott Parsons, a Harvard professor who studied Weber's work and translated much of it into English. We'll look first at Weber's contributions. Then we will examine how Parsons built on Weber's ideas to develop a simple yet elegant framework for understanding social systems.

Verstehen: Understanding Means and Ends

Weber used the German word *verstehen,* "understanding," to describe a process of examining the relationship between means and ends. He argued that it is not possible to have a clear understanding of social phenomena without looking at both actions and their consequences.[3] This might seem obvious, yet what passed for management (as well as social science) in the nineteenth and early twentieth centuries was often a list of how people *ought* to act and how organizations *ought* to function.

In 1916, in France, Henrí Fayol, then the director of mines, wrote the first book of "principles of management."[4] He did not describe how administrators and managers acted, based on objective observation. Instead, he detailed how they *ought* to act, based on his experience, to get the best results. In the United States, various scholars and practitioners wrote similar texts. Their work came to be known as the "principles" school of management.[5] There is nothing inherently wrong with ideals or principles. However, simply stating ideal conditions, what ought to exist, or principles, how one ought to manage an organization, is unrealistic, in light of human nature. What's more, it ignores the important question of what the consequences might be if these ideals and principles are or are not implemented.

Weber was interested in what really goes on in organizations, rather than what we would like to happen or what we believe should happen. That's why he insisted that understanding actions in organizations requires that one examine the larger context and include a focus on the consequences of actions. We must look at what is done and what the outcomes are. We can then identify the links between what we do and the results we get. This sort of means-ends analysis has become so important that we rarely think of it as a basic approach to social science. That is, however, exactly what it is, and it was another contribution from Max Weber.[6] However, to fully understand the social context, another sociologist, Talcott Parsons, determined that another aspect, besides means and ends, must be examined.[7]

Boundaries: Internal and External

Many in the field consider Talcott Parsons to be the most important sociologist of the twentieth century. His "theory of action" is too complex to summarize here, however, and quoting excerpts from his writings probably would not help. When he died in 1979 *Time* magazine published a brief extract from his writing, to show how difficult it is to understand Parsons. Fortunately, the basic concepts that form the foundation of Parsons' theory are elegant in their simplicity.

Parsons developed the most advanced and complete form of his theory in the 1950s.[8] A new way of thinking about social organization had started to catch on. This new approach was based on *general systems theory*.[9] The idea is that all organizations are systems. That is, a variety of coordinated activities take place within an organization, aimed at transforming "inputs"—which may be physical raw materials or intangibles like information—into some product or "output." Of course, many events, activities, and other systems exist outside the organizational system. A *boundary* separates these internal and external patterns of action.

Boundaries can, of course, be walls made of bricks but they can also be walls made of ideas and assumptions. What, for example, makes you feel part of a church or social organization? Is it because you meet at a certain, regular time in a particular building? Or, is it because all of those who belong to the organization share certain beliefs and views?

We think of ourselves as members of an organization, separate from other people and organizations in our society. This is because of the way we see and think about issues that relate to that organization, not just because we all work in a particular building or on a particular type of work. These latter factors are not irrelevant. They are, however, only part of what makes up the boundary that separates those inside an organization from those outside.

The notion of a boundary—mental and social, as well as physical—is what Parsons added to Weber's means-ends analysis. The result is a simple model that crosscuts means-ends with inside-outside. This framework, Parsons argued, could be used to analyze and understand the actions that go on in any organization. Table 8-1 shows how Parsons combined Weber's distinction

TABLE 8-1	The Action Framework	
	Means	**Ends**
Outside	Actions that involve dealing with things outside the organization in order to attain goals	Actions that are directly concerned with producing outcomes or achieving goals
Inside	Actions to define values and beliefs that determine how actions in the other three areas are carried out	Actions that involve coordinating the ongoing work of individuals and groups

of means and ends with the systems theory view of inside and outside. The result is a four-box model known as Parsons' "action framework." By carefully examining each of the four boxes, we can get a much better understanding of the nature of the organizational context.

Before considering the four boxes in detail it may be helpful to think first about your own organization. Answer the eight questions that follow in the Organizational Context Questionnaire. We will show how to score the questionnaire after exploring in more detail the aspects of organizational context the OCQ measures.

Organizational Context Questionnaire

This short questionnaire is intended to help illustrate concretely certain aspects of the context of an organization. Please note that in responding to the statements below you must refer to a *specific* organization. This inventory is not a test of your own beliefs or views but is, rather, a report on certain aspects of your organization.

Directions: For each of the statements below, select the alternative that most accurately describes the organization you are thinking of. Some items call for judgments on your part; try to be as honest and accurate as you can in your descriptions.

Use the following key: **C** = Completely true
M = Mostly true
P = Partly true
S = Slightly true
N = Not at all true

1. This organization has clearly demonstrated that it
    can adapt to changing conditions as needed.   **C M P S N**
2. Goals in this organization are always defined in terms
    of the desires and needs of clients and customers.   **C M P S N**
3. Coordination among individuals and units in this
    organization is exceptionally high and effective.   **C M P S N**
4. This organization has a long history of maintaining
    a stable pattern of shared values, beliefs,
    and behavioral norms.   **C M P S N**
5. When changes are necessary, everyone in this
    organization has a clear idea of what sort
    of changes are—and are not—acceptable.   **C M P S N**
6. In this organization, people do the best they can;
    there is little pressure to strive for specific goals.   **C M P S N**
7. People in this organization have clear concepts
    of their own roles and how they relate to the roles
    of others.   **C M P S N**
8. In this organization, everyone believes strongly
    in a set of shared basic values about how people
    should work together to solve common problems
    and reach shared objectives.   **C M P S N**

Four Crucial Organizational Functions

Each of the four boxes of Parsons' Action Framework (Table 8-1) describes certain actions that are important for organizational functioning. Parsons called this the functional perspective. His four boxes refer to four key functions that all organizations must perform to be effective and survive. These functions are shown in Table 8-2; we will briefly explore each.

The actions in the upper left box, concerned with external means, relate to coping with change in the outside environment. Parsons called this "adaptation" but we refer to this function as *change*. All organizations must find ways to deal with change, and most change comes from the organizational environment.

Actions in the top right box, external ends, have to do with the product an organization puts out for clients or customers. Parsons labeled this function "goal attainment." We simply call it *goals*.

TABLE 8-2	**Functions of the Action Framework**	
	Means	**Ends**
Outside	**Change.** Actions that involve dealing with things outside the organization in order to attain goals	**Goals.** Actions that are directly concerned with producing outcomes or achieving goals
Inside	**Culture.** Actions that define and support values and beliefs that determine how actions in the other three areas are carried out	**Teamwork.** Actions that involve coordinating the ongoing work of individuals and groups

The bottom right box, internal ends, describes actions within the organization that are directed toward coordinating the activities of individuals and groups. The actions represented by this box deal with what Parsons called "integration" of various organizational activities. We label this function *teamwork*.

Finally, the box on the bottom left, internal means, contains actions designed to establish and support certain values and beliefs within the organization. In other words, this box concerns the organization's *culture,* the "way we do things around here." The values and beliefs that make up culture maintain the way things happen. That's why Parsons labeled this function "pattern maintenance." The actions in this box maintain the patterns of action in the other three boxes.

We don't talk much about our values and beliefs; we usually take them for granted. That's why Parsons called this pattern maintenance function "latent" or hidden. There is a reason for "hiding" the pattern maintenance function. This function maintains the stability of the pattern of organizational action. If we fool around with that too much we could produce undesired changes, the opposite of maintaining stability. Rather than use Parsons' label, "latent pattern maintenance," we simply call the function represented by this box *culture.*

In sum, Parsons' action framework identifies four key issues faced by people in organizations. They are

❖ **how people deal with external forces and the need to** *change;*

❖ the nature of organizational *goals*, how they are defined, and
their importance;

❖ how people *work together* to get the job done; and

❖ the degree to which people in the organization generally
agree on the important *values and beliefs* that should guide
their actions.

The Organizational Context Questionnaire gives a rough idea
of how these issues play out in your own organization. Use the
instructions that follow to score your answers.

Scoring the Organizational Context Questionnaire

Transfer your responses to the questions on the Organizational Context
Questionnaire to the scoring grid below, by circling the number that corre-
sponds to the letter of the response you selected. When you have circled the
appropriate numbers, add the two circled numbers in each column and enter
the totals in the empty boxes at the bottom of the columns.

1. C = 5
  M = 4
  P = 3
  S = 2
  N = 1
	2. C = 5
	  M = 4
	  P = 3
	  S = 2
	  N = 1
		3. C = 5
		  M = 4
		  P = 3
		  S = 2
		  N = 1
			4. C = 5
			  M = 4
			  P = 3
			  S = 2
			  N = 1

5. C = 5
  M = 4
  P = 3
  S = 2
  N = 1
	6. C = 1
	  M = 2
	  P = 3
	  S = 4
	  N = 5
		7. C = 5
		  M = 4
		  P = 3
		  S = 2
		  N = 1
			8. C = 5
			  M = 4
			  P = 3
			  S = 2
			  N = 1

Totals			
Change	Goals	Teamwork	Culture

Your scores can range from 2 to 10 on each of the four functions
that make up the organizational context. The higher the score, the
better your organization is doing about these four crucial functions.

The three issues concerning change, results, and teamwork are all
focused in the concept of organizational culture. To see how transformational leaders deal with—actually construct—the organizational context, we need to look more closely at the nature of culture.

Culture Is the Key

The fourth function, culture, is so important because it has tremendous effects on the other three functions. Culture determines the way the other functions are carried out and how well they are performed. The organizational psychologist Edgar Schein has said that it may be that the only really important thing leaders do is construct culture. That is, leaders somehow help to define and inculcate certain shared values and beliefs among organizational members. Values define what is right or wrong, good or bad. Beliefs define what people expect to happen as a consequence of their actions. The values and beliefs shared by people in an organization are the essence of that organization's culture.

Constructing culture means defining and supporting certain values, assumptions, and beliefs. That is, we make choices in how to go about dealing with change, achieving goals, and working together. Certain values are more or less helpful in support of these key functions. That is, the assumptions one makes, the beliefs one holds, and the values one lives by make a difference in how one approaches the typical problems and issues of organizational life. Let's consider some of the values and beliefs that act in support of or in opposition to effective performance of each of the four organizational functions.

Values About Change

Consider two specific beliefs about change. The first goes like this: "We really just have to go along with outside forces; what we do can't make much of a difference." Such a belief has clear implications for action—or, rather, for inaction. After all, why bother? If people choose to do anything at all, they are likely to concentrate on maintaining the status quo. This belief leads people to take a passive approach to change.

Contrast this outlook with the belief, "We can control our own destiny." When organization members hold this belief, they will probably assume that they can influence what is going on in the organization. They believe that their actions can and will have certain desired consequences. Such persons are likely to take an active stance when confronted with the need for change.

What if our assumptions are wrong? What if we assume that we can have a great deal of influence, perhaps even control, over the environment when, in fact, we are largely at the mercy of the environment or can at best have only a slight effect on it? Assuming that we can control (or have some control) over the environment may lead us to take actions aimed at exerting such control. Similarly, assuming that we cannot control the environment is likely to lead to inaction, since any actions are, in this view, pointless.

If we assume that we can control the environment by our actions, but are wrong, we might engage in pointless activity with no positive effect. If we assume that we can't control the environment, but are wrong, we'd fail to engage in actions that could result in desirable outcomes. But these are not equivalent errors. In the first case, even if our actions are unlikely to have the hoped-for effects, they still might have *some* effects. In the second case, we know (in hindsight) that actions could have had results. It is generally better to do something rather than nothing, because action just might have a positive effect. There's even more to the advantage of action over inaction. Often, what people expect becomes more likely in fact. This is called a "self-fulfilling prophecy."

Our point, then, is that some assumptions are better than others. This is not necessarily because they are more accurate. Rather, it is because these better assumptions inspire hope and a willingness to act, even in circumstances in which one's actions might, in an objective sense, seem unlikely to lead to positive outcomes.

In Chapter Four we saw that believing we control our own fate can be beneficial even when not, objectively, accurate. Some assumptions, based on values or beliefs, are more likely to result in effective organizational functioning, even if the assumptions aren't correct.

Beliefs concerning change and adaptation are the organizational analog of self-confidence, the belief that one's destiny is a matter of self-control. Like self-confidence, belief that we (organization members) can have some effect on our environment could lead us to act. And, even if it's unlikely, our actions just might result in positive outcomes. In contrast, it's certain that inaction will have no benefit.

Values About Goals

The subject of organizational goals is more complicated than you might think. On the surface it seems pretty obvious; an oil company's goal is to produce and sell a lot of gasoline (and make a big profit), isn't it? But while these "overt" goals are not irrelevant, we often find other, less obvious goals that are just as or even more important, if we look closely. For example, an investigative reporter recently described how the top executives of a major American oil company had the important but hidden goal of obtaining huge personal fortunes.[10] They did this through secret deals with government officials in Kazakhstan and Iran. They contrived to move oil illegally from central Asian fields through Iranian ports. Their goal was not to make more gasoline and thus earn more profits for investors. It was, simply stated, to personally benefit themselves by engaging in illicit activities. (Their partners, the dictator of Kazakhstan and government of Iran, also benefited, of course.)

The central issue about goals is really a question of values. That question was put simply and clearly by the sociologist Peter Blau, who asked *Cui bono,* which is Latin for "Who benefits?"[11] Is the aim of organizational outcomes to benefit members of the organization (individually or collectively), or is the goal to benefit clients and customers? This is a matter of choice. The choice depends on values. Is benefit to organization members valued above all else? Or, is benefit to clients and customers the primary value? Such choices are rarely acknowledged. Yet it is clear that these value choices make a difference. When goals are chosen to benefit a particular group, goal attainment strategies will be consistent with those goals.

Values About Teamwork

In any organization the work of individuals and groups must be coordinated, so that the various parts form a "whole." The need to effectively coordinate the work of individuals and teams is a basic fact of organizational life—and survival. But how the work of individuals and groups is coordinated depends on values.

For example, a value shared by most organizational members might be "everyone out for him- or herself." In that case, coordination will have to rely on various mechanisms—rules and regulations—to make sure that the overriding job gets done. Alternatively, the central value could be "we're all in this together." Coordination will be easier to attain and may rely more on informal processes. When individuals or team members don't have to be concerned about getting "stabbed in the back" or otherwise taken advantage of, they can cooperate more comfortably (and devote more energy to the work itself).

Cultural Values

Constructing the organization's culture means identifying, instilling, and supporting the sort of values that facilitate effective operation of the four functions. But how, then, is culture itself "managed" by transformational leaders? There are two parts to our answer. We deal with one part in Chapter Nine, where we will describe in detail how leaders define values, make them part of the organization's operating system, and act to support those values.

For the moment, however, let us consider the other part of the answer to how culture is managed. Transformational leaders manage culture by identifying and demonstrating the importance of shared values. These are values that everyone agrees to and that guide everyone's actions.

Of course, diversity and even disagreement can be productive. Good leaders don't instill a value that calls for everyone to be the same, to think the same way, or act the same way. Ideally, there should be an emphasis on common beliefs to guide action. But there should, at the same time, be encouragement for diverse views and approaches to problems. This approach is summarized by the saying, "Many paths but one direction." That is, it is possible to disagree with others on what course of action to take or what would work best, and to advocate for different approaches, while agreeing on the values that define common aims and orientations.

In sum, there is one overarching cultural value that any transformational leader must define and gain widespread acceptance for. That value states, in essence, that values are not debatable or individual; they are "ours," shared by all who want to be a part of the organization. "We expect everyone to stick to a common core of values and beliefs" is itself a value. This value supports and

strengthens the culture function. Other specific values support
the three remaining functions described in Table 8-2: change,
goals, and teamwork.

Of course, strong agreement on common values and beliefs
will make values and beliefs that lead to ineffective change, poor
results, and inadequate teamwork even more dysfunctional.
That's why cultural strength alone, the degree to which the members of the organization share a common set of values and beliefs,
is a poor predictor of organizational effectiveness. Shared values
and beliefs can support increased organizational effectiveness but
they can also impair effectiveness. When everyone holds to the
same flawed beliefs, their combined efforts may lead to disaster.
The consequences of a strong organizational culture depend on
the specific values and beliefs that culture is built on.

What about the specific values that define how people should
deal with change, achieve goals, or work together? Is there a set
of specific values we could list that would strengthen each of these
organizational functions? No.

Certainly some values make effective change, goal attainment,
and teamwork more likely, and other values make such effectiveness more difficult. However, no set of specific values characterizes all effective organizations. Exceptional organizations differ
widely in specific values. Still, it would surprise us to find a highly
effective organization in which the members did not share a
belief in the importance of a strong shared culture defined by certain specific values.

Summary

Culture is key to organizational functioning. The values and
beliefs generally shared by people in an organization define the
organization's culture. Some values and beliefs are more likely to
have positive effects than others. It is the role of leaders to define
and develop values and beliefs that support effective organizational functioning. Transformational leaders must develop within
their organizations a common belief in the importance of adher-
ence to this set of shared values. How do they do this? That's the
next question we'll address, in Chapter Nine.

NINE

How Transformational Leaders Construct the Cultural Context

When the leader knows how things happen, people deal effectively with change, with their goals, and with one another all by themselves. ·

Tao Te Ching, **Chapter 37**

Chapter Eight introduced and defined the organizational context. We described the four key functions that create the context. Finally, we focused in particular on how the organizational culture defines and maintains these functions. In this chapter we will explore just how leaders construct culture.

Three Keys to Constructing Culture

In his book *Organizational Culture and Leadership,* the noted organizational psychologist and consultant Edgar Schein identified a variety of ways that leaders construct culture.[1] He said, for example, that "what leaders pay attention to" partly determines cultural values. Some of the methods he described are, in our view, especially important. What we and Schein agree on most, however, is that leaders do not create culture in the ways popularized by many management consultants. Developing rituals and ceremonies, a strategy advanced by many consultants to top management, does not construct culture. Neither is culture defined by storytelling or identifying organizational "heros." Some see these methods as dramatic and inspiring, but we think of them as heavy-handed efforts to impose culture. Like Schein, we believe these methods may be useful for reinforcing existing cultural values. They are not, however, especially useful for creating or changing culture. How, then, do leaders go about constructing organizational culture?

There are three basic ways that leaders construct culture, that is, define values and beliefs and make them "live" in the actions of people in an organization:

- ❖ *First,* leaders (with the involvement of others) define an explicit *organizational philosophy,* a clear, brief statement of values and beliefs.

- ❖ *Next,* leaders work with others to determine *policies,* develop *programs* and institute *procedures* that put the philosophy into action.

- ❖ *Finally,* leaders *model* values and beliefs by their moment-to-moment *actions* and their consistent *practices.*

We will look at each of these three culture-building processes in more detail.

An Organizational Philosophy

Leaders work with others to define a philosophy that incorporates explicit values and beliefs. This definition should be a clear, simple, value-based statement of organizational purpose or mission that everyone understands. Formulating such a statement is, however, anything but simple.

A philosophy does not spring fully formed from the brow of the leader. Leaders must involve many others throughout the organization. They must solicit others' thoughts and ideas. In doing so, they identify important shared values. They also uncover values and beliefs that people might not realize they share. Moreover, they learn what values are absent yet necessary to sustain the sort of culture they want to build.

An organizational philosophy must also be brief. For example, Johnson & Johnson's, developed many years ago, is just one page long. It's reviewed every few years and revised to make sure it covers new developments and concerns. This updating process also reminds people of the values defined by what they call the "credo." Nevertheless, if the result was seen only in plaques hung on office walls throughout the company the effect, if any, would be slight. The next two leadership actions breathe life into the values and beliefs that define the organization's culture.

Policies and Programs

Johnson & Johnson is a diversified organization that concentrates on health care products and equipment. In September 1982 there was a terrible incident involving the company's well-known pain reliever, Tylenol. Seven people in the Chicago area died after taking Tylenol, one of the firm's most important products. Someone had put cyanide into Tylenol capsules in a number of bottles. Each bottle had been put back on the shelf in a different store.

J&J immediately removed all Tylenol from all stores in the United States. This was a costly decision. Some thought the move wasn't necessary. In fact, it turned out that this was an isolated event. No other Tylenol poisonings occurred anywhere in the United States.[2]

The organization's founder, Robert Wood Johnson, had expressed, in the credo (the company philosophy) that we mentioned above, the central concern for health of customers. This primary value was explicitly stated in the very first version of the credo; it has never changed. Clearly, the credo is not simply a statement of ideals or a plaque on the wall. It drives policy and guides crucial decisions.

In the Tylenol poisoning case quick action was possible because a policy guided the decision. That policy was based on and reflected the value of concern for health of customers. Some industry analysts were concerned that Johnson & Johnson would lose its dominant market share for non-aspirin pain relievers. Those analysts would have advised a more conservative response, perhaps taking stock off shelves only in Chicago. Indeed, for a while sales were down (especially since the company had taken the product off the market). Nevertheless, today Tylenol is not only the continued market leader, its sales volume has dramatically multiplied.

Value-based policies and programs guide actions that define and thus construct an organization's culture. Several years ago we had lunch with an individual who had recently become CEO of a small firm. He was excited about his new opportunity, especially the chance to build the sort of culture he thought would serve the firm and its clients well. He explained that he'd just been to a seminar conducted by a well-known consultant. In that seminar he'd learned how to design ceremonies and rituals that he was assured would define his organization's culture and instill the values behind it.

We listened and then asked, "John, what was the very first thing you did after accepting your position?" John thought for a moment and said, "Well, I guess the first thing was to call two people I'd worked with before, in another company. I really respected them and thought they could make important contributions working with me in this new job. So, I asked each if they would consider joining the company." We asked John why he thought they'd be so helpful. He responded that it was probably because he knew them so well that he understood not only what they could do but what they stood for. "In other words," one of us said, "you felt that you shared important values with these individuals." "Exactly!" said John.

What John had done was to select people who already shared his values and beliefs to fill key roles in the organization. Edgar Schein observes that one of the most powerful ways to define the values and beliefs that create culture is to select and hire people who share those values to begin with. We agree. This applies not just to executive roles but to positions throughout an organization. An organization's culture can be defined, in part, by hiring and promotion policies that take into account values consistent with the philosophy, not just technical knowledge and skill.

For example, if the aim is to develop effective self-managed teams, it would make sense to screen and hire employees who have strong, positive values toward teamwork. Moreover, organizational reward systems should recognize cooperation rather than emphasizing individual achievement. This is important if the value of cooperation is part of the organization's philosophy and is to become an integral part of the culture. In that case, reward systems that set employees up to compete with one another for a limited reward pool can undercut and weaken the culture.

Self-managed teams must also have access to information to operate effectively. If open information is to be an operational value, then "open book" financial and accounting policies make sense. The traditional "closed book" policy provides information only on a need-to-know basis. That's likely to prevent the value of open information from becoming an operational reality and may hamstring self-managed teamwork. The way information systems are structured will also either support or stifle this value.

Some, like our friend John, are led to believe that rites, rituals, and ceremonies designed by leaders can define an organization's culture. They think that such methods can express certain values and beliefs and encourage the organization's members to accept them. Others favor fad-like applications such as team-building training to inculcate values like cooperation and a sense that "we're all in this together."[3] But these approaches don't construct culture. Policies, programs, and organizational systems that carry out "standard operating procedures" are what really build organizational cultures. These traditional aspects of organizational operations may not be very exciting. They are, however, absolutely crucial for constructing culture.

Leadership Practices

Albert Schweitzer once said, "Example is not the main thing in influencing others . . . it is the *only* thing." Leaders inculcate values and beliefs through their own personal practices. They model organizational values and beliefs by living by them, constantly and consistently. This is one reason that the leadership behaviors we described in Chapter Two are so important. Many think of these behaviors as tools leaders use to explain their vision to followers and convince them to carry out that vision. There is some truth to this. Just as important, leaders use these behaviors to display and illustrate the values and beliefs on which visions are founded.

We began in Chapter One with an explanation of the difference between transactional (or managerial) behavior and transformational leadership. Burns, whose groundbreaking ideas are the foundation for our understanding of leadership, eventually realized that transactional and transformational leadership are not exclusive of one another.

In fact, to be an effective transformational leader, one *must* be a good manager—a transactional leader. Transformational leaders use everyday managerial activities—committee meetings, for example—as opportunities to communicate their values to others.

That is, effective leaders show how their values guide their actions. For example, in a meeting the leader may facilitate a decision-making process while making it clear that final authority and responsibility rests with the group. By doing this the leader instills the value of empowerment in what might otherwise have been nothing more than a bureaucratic process.

One of our favorite examples of a management activity used to define and express cultural values comes from a study of time use by school principals.[4] This was a research study designed to see how principals allocated their time and activities. The researchers gave participating principals beepers to carry around. The beepers went off at random (all at the same time), to get a sample of the principals' daily activities. Every time the beepers went off each principal took an index card and wrote down, briefly, what he or she was doing. At the end of each day the principals reviewed the cards and entered their activities in a journal, giving more detail.

The study lasted a week. By week's end, as you might imagine, the principals were pretty tired of recording their actions! On one day during the week the beepers went off at about 3 p.m. You can probably guess what most school principals were doing at that time of day: supervising loading of buses that take the children home. One principal wrote on the card, "Supervising bus loading." Another, however, wrote "Encouraging kids to do their homework well as they get on the school bus to go home." Both principals were carrying out management activities, and probably doing that effectively. The second, though, was doing a lot more, by overlaying a value-defining culture-building activity on the routine managerial action.

Whenever possible, transformational leaders take advantage of opportunities to use managerial actions to build culture. They do so by overlaying value-inculcating actions upon ordinary bureaucratic management activities. Without a sound base of management skill this would not be possible.

Culture: The Context Transformational Leaders Construct

The analytic approaches first defined by sociologists Max Weber and Talcott Parsons gave us the basis for understanding four organizational functions necessary for long-term survival. These are: managing change, managing results, managing coordination, and managing culture. We saw that culture is the essence of the organizational context.

The old managerial approaches to leadership, when they recognized the context at all, tried to identify the specific organizational context that called for one or another style of management. Management (or transactional leadership) is about *adapting* to the existing context. In contrast, transformational leadership is about *creating* the context.

Leaders construct cultures that foster effective management of change. They do this by defining and inculcating in organization members the belief that they can affect, if not control, their environment (which includes, for example, government regulation, market competition, and technological change). Leaders build cultures that enable the organization to achieve its goals effectively. This is done by instilling values of the importance of achievement and of meeting the needs of the customer. Effective leaders design cultures that help individuals, teams, departments, and divisions work together effectively, by sharing the value of cooperation. Finally, successful leaders create cultures that are self-sustaining, due to the strength of the above, and other, shared values.

Transformational leaders do all this by, first, defining a meaningful organizational philosophy. Such a philosophy is based on clear values, not banal slogans. They then develop policies, programs, and procedures based on the values and beliefs that underlie that philosophy. Finally, by consistent actions that are directly linked to those values and beliefs leaders show how the organizational philosophy guides their own behavior.

Leadership that matters—transformational leadership—is not about defining a goal-based "vision" and then convincing followers to do what they must to achieve the leader's goals and realize the leader's vision. That sort of leadership is transactional or managerial leadership. It is done by engaging in transactions with followers who receive (or, sometimes, are merely promised) certain rewards for achieving the leader's clearly defined goals.

Summary

Transformational leaders create organizational cultures that empower followers to achieve goals that they share. Followers "own" these goals because they have had a role in defining them— and in constructing the organization's culture. This sort of leadership matters not just because it results in organizational transformation. It also transforms individuals, followers. In Chapter Two we noted that James McGregor Burns had said that through this form of leadership both leaders and followers are raised to new heights of achievement and moral development. We will explore that transformation in more depth in the next chapter.

Chapter
TEN

Six Paradoxes of Leadership: Transforming Followers

People don't change and improve by listening to scholars . . . .
Good leaders are the best teachers, for they need followers to
teach and to serve.

                                    Tao Te Ching, **Chapters 19 and 27**

In Chapter Nine we raised the issue of how transformational leaders transform organizations. We identified three specific strategies. First, these leaders, with the involvement of followers, define key values as part of an organizational philosophy. They then design and implement organizational policies, programs, and procedures based on those values. Finally, transformational leaders model the values with their own behavior. In these ways transformational leaders, working with followers, construct an organization's culture.

Earlier, we said that transformational leaders transform people as well as organizations. In fact, transforming followers is a crucial aspect of transforming the organization. Leaders cannot engineer all of the steps in organizational transformation by themselves. For cultural transformation to be successful leaders must have the active help of many organization members. The followers must themselves have the necessary knowledge, skills, and abilities. Thus, leaders must transform followers so that followers can work with leaders to transform the organization.

Just what do we mean by "transforming followers"? How are followers transformed? From what are they transformed? And to what? These are the questions we address in this chapter.

129

The Paradoxes of Transformational Leadership

In Chapters Four, Five, Six, and Seven we identified the crucial personal characteristics required for transformational leadership: confidence, an empowerment orientation, and cognitive capability ("vision"). Transformational leaders require self-confidence; otherwise, they would never bother trying to lead. They require what we've called a "prosocial" orientation toward power and influence. That is, while they must have a strong need for power, that's not enough. They must also know how to use power and influence to attain goals that benefit others and not just themselves. Finally, transformational leaders must have vision. They must be able to see and understand complex cause-and-effect relationships that sometimes take years to work out. These requirements for transformational leadership come with certain built-in paradoxes.

In comparison, there are few paradoxes in transactional leadership. Good transactional leaders define clear tasks and goals. They contract with followers as to the payment or reward followers will receive for carrying out these tasks and reaching the defined goals. This calls for good communication skills as well as a concern for fairness. Overall, however, the requirements imposed on transformational leaders are quite different from those needed for transactional leadership.

Like transactional leaders, transformational leaders must meet certain requirements to establish effective leader-follower relationships. For transformational leaders, however, these requirements have certain paradoxical aspects. Some of these paradoxes are clear; others are harder to see. We will examine six paradoxes of transformational leadership. Each centers on the questions we just raised: What do we mean by transforming followers? How are followers transformed? From what are they transformed? And to what?

The Paradoxes of Self-Confidence

Paradox One: *Transformational leaders have a high degree of self-confidence. It is this self-confidence that enables them to act. However, if leaders rely on their own actions alone, rather than the actions of followers, they are likely to fail as leaders.*

In Chapter Six we mentioned Karl Wallenda, of the acrobat troupe "The Flying Wallendas." His inability to allow others in the troupe—his own family members—to share in the work of setting up and testing rigging may have been a central factor in his fall to his death.[1] Paradoxically, Wallenda's evident self-confidence, his insistence on doing it all himself, resulted in tragic failure.

This paradox holds true, though perhaps in less dramatic ways, in most organizations. Leaders who insist on trying to "do it all" almost inevitably burn out. This is no surprise; in complex organizations goals and results are achieved through the efforts of many people, not by a leader who does it all. The challenge of leadership is not to "do it" but to enable others to act, to get things done.

How can a leader enable followers to act, and act effectively? In Chapter Six we showed that leaders are not likely to act unless they believe that their actions will yield results. Similarly, followers are unlikely to take actions if they do not have the conviction that the outcomes are under their control. How do followers come to possess the self-confidence that enables them to take effective action?

We find that leaders provide the opportunities for followers to learn that they can act to control outcomes. Peter Senge has observed that an important new role for leaders is that of *teacher.*[2] This means that leaders must teach followers that their actions can produce results, that followers can control their actions and outcomes. How do leaders do this?

One common notion is that a person develops confidence and self-esteem by hearing that he or she can do it, that she or he is capable and can succeed. But this sort of inspirational encouragement does not really produce confident followers.[3] Leaders teach self-confidence through actions, not just words. They develop confidence in followers by creating opportunities for followers to do so. It is only through real experience that followers gain this crucial sense of self-confidence.

Leaders design experiences for followers in three major ways. First, leaders provide opportunities for training, through traditional training and development activities. This gives followers the knowledge and skills needed to build confidence through the experience of success.

Second, leaders carefully structure what might be called "learning assignments." These are challenging assignments that the leader knows the follower is able to complete successfully (though perhaps with assistance or coaching). By doing and succeeding, followers develop a personal sense of competence and capability—they become more confident in themselves. Followers come to believe that they can accomplish even difficult assignments.

Finally, leaders work one-on-one with followers. In these coaching sessions they guide followers in solving a problem or accomplishing a task. By successfully achieving a specific, difficult goal the follower becomes more confident of being able to do so. The next time, she or he can take on the problem alone, rather than with the guidance of a coach.

In sum, leaders become teachers when they create opportunities for followers to engage in meaningful tasks in which they, the followers, achieve success. This means that the leader must make sure that the follower has the ability to succeed, as well as the knowledge and resources needed to do the job. It is the direct and real experience of success, of acting and achieving, that builds confidence.

So there is a second, and more subtle, paradox of confident leadership:

Paradox Two: *Transformational leaders must have a high degree of self-confidence if they are to take effective leadership action. Even more important, they need such confidence to instill self-confidence in followers who carry out organizational tasks and achieve organizational goals.*

Several years ago we were privileged to meet, in Rangoon, Burma, with Aung San Suu Kyi, who was awarded the 1991 Nobel Peace Prize for her determined efforts to bring democracy to her native land. Despite being held under house arrest since the victory of her party, the National League for Democracy, in the 1990 elections, she has worked tirelessly to develop the basis for a democratic Burma.

In our interview we asked Suu Kyi how she could develop in her followers the confidence and capability for self-direction that are necessary in a democracy, when their activities were so limited and circumscribed by Burma's military rulers. She pointed out that such capabilities were being developed through the actions that followers were empowered to take. Often, she said, these actions were small, such as delivering messages to small groups in the countryside or simply opening the NLD office daily. Other actions involved organizing and managing arrangements for the weekly speeches she delivered from inside the gates of her home prison to crowds that would gather outside in the streets to see and hear her.

None of these empowered actions were without danger. The State Law and Order Restoration Council—SLORC, the arm of Burma's military dictators—might arrest and imprison them at any moment, and had done so on many occasions. However, she explained, responsibility for effectively and successfully carrying out even these small—though often dangerous—actions would help build in followers the confidence to take more important actions on their own initiative, when the time came.

Transformational leaders don't need self-confidence simply to act, to achieve successful outcomes. They need it to be able to teach self-confidence to others. Successful leaders are those who teach followers to be confident so that they (followers) can get the job done and be successful. Teaching people that they can control their own destinies can accomplish great things in organizations. Only those who have learned this lesson themselves can teach it to others.

The Paradoxes of Power

Truly central to transformational leadership is the way these leaders understand and use power and influence. We saw in Chapters Four and Five that leaders invariably have a high need for power. We also saw that this need can be expressed in either of two ways. It can come out as dominance and control over others. Or, leaders can use it to share influence with others, to achieve outcomes that benefit everyone. Thus, the most obvious paradox of power is

> **Paradox Three:** *Transformational leaders must have a high need for power. This is what motivates them to lead. However, this same need drives both a Gandhi and a Hitler.*

There is, of course, a crucial difference between the way a charismatic monster like Hitler and a transformational leader such as Gandhi use power. It has, in part, to do with the leader's role in safeguarding how power is used in the organization. Peter Senge identifies this as a new leadership role: that of *steward.*[4]

The term "steward" refers to the concept of power directed toward the service of others, not simply used to satisfy personal desires. Transformational leaders do not use power to control and dominate others. Equally important, they prevent others from using power in this dangerous and damaging way. An important aspect of the role of steward is safeguarding power, that is, preventing organizationally dysfunctional uses of power.

Transformational leaders make it difficult for individuals to gain and exercise personalized power. We have seen, in Chapter Eight, how transformational leaders construct organizational cultures. Such cultures enable organizations to adapt to change effectively, to better achieve goals, to coordinate internal operations effectively, and to sustain themselves. Sustainability also depends on preventing the sort of malignant narcissists we described in Chapter Five from getting into positions of power. Effective, sustainable cultures also have values and beliefs that work to root out such individuals. Organizational cultures constructed by transformational leaders make it difficult to gain or use power for self-aggrandizement.

Transformational leaders also act as stewards by developing in followers a prosocial power orientation. They do this by empowering them.[5] They give followers authority to accomplish defined goals—to take responsibility, to take action, and to experience success—rather than simply requiring them to behave as the leader has directed. This is part of the leader's role as teacher of confidence. But there is more to empowerment than that. By creating opportunities for followers to take *responsible* action, transformational leaders teach followers how to use power and influence in a positive way, to benefit others and not just themselves.

The experiences of and opportunities for empowerment that transformational leaders typically construct involve not just one follower but several. This sort of empowerment does not simply mean that the leader tells one follower, "You are now in charge; take control!" Rather, the leader will explain and, more important, model how to share influence, how to use power *with* instead of *over* others. The leader may even arrange to switch roles with the follower. This not only gives followers an opportunity for leadership and learning, but shows that good leadership includes good followership.

Finally, transformational leaders model self-control. That is, they show followers that having patience is both possible and desirable. They reject immediate gratification through the use of power. This way, leaders teach followers to control their impulsive needs by modeling the effective use of power and influence.

Understanding the real paradox of power, then, begins by realizing that transformational leaders use power to benefit the organization and its members, rather than to satisfy their own desires. A less obvious aspect of this paradox of power is that transformational leaders strive not merely to attain power but to "give it away." They spread power and influence throughout the organization. In this way, the organization becomes one in which everyone feels more powerful and everyone has a sense of being able to influence what happens. This sense of high control by organization members is characteristic of high-performing organizations.

Perhaps the most paradoxical aspect of power for transformational leaders is that rather than using power themselves—and in addition to simply empowering others—these leaders show others how to use power and influence in ways that benefit the organization. As stewards of power, transformational leaders recognize the importance of developing in followers the same sense of stewardship, of prosocial use of power and influence, that they have themselves.

Paradox Four: *Transformational leaders have a strong need for power. They want power to use it to benefit others and the organization, not just to benefit themselves. However, the most important way that leaders use power is to share it, by empowering followers and teaching them how to use power in organizationally productive ways.*

The Paradoxes of Thought

The third personal characteristic of transformational leaders is cognitive capability, what some call vision. This ability does not mean that leaders can predict the future. Vision does not give leaders a view of the future. Rather, it enables transformational leaders to think through ways to *construct* the future that they—and followers—want. This is why Peter Senge refers to a third and final new role of leaders as that of *architect,* designer of organizational futures.

Paradox Five: *Transformational leaders must have a high level of cognitive capability, the ability to understand complex chains of cause and effect that happen over relatively long spans of time. This is what we mean by "vision." However, they don't use this ability to create a vision that is a prediction of what will happen. Instead, they use vision to decide what actions they must take to make happen the outcomes they desire.*

In Chapter Seven we argued that organizational leadership calls for exceptional people who can envision complex patterns of events, of cause and effect, over long periods of time. This ability is not used (as some leadership writers seem to believe) to develop predictions or to construct a future image of the organization. Transformational leaders do not sell visions to followers to inspire them to act to attain these visions. The simple paradox of vision is that leaders use their cognitive ability to figure out what actions will lead to desired outcomes. However, a deeper paradox of vision is that the leader's chief role is *not* to tell followers what actions to take to produce long-range results.

If the leader's role were to develop a blueprint for the future, we would be speaking of a very different sort of leadership. It would fit not with our notion of transformational leadership. It would, however, match the view of those who think the leader's role is to come up with a personal vision. Such leaders then present that vision to followers in ways so exciting, so inspiring, that followers are motivated to do whatever they can to achieve the leader's vision. Certainly this does happen, but it is not what we mean by vision in transformational leadership.

In our view the underlying values and beliefs that shape an organization's culture guide an organizational vision. The vision, therefore, is not just the leader's. It also comes from and belongs to the members of the organization. When followers are, in part, the source of the vision, they are more willing to carry out the organization's mission and vision. But their role is not simply to carry out actions that the leader envisions. Rather, followers must themselves have adequate cognitive capability—a degree of vision sufficient to help enact and realize an organizational vision.

This is the far more subtle paradox of thought:

Paradox Six: *Transformational leaders must have a high level of cognitive capability to construct the organization's future. However, it is followers—in whom leaders help to develop increased cognitive capability—who think through, identify, and take the specific day-to-day, week-to-week, month-to-month, and even year-to-year actions that result in the desired future outcomes and results.*

Although the leader must have the vision, the cognitive capability, needed to construct the organization's future, it is followers who do the "heavy lifting." Followers must be engaged in the work of constructing the future. To do this, followers must have adequate cognitive capability. And leaders must act to develop that capability in followers.

As we have discussed, the leader's chief tool in follower development is giving followers good opportunities for experience and learning. Transformational leaders who want to get followers to become more capable of long-term planning and thinking give them assignments that last longer and are increasingly complicated. Leaders also provide opportunities for prioritizing and scheduling, over longer time spans and involving more complex circumstances. Transformational leaders will work with followers on long-term projects and leave followers alone to carry out short-term day-to-day affairs.

What About Leaders' Own Transformation?

So far we've discussed in some detail how it is that followers are, through the actions of transformational leaders, raised (as James McGregor Burns says) to new heights of achievement and moral development. What about the leaders themselves? Surely there is some need, as well as some means, for their own development.

Of course, the logic of our argument in this chapter suggests that a major means for developing transformational leaders is the process of follower development. That is, as followers develop in themselves the three personal characteristics of transformational leaders they, the followers, become leaders themselves.

Developing followers into transformational leaders is neither quick nor easy. For one thing, as followers develop leadership skills and characteristics they are likely to first focus on their own goals as achievers and managers. Transformational leaders don't just appear fully developed. And what if an organization has few or no transformational leaders to begin with? Which comes first, the chicken (the transformational leader who develops new transformational leaders) or the egg (a transformational leader who has developed from a follower)?

The development of new leaders by existing transformational leaders might be a useful long-term answer. However, it skirts the issue of what to do *now*. The immediate answer has two parts: self-development, and participation in formal leadership development programs.

Self-Development

Those who have some awareness of the nature of transformational leadership, some of the leadership skills described in Chapter Three, and a start on the personal characteristics detailed in Chapters Four through Seven are well prepared for self-development. That is, they can design opportunities for experiencing success themselves. An aspiring transformational leader may also take part in projects and work activities in which there is a need for mutual influence and a sharing of power. An explicit focus on long-term aims and outcomes will also help stretch an individual's time perspective and encourage more complex thinking and planning.

Leadership Development Programs

Books have been written advocating, criticizing, and evaluating leadership development, both in general and about specific programs. There is, however, very little solid research that tells whether or to what extent leadership development programs work. We have been involved in three rigorous research studies to examine the effects of leadership development efforts. On that basis we can offer some thoughts about developing transformational leaders.

One of these studies was conducted by our doctorial student, Brad Lafferty, at the premier training academy for U.S. Air Force officers, the Air Command and Staff College (ACSC), part of Air

University in Montgomery, Alabama.[6] This ten-month residential program centers on leadership development. No individual has ever been promoted to Air Force general staff officer without successfully completing this program. Just before our study the program had been redesigned to focus particularly on transformational leadership.

For the next several years, we administered a research-based, validated leadership assessment questionnaire, The Leadership Profile (TLP), before and after the program.[7] The results were clear: The training program did make a difference. We can say with a reasonable degree of certainty that the training caused improvement in scores on a validated transformational leadership assessment test. (In Chapter Eleven we will discuss, in more detail, research that used this test to study the relationship between transformational leadership and performance outcomes.) Moreover, these scores continued to improve when program graduates went back "on the job" (though not as much as the initial post-training improvement).[8]

Still another program we were involved in occurred over a six-year period. Each year, the Ohio Vocational Education Leadership Institute (OVELI) selected a group of 20 to 25 young people to participate in a leadership program.[9] These individuals were chosen for their potential as future leaders in the field of vocational education in Ohio. They met for one weekend a month over the course of a year. The sessions included presentations, discussions, and structured learning activities. The content dealt with a wide range of material relating to vocational education. This included, but was not limited to, transformational leadership. In the early summer the group spent ten days in Washington, D.C., learning the political ins and outs of federal programs relating to and supporting vocational education.

The training year started with a version of the same leadership assessment used in the Air Force study. In this case, however, the trainees received individual feedback reports, in a workshop held during their February weekend. They received feedback based on assessment data from others, as well as a self-assessment questionnaire. This was the only one of their sessions that was explicitly focused on transformational leadership (although participants kept journals and engaged in planned personal activities and goals related to leadership).

At year's end trainees again completed the assessment. We participated in this program for five years in a row, so we collected a considerable amount of data. The research design was similar to the one we used in the Air Force study: Each successive group served as a "control" on the preceding training group. This allowed us to make strong conclusions about the effects of the training.

The results showed that the program did cause significant increases in transformational leadership, though these were not as great as for the Air Force officers. But the most interesting result was that the trainees whose self-assessment scores initially differed from the assessments of others were, at the end of the year, much closer in agreement. (The increase was statistically significant.) By year's end the trainees had made important gains in "self-awareness."

Self-awareness is a central element of emotional intelligence, or "EI." This concept was pioneered by Daniel Goleman, who defines EI as "the capacity for recognizing our own feelings and those of others, for motivating ourselves, and for managing emotions well in ourselves and in our relationships."[10] Considerable research suggests that EI is crucially important for effectiveness in life in general as well as for leaders in organizations.[11]

Our research study demonstrated that key aspects of transformational leadership can be developed. The gains were, moreover, directly attributable to a training program. Important aspects of the OVELI program were the inclusion of specific leadership assessment feedback to participants, the long-term program design, and the opportunity for reflection.

But is it the feedback that really made the difference? Jim Stryker tried to answer that with a true experiment, that is, involving random assignment of participants to experimental "treatment" and "control" groups.[12] In a medium-sized firm with about 120 supervisors, he divided the supervisors at random into three groups. All three groups were assessed using the same transformational leadership assessment questionnaire (the TLP) mentioned above. Stryker obtained both self-assessments and assessments by others, of all the supervisors in the study.

The first group received a detailed leadership assessment feedback report in a half-day workshop. Each participant also received brief but individual and private counseling. The second group of

40 supervisors received only a written feedback report. And the third group received nothing. They were told that everyone would eventually receive personal feedback but that the feedback sessions would be staggered over several months (which was, in fact, the case). This third group served as a control on the two experimental groups. Because supervisors had been assigned to groups at random, we could assume that all three groups had started out about the same.

Three months after the initial assessment and the feedback workshops everyone was assessed again. Stryker expected that those in the group that got feedback and the workshop would improve the most. He thought that those in the feedback-only group would improve some, but not as much. He predicted that there would be no improvement for those in the group that received no feedback or training. He was wrong on all counts.

There were no changes in either of the feedback groups, with or without the training workshop. What's more, there were some slight but significant improvements among the *untrained* supervisors who got no feedback.

On further investigation, Stryker concluded that the failure to find any change as a result of training and feedback was due at least in part to top management's open lack of support for the program. Few of those in either experimental group took advantage of opportunities Stryker provided for making and acting on development plans based on the feedback. Top managers had told them not to bother! He attributed the improvements among untrained supervisors to their putting on a positive face in the absence of any evidence as to their actual leadership assessment. (These supervisors knew, of course, that other supervisors had received feedback and, in some cases, training workshops.)

Keys to Successful Leadership Development Programs

Two of the three programs we studied had clear success, in terms of improvements in transformational leadership that we can attribute directly to the training. What made these programs work while the third, which more closely resembled traditional leadership training, failed? We think there were three factors.

Long-term learning.   Few today would argue that leadership is a simple skill easily learned in a two- or three-day workshop, much less from a four-hour briefing session. Even so, most leadership training consists of short seminars ranging from a day to a week. Stryker's study clearly demonstrated the folly of trying to develop leadership on a short-term one-shot basis. The results of the other two efforts we've described show that there can be substantial outcomes from long-term learning.

Work-context linkage.   One common characteristic of the two successful programs that we've described was their intense focus on the organization or the work itself. These programs focused on content, rather than on abstract concepts or general skills. Both had a strong transformational leadership element. However, the aim was not simply to become a better leader but to become a better Air Force leader or a better vocational education leader. The program that failed had very little contact time with participants. Most of the training time was spent on the basic concepts and measures rather than on what they meant in the context of the participants' own work and organization. The lesson seems clear: Effective leadership training requires a strong focus on the context and content of the leader's work and organization.

A reflective focus.   The OVELI study most clearly displays what we consider the third key to effective leadership training: a focus on increasing participants' capacity to reflect on their own leadership learning. It is no surprise that Jay Conger, when he examined a variety of executive leadership development programs, concluded that the best ones involved participants in "back home" assignments followed by additional seminars.[13] Such reflective learning happens in at least two ways. It occurs, first, in participants comparing how they see themselves to how others see them. Second, it happens as participants plan developmental activities, engage in those actions, and then observe the consequences. They can then reflect and learn from their experience. They repeat this cycle as they go from seminar activity to actual work experience to observe and reflect on outcomes and then back to seminar experiences. Leadership assessment feedback from others is an essential part of the reflective learning process. So is the link between leadership learning and the work context. And the time needed to obtain such information, from actions and from others, and to reflect and learn from it, is not short.

Summary

At the beginning of this chapter, we said that we would address several issues:

- What do we mean by transforming followers?
- How are followers transformed?
- From what are they transformed? And to what?

What we mean by transforming followers should now be clear. Followers become more self-confident. They also become more able to function at a higher level of power need development. That is, they are oriented toward the prosocial rather than the personalized use of power. Finally, followers become more able to use and expand their vision. They increase their level of cognitive capability. They can understand and enact more complicated cause-and-effect chains that result in desired outcomes.

We have also described how followers are transformed. The simple answer is "by leaders." In fact, the process is often complex and difficult. Leaders must not merely support traditional training and development opportunities. They must, themselves, construct such learning opportunities. This process enables followers to develop self-confidence; a prosocial power orientation and the skills to apply it; and, to the greatest degree possible, their cognitive capabilities.

The last two questions are really the keys. If you have been following the argument made in this chapter you will see that followers can be transformed from subordinates who take and carry out orders into self-directed leaders. A central task of transformational leaders is the transformation of followers into leaders.

The research we have mentioned in this chapter is consistent in showing that it is possible to increase individuals' capacity for transformational leadership. But we have yet to show that such leadership has any real benefit for an organization. That is the focus of the next chapter.

Chapter

ELEVEN

How Do We Know Leadership Matters? The Research Evidence

The fundamental principle works regardless of our wishes or preferences. . . . Effective leaders don't put on a show of being great but, knowing how things work, they can achieve great things.
                    Tao Te Ching, **Chapters 5 and 34**

We have until now implicitly asked you to accept the word of James McGregor Burns, and our word, as well, about the effects of transformational leadership. Burns asserted that this sort of leadership raises leaders and followers together to new heights of achievement and moral development. In prior chapters, we've tried to show what he and we mean by this.

Transformational leaders create organizational conditions in which organization members can develop their own leadership capabilities. These followers learn new behavioral skills and develop the three personal characteristics of transformational leadership within themselves. This seems to us a form of moral development. Leaders, too, develop in this process. They improve their own skills and characteristics; even more, transformational leaders develop morally, in constructing organizational cultures that benefit others. Thus they create meaning in their own lives and an organizational context in which others can make their own meaning.

What about achievement? Do transformational leaders really achieve exceptional results, not just morally but in terms of traditional, "hard" criteria of productivity and performance? Yes, they do. In this chapter we present capsule summaries of rigorous research results. We will share some examples of the bottom-line contributions that can result from effective transformational leadership.

Throughout this book we have tried to give meaningful examples of transformational leadership and its effects. We've used specific, real-life examples. We have also mentioned some of the research we and others have done. In this chapter, however, we present no stories or anecdotes. Instead, we examine solid research evidence based on sound research designs and formal statistical tests.

Our aim here is not to provide a detailed and in-depth review of all the research studies we and our associates have conducted.[1] Rather, we want to share a sample of our research results. These research outcomes show that transformational leadership is associated with various hard measures of performance.

We will discuss research done in factories, retail stores, hospitals, schools, and banks—a wide range of organizations. In all of these studies we looked for hard indicators of productivity and performance. How, you might ask, did we identify transformational leaders and assess transformational leadership? We used a leadership assessment questionnaire that we have developed and refined over two decades.

The Leadership Profile[2]

Originally we called our measure the "Leader Behavior Questionnaire," because our focus was on the specific leadership behaviors we described in Chapter Three. As we explained in that chapter, though, we soon realized that there is more to transformational leadership than certain behavioral skills and practices. Thus, we added assessments of personal characteristics. Finally, we developed measures of transactional leadership as part of a comprehensive assessment, The Leadership Profile, or TLP.

Although we continue to refine and fine-tune the TLP, we have made no major changes since 1998. The questionnaire has fifty items that form ten separate "scales." Each scale measures a particular behavior or characteristic. We have shown that the five items that make up each scale hang together well, to assess a single aspect of leadership. Moreover, the fifty items tend to sort out, statistically, into the scale categories we designed them to measure. In sum, the TLP has good psychometric properties. It is a reliable assessment instrument with evidence that it measures what it claims to.

The TLP is an example of what is commonly called a "360-degree" assessment instrument. That is, the TLP is completed by the person being assessed as well as by several others who have the opportunity and experience necessary to provide accurate observations of the person being assessed. Most of our research studies used data obtained from both the leader and from observers.

Research and Results

We will review seven studies. These are some of the most important research studies conducted using the TLP. The studies were designed and conducted by us, under our supervision or (in two cases) with our advice.[3] In each study we were looking for the relationship between transformational leadership, as assessed by the TLP, and measures of individual and organizational performance.

Leadership and Attention to Performance

You might think that if transformational leadership is related to performance, transformational leaders would be likely to pay special attention to various aspects of performance. Do transformational leaders pay more attention to things like productivity, stability, efficiency, quality, growth, morale, and profit than leaders who are not transformational? One of our students conducted a study to see if they do.[4]

He found that the more transformational leaders (those who score higher on the TLP) report that they pay attention to a larger number of performance criteria, compared to leaders who score lower on transformational leadership. This relationship was strong and statistically significant.

Of course, paying attention is one thing. Does it, however, translate into effective organizational performance? This is the question addressed by the other studies we will summarize here.

Leadership and Student Performance in High Schools

School performance is usually measured by students' scores on standardized achievement tests. A doctoral research student in California identified two groups of high schools in southern California.[5] One group of 30 schools was characterized by low scores on the California Achievement Test (CAT). This is a standardized test of student performance in reading, writing, and math that takes into account such factors as the economic status of students. The second group of 30 schools had students with high CAT scores.

The researcher used an early version of the TLP, called the Leader Behavior Questionnaire (LBQ). This assessment only measured transformational leaders' behaviors. It did not measure any of the three characteristics. Principals of the high-performance schools scored significantly higher on the transformational leadership behaviors (as defined in Chapter Three) than the principals of the low-performance schools.

This study was one of the first to show a clear and strong association between transformational leadership behavior and organizational performance outcomes. When their principal was more of a transformational leader, high school students were likely to score higher on achievement tests.

District Managers' Leadership and Performance in a Bank

Several years ago we and two colleagues conducted a research study in National Australia Bank, the largest bank in Australia. NAB has over A\$100 billion in assets and subsidiaries in the United States, the U.K., and Ireland.[6] At the time of our study the bank had 33 districts in Australia, each with a district manager. Most managers were responsible for between 5 and 12 bank branches. District managers reported to state managers. (Like the United States, Australia is divided into states; the bank had a manager for each state.)

LBQ data were collected from several of each district manager's direct reports. The group human resources manager of executive development assessed each manager's performance. This individual had access to the following information:

- the district managers' performance appraisals;
- senior bank executives' performance ratings of the district managers; and,
- the degree to which district managers' had attained specific financial performance targets.

Based on these criteria, the group human resources manager sorted the 33 district managers into four performance categories: top, upper middle, lower middle, and bottom.

We also collected data, separately, on the culture of each district, based on information from employees in district banks. We used another questionnaire, the Organizational Culture Assessment Questionnaire (OCAQ).[7] The OCAQ measures the extent to which organizational values support effective performance of the four organizational functions we described in Chapter Eight: change, goals, teamwork, and culture. Those who were asked to complete this assessment were not the individuals who gave their views about the division manager's leadership. (That reduced the chance of finding a relationship between culture and leadership that existed only as a result of the same person responding to questions about culture and about leadership.)

We have particular confidence in these results because all of the measures were independent of one another. There was no possibility that the leadership measure could affect ("contaminate") the performance assessment or the culture scores. And none of the measures were based on the reports of the leaders— the division managers—themselves. We got all our information from the leaders' superiors, from their direct reports, or from company records.

The district managers who were ranked in the top performance group not only had the highest transformational leadership behavior scores, they also received the highest organizational culture scores. Most of the differences in leadership and culture scores between performance groups were statistically significant. Higher leadership scores were always associated with higher performance ratings. Higher culture scores were always associated with higher performance ratings. Higher leadership scores were always associated with higher culture scores. In summary, we found consistent across-the-board positive relationships between transformational leadership and the leader's performance ratings, and between transformational leadership and the culture of the leader's district.

Leadership and Performance in Retail Stores

A doctoral student supervised by one of us conducted a study of the relationship between store managers' leadership and store performance. She did her research in 69 of the 72 stores in a major eastern U.S. retail chain.[8] Performance data included a measure of theft ("shrinkage") and a measure of profit that considered the store's size and budget.

There was a significant positive relationship between profit and transformational leadership behaviors (assessed using the LBQ). There was also a significant negative relationship between transformational leadership characteristics and theft. That is, the more transformational the leader, the less theft in the store. We were surprised that a more extensive pattern of relationships did not appear. However, when we looked at a subgroup of 22 managers, we found some striking results.

These 22 managers all had LBQ self-assessment scores that agreed with LBQ scores reported by others about them. In other words, these managers were the ones who understood how others saw them. They were, therefore, what we might call "self-aware." Such self-awareness is a key factor in emotional intelligence.[9]

We examined the relationships between leadership and store performance for this group of 22 self-aware managers. We found that the relationships were much stronger than the overall leadership-performance relationship for all 69 managers and stores. What's more, for this group, we found significant relationships between the *total* transformational leadership score and profit, as well as between transformational *behavior* and profit. As before, we found a significant negative relationship between transformational leadership behavior scores and theft. We also saw a significant negative relationship between transformational leadership *total* scores and theft.

This study is valuable for two reasons. First, it showed clear and strong relationships between transformational leadership and hard measures of performance in retailing. Second, the study showed that leaders' self-awareness, defined as agreement between leaders' self-perceptions and others' perceptions of the leader, is important.

CEO Leadership and Performance in Hospitals

Another of our students examined the relationship between the transformational leadership scores of CEOs of hospitals and bottom-line hospital performance measures: operating margin and the improvement in patient satisfaction scores over the previous year's scores.[10] (All the CEOs had been in their positions more than a year.)

The study included only 12 hospitals. This is a very small number of hospitals to use for a statistically rigorous study. Even so, we found a very large and statistically significant correlation between improvement in patient satisfaction and CEOs' self-reports of their transformational leadership characteristics. That is, hospitals led by CEOs with higher transformational leadership scores were also likely to have patient satisfaction scores that were on the rise. The same relationship held when the researcher examined the relationship between performance and subordinates' ratings of the CEOs' transformational leadership.

As in the study of retail stores, we looked next at the results for those CEOs whose perceptions of their own leadership were consistent with others' perceptions. We found a strong relationship between transformational leadership scores and operating margin (a financial performance measure used in nonprofit firms that is analogous to profit in for-profit organizations) for self-aware leaders (whose self-assessments agreed with others' assessments of them).

Hospitals with CEOs who scored higher on transformational leadership also had larger operating margins, a clear economic performance indicator. Because of the small number of CEOs involved, these relationships were not statistically significant. However, it was interesting to see that there was a large and statistically significant negative relationship between leadership and operating margin for those CEOs whose leadership self-assessments were inconsistent with the assessments of others. That is, CEOs who were less self-aware were significantly more likely to head hospitals with smaller operating margins.

We also examined a third performance measure, the hospital's score on the accreditation assessment administered by the national hospital accrediting agency, the Joint Commission on Accreditation of Hospital Organizations. An unacceptably low score means that the hospital loses accreditation and must cease operation. The same pattern of relationships—positive for CEOs whose perceptions were consistent with those of others and negative for those whose scores were not—held when we calculated the relationships between CEOs' leadership and the hospitals' accreditation scores.

In sum, despite the small number of CEOs and hospitals in the study, we found clear patterns of relationships between CEOs' transformational leadership and organizational performance outcome measures. Many of these relationships were statistically significant.[11]

Leadership and Performance of Engineering Development Teams

One of our doctoral students examined the performance of engineers in development teams in a large organization.[12] The team leader's superior assessed team performance. Team members assessed their team leader's leadership using the TLP.

All measures of transformational leadership behavior and transformational leadership characteristics were strongly and statistically significantly associated with team performance. The impressive pattern of relationships we found strongly suggests that transformational leadership makes a bottom-line difference in team performance.

Leadership and Fiscal Sustainability in Health Care Systems

A Case Western Reserve University doctoral student, himself CEO of a health care-related organization, examined the relationship between transformational leadership and financial sustainability. The latter is an indicator of anticipated long-term organizational survival. Eric Harter, the researcher, developed a financial database comprising 900 health care organizations that were publicly traded on the American Stock Exchange and on NASDAQ. He included an additional 20 privately held firms for which he could secure financial data. He was able to make clear judgments of fiscal sustainability for 272 of the firms, which became the target population.

A total of 35 of these organizations participated in the research study. The CEO of each, and key senior executives reporting to the CEO, completed the TLP forms. The average annual income for these firms was $658 million, ranging from $18 million to $3.8 billion. Harter classified 13 of the 35 firms as financially sustainable. He judged another 11 to be weakly sustainable. The remaining 11 were rated not sustainable, based on review of financial records.

The sustainable and weakly sustainable organizations did not differ greatly in terms of CEOs' transformational leadership scores. There were, however, clear differences between the weakly sustainable and the nonsustainable firms. CEOs of nonsustainable firms scored significantly lower on transformational leadership. That is, the CEOs of the weakly sustainable firms were significantly more transformational than their peers in nonsustainable organizations.

The differences observed were even more striking when Harter examined CEOs' transformational leadership scores as reported by executives who worked for these CEOs. There were statistically significant differences, favoring the CEOs of the more sustainable firms, on nine of the ten leadership dimensions assessed by the TLP. Moreover, these executive subordinates rated the CEOs of sustainable firms significantly higher in all three areas of leadership—transactional, transformational behavior, and transformational characteristics—compared to CEOs of nonsustainable organizations.

Finally, the researcher examined the effect of self-awareness on the relationship between transformational leadership and performance. That is, he looked at differences between how the CEOs saw themselves and how their executive subordinates saw them. For the sustainable organizations there were no differences. The CEOs were in agreement with senior executives who worked for them in how they perceived the CEOs' leadership. The results were different when CEOs' leadership self-reports were compared with assessments of them by the executives reporting to them in the nonsustainable firms. In these cases there were statistically significant differences between CEOs' leadership self-perceptions and the perceptions others had of them.

In summary, this study yielded two important results. First, the nonsustainable firms were lacking in CEOs' transformational leadership, as compared with CEOs in sustainable firms. Second, the nonsustainable firms were led by CEOs whose perceptions of their own leadership were substantially in conflict with how others saw them.

Okay, Okay, So It Works! But *How Well* Does It Work?

We have reviewed only a sample of the more than two dozen research studies we have been involved in. These studies examined relationships between leaders' transformational leadership scores and bottom-line performance criteria. They used The Leadership Profile (or its predecessor, the Leader Behavior Questionnaire) to identify a variety of statistically significant relationships between transformational leadership and measures of performance.

We found significant relationships between transformational leadership and performance of the leaders (in banks). There were also significant relationships between transformational leadership and the performance of those who reported to the leaders (in engineering development teams). Finally, we observed significant relationships between leaders' transformational leadership and their organizations' performance (in retail stores, in schools, and in hospitals). Nevertheless, although such relationships exist and are statistically significant, one might still ask whether they are important.

With a very large sample and a carefully designed and controlled research study, relationships that are quite small, even trivial, can be statistically significant. It's only reasonable to ask whether the relationships we find between transformational leadership and performance outcomes are large enough or strong enough to make much difference.

In fact, the relationships between leadership and performance outcomes that we typically find *are* big enough to be of practical use. In our report of research results we have purposely avoided presenting tables of statistics and correlation coefficients. (If you are so inclined, you can examine many of the research studies we have described, and the others listed in Appendix One and in libraries. Copies of doctoral dissertations can be purchased on the internet, and we will be glad to e-mail copies of most of the reports we have presented at national and international professional conferences.) The size of the statistically significant correlations we find is generally moderate. That means that by knowing a leader's transformational leadership score, we can predict somewhere between 10 and 30 percent of the variation in performance.

This range may seem low on the bottom end. However, think of it this way: What would it be worth if a baseball team manager could increase a player's batting average by 10 percent, say from .250 to .350 or from .300 to .400? Clearly, this would mean a significant performance gain—and advantage—for the team.

There are, of course, limits to the meaning of quantitative research results. Although we have tried hard to quantify our measures of leadership and performance, the fact is that leadership cannot be precisely quantified. For example, Max De Pree, former CEO of Herman Miller, manufacturer of high-quality office furniture, is generally considered to be a transformational leader. He certainly has been a successful one. Despite being one of the smallest firms in the Fortune 500, Herman Miller has consistently reported one of the highest returns on investment. Several years ago, De Pree wrote a well-received book, *Leadership Is an Art*.[13]

Although there are no guarantees, we know roughly how much of a difference transformational leadership makes. In terms of bottom-line measures, our conservative estimate is that transformational leadership accounts for between 5 and 25 percent of performance results. If a 5 percent profit increase seems small, note that it is about the average total profit for some market sectors (supermarkets, for example). And of course, few would argue that a 25 percent difference in profitability does not matter much.

In sum, there is clear evidence that transformational leadership matters. This is true in the scientific and academic sense. However, performance is not the only reason that transformational leadership matters. Such leadership matters because it makes a practical, meaningful difference in people's lives.

Summary

The research studies we've reviewed consistently demonstrate significant and meaningful relationships between transformational leadership and performance. These studies used many different performance measures. They covered a wide range of organizations, public and private, service and manufacturing. We found that leaders' transformational leadership scores were strongly and significantly related to performance and productivity in schools and in engineering teams. Transformational leadership was related to higher sales and less theft in retail stores. It predicted gross measures of performance in hospitals, both "soft" (patient satisfaction) and "hard" (financial performance). These wide-ranging and consistently strong relationships provide solid support to our argument that transformational leadership matters.

Before congratulating ourselves on the set of striking research results we have just reported, we should mention some limitations. None of the research studies we reviewed proves that transformational leadership *causes* high performance. It could be that high-performing groups and organizations attract transformational leaders. Nevertheless, the variety, strength, and consistency of the relationships we've identified suggest that there may well be a cause-and-effect relationship between transformational leadership and performance outcomes.

In the next chapter we will speculate a bit on just how transformational leadership matters with regard to several important issues. These issues include gender, empowerment, turbulent times, and globalization.

Chapter

TWELVE

Issues in Leadership: Implications for Transformational Leaders

There are enough "special issues" in leadership to fill several books. Certain issues, however, stand out to us. The four issues we will examine in this chapter are clearly important: women's leadership, how empowerment works, uncertainty and ambiguity in organizations, and globalization. Moreover, each has an important connection to transformational leadership.

The first issue we will discuss is gender. That is, does gender make a difference? Are male and female transformational leaders essentially the same, other than gender? Are women as effective—or, perhaps, more effective—as transformational leaders than men? We have some interesting evidence that addresses these questions.

The second issue concerns empowerment, a term that has become so common in the management literature as to be almost meaningless. Nevertheless, empowerment is a central issue for transformational leadership, as we explained in Chapters Four and Five. How an individual's need for power develops will determine, to some degree, the sort of a leader that person will be. Will a person become an exceptional transformational leader or a charismatic but narcissistic tyrant? A good manager or an empowered follower? Or, is an individual so desperate for a sense of power and control that total dependency on a leader appears a desirable option? Finally, just how does empowerment work?

Again, we have empirical data that helps explain how empowerment works for transformational leaders.

A third issue concerns the role of leaders in turbulent times. As we prepare this book for publication, the United States is coming out of a state of shock. That shock is commonly referred to as 9-11. It was the result of the first foreign attack on American soil in more than fifty years and the first attack on the continental United States since the war of 1812. We believe that transformational leaders have an important role to play in such times of great uncertainty and distressing ambiguity.

Finally, we think it is important to address the issue of leadership in the new, global economy. Globalization is one of the most important forces of the twenty-first century. In his best-selling book *The Lexus and the Olive Tree,* Pulitzer Prize-winning author and observer Thomas Friedman gives what we believe to be the best and clearest framework available for understanding globalization.[1] His key points parallel the issues central to transformational leadership. We want to share this with you because we believe it adds broader perspective to our belief about transformational leadership. Such leadership—leadership that matters— is crucially important not just for organizations but for our society in a new world economic order.

Leadership and Gender

The effective leader uses both the masculine and the feminine in nature.

                                    Tao Te Ching, **Chapter 28**

The process of revising our leadership assessment questionnaire, The Leadership Profile (TLP), gave us the opportunity to study leadership differences between men and women leaders. Those who were part of our research study were all CEOs or senior executives.[2] They were all members of the American Management Association and were CEOs or executives of mid-sized corporations.

Of 4000 male and 4000 female CEOs and senior executives randomly sampled from AMA lists approximately 750 men and 750 women returned our questionnaire. This response rate of almost 20 percent is generally considered good for a study of this sort. Moreover, this unusually large sample, in absolute numbers, increases the reliability of our results. That is, the large number of individuals involved in this research study allows us to draw strong conclusions regarding statistical significance. (At the same time, we must be wary of "differences" that, while statistically significant, are for practical purposes quite trivial.)

In addition to the TLP, the executives completed a questionnaire on androgyny, the extent to which a person balances task instrumental roles and expressive behavior. The former role activities are traditionally seen as masculine and the latter feminine. A person who balances the two role behaviors well is termed "androgynous." An emphasis on one or the other suggests a preference for stereotypically male or female roles.

Those responding to our questionnaires also reported on various personal background characteristics, such as their marital status and whether they owned the business. We also asked about characteristics of their organizations, such as type of industry and size of the organization.

Male-Female Differences in Transformational Leadership

We found only a few small differences between the transformational leadership of male and female CEOs/executives. Female CEOs and executives, for example, reported a slightly greater concern for administering rewards equitably than did their male counterparts. However, although the difference was statistically significant, it was so small as to be trivial, from a practical viewpoint. Nonetheless, equitable distribution of rewards is an important measure of managerial (transactional leadership) effectiveness.

Women also reported a significantly higher level of respect and concern for others than did the men in our study. As with reward equity, this difference, too, was quite small. Although statistically significant, the difference has no practical meaning. Yet concern for others is surely an important factor in creating meaning in organizations. Such concern, expressed by actions such as showing respect toward others in daily interactions, is one of several behaviors characteristic of effective transformational leaders.

The final significant male/female difference we found was in the extent to which leaders report that they involve and empower subordinates. Women CEOs and senior executives again scored slightly but significantly higher than men. Again, this difference was so small that it is meaningless for all practical purposes. All the same, as we detailed in Chapters Four and Nine, a positive empowerment orientation is an important personal characteristic of effective transformational leaders.

In sum, we did not find a strong pattern of differences between men and women leaders. We did observe a slight (but statistically significant) trend favoring women in areas crucial to both traditional management and to executive leadership. Our findings are consistent with past research that suggests specific ways in which women leaders act differently and more effectively than men. Such past research, however, has never shown strong differences or clear patterns of differences. Neither did our own research results.

Male-Female Differences in Androgyny

No differences were found. Although men scored slightly higher than women on task instrumental ("masculine") aspects of their roles, this difference was very small and was not statistically significant. And, although women CEOs and senior executives scored slightly higher than men on interpersonal expressiveness ("feminine") aspects of their roles, this difference, too, was insignificant. There was no difference between men and women on androgyny, the blending of the two role patterns. There was, however, a strong and highly significant positive relationship between transformational leadership scores (of men *and* of women) and androgyny, the balance of the two role sets.

Personal Characteristics

We asked a number of background questions, including one about marital status. In one of the earliest studies of transformational leaders, Bennis and Nanus[3] reported that the exceptional executives they studied displayed, in their personal relationship histories, a high degree of commitment and constancy. They suggested that this was shown by the fact that these leaders (both male and female) were invariably in long-term relationships and had been married just once. To see if this held true for the leaders we studied, we separated the men and women in our study into two groups. One group consisted of those who had been married just once and were still married. The other group included everyone else. We found that the former group—married just once—had significantly higher transformational leadership scores than the latter group. It appears that exceptional leadership goes hand-in-hand with strong personal commitment.

Gender and Ownership

After reviewing these analyses, we were disappointed that we had not identified any clear differences between male and female CEOs. We were not, however, surprised. Books on women's leadership have typically pointed out that the route to success for executive women is to learn to "play the game" as men do. In her book *The Female Advantage,* Sally Helgesen suggests that this may be changing.[4] She did extensive, in-depth observation of several women leaders and characterized them with some of the same terms we used in describing transformational leaders (caring and sharing, for example). We had expected to find results more consistent with Helgesen's, rather than the lack of real differences that we actually saw.

Dr. Cheryl Tibus, then a student, suggested another analysis.[5] She knew that there were biographical/background data attached to the questionnaire responses and suggested looking at whether ownership made a difference. We split the CEOs and executives into four groups: (1) men who owned at least 51 percent of the business; (2) all the other men in our sample (who did not have a majority ownership stake in the business); (3) women who owned at least 51 percent of the business; and, (4) women who did not have a majority ownership stake.

The results were striking: Women business owners had transformational leadership scores that were significantly higher than women who were not owners. The women business owners did not, however, differ from men business owners or men business executives. Neither did the men business owners differ greatly from men business executives.

Conclusions

These results confirm what many have suggested but rarely demonstrated with statistical proof: There *are* some differences between men and women as leaders, that is, as CEOs and senior executives. Stereotypical "differences," such as a greater tendency by women leaders to express respect and caring for others, were either absent or, when present, were trivial (even if statistically significant). However, when we accounted for *ownership*, we found an important difference. The women business owners appear to be far more capable as exceptional, transformational leaders than nonowner women business executives.

It might be that when a woman is in a position of ownership, she is better able to resist simply conforming to male leadership norms. She may then be more likely to make effective use of her transformational leadership skills and characteristics. Of course, this is just one possible interpretation. It is, however, consistent with Helgesen's argument. Regardless of the reason, our results clearly demonstrate that ownership makes a difference in the extent to which women CEOs and executives see themselves as transformational leaders.

Research, as we showed in Chapter Eleven, has consistently demonstrated significant performance advantages for organizations with transformational leaders. If women are more naturally inclined toward this form of leadership than men, organizations not owned by women might improve both leadership and performance by finding ways to draw out the transformational leadership abilities of women who are senior executives. For example, women in such positions might be guided to women business owners as models. They could then learn to exhibit a greater degree of transformational leadership. Those women leadership models might even serve as guides to better leadership for male CEOs and executives.

Empowering Leadership

Great leaders give others opportunities, not orders.
                              Tao Te Ching, **Chapter 68**

In Chapter Three we described one important transformational leadership behavior as "creating empowering opportunities." This behavior is obviously related to the leadership characteristic we explored in considerable detail in Chapter Four: empowerment orientation. It is not too strong a statement to say that the very core of transformational leadership is based on empowerment. But what *is* empowerment?

The term "empowerment" has been thrown around so much and so loosely that it has become a buzzword that can mean almost anything. If you follow the cartoon "Dilbert" you may recall that Dilbert's pointy-haired manager once declared they were all empowered. Instead of improved performance the result was confusion. Dilbert asked the boss whether empowerment meant that the employees could now exercise initiative and make decisions on their own without going through many levels of approval. The boss responded, "No, it's just a new word we use to blame you for not doing what we tell you not to do." Clearly we need a better definition of empowerment!

Thomas Jefferson said, "Educate to empower." In his view, empowerment results from teaching people things they can do to become less dependent on others and more independent. Although this idea gives us a hint of how empowerment works, it still tells us very little about the underlying nature of empowerment. Fortunately, some of our recent research does provide some clues, if not the final answer, to the question, "What is empowerment?"

In Chapter Eleven we described research that showed a clear and strong relationship between transformational leadership and team performance in engineering development teams.[6] That study also examined empowerment and how it worked.

The model of empowerment used was based on two major research streams. One stream centers on the perceptions and feelings of empowerment that individuals report. This approach concentrates on what might be called "psychological empowerment." The other approach focuses on the organizational conditions of empowerment. It deals with what we might call "structural empowerment." In the study we described, the researcher, Seth Silver, wanted to see how transformational leadership was related to each of these two aspects of empowerment. He also wished to examine the relationships between transformational leadership and the performance of individuals and teams.

You may recall that the team performance measures were based on actual performance goals and the judgments of the team leaders' managers. The team leaders completed TLP self-assessments.

They also rated individual team members' performance. Team members reported on their team leaders' transformational leadership using the TLP. They also completed empowerment questionnaires to measure their feelings of empowerment and to assess whether certain organizational empowerment structures were in place.

Ken Blanchard and his associates describe "empowerment structures" in their best-selling books *Empowerment Takes More Than a Minute* and *The Three Keys to Empowerment.*[7] The three keys explain how organizations create empowerment structures in three important ways.

First, there is extensive sharing of accurate information throughout the organization. Blanchard and his colleagues observe that people without information cannot act responsibly. In contrast, they note, people who have the information they need to make good decisions are almost compelled to act responsibly.

Second, teams, groups, departments, and divisions gain autonomy by having clearly defined boundaries. These boundaries refer, of course, to roles—who does what—and to goals (what, when, where, and how we do what we do). Boundary definitions also specify purpose—the business we're in—and values—operational guidelines.

Third, self-managed teams replace traditional hierarchical management. This sort of team operation increases team members' satisfaction and commitment. What's more, it makes decision making more efficient, reduces operating costs, and improves quality.

Three questionnaires were used in this research study. One was, of course, our TLP. The second was a validated measure of psychological empowerment. The third was a measure of the three structural empowerment dimensions developed by Ken Blanchard and his associates.

We reported in Chapter Eleven that this research study found strong and significant relationships between team leaders' transformational leadership scores and measures of team performance. There were also significant relationships between each of the three dimensions of structural empowerment and team performance.

There were few associations between psychological empowerment and team performance. Psychological empowerment was, however, significantly related to *individual* performance measures. This makes good sense. Those aspects of empowerment that relate to group structures and processes are associated with team performance. Those aspects of empowerment related to individual feelings and perceptions are associated with individual performance measures.

Both leadership and empowerment are, then, related to performance outcomes. What's more, each—leadership and empowerment—makes a separate and independent contribution to performance. What we need next is a long-term study to see if our expectation is correct—that transformational leaders construct a culture of empowerment which then leads to performance improvements.

This research shows quite clearly that transformational leadership, empowerment, and performance (individual as well as team) are all intimately interrelated. The results also show that empowerment is not a simple process and involves much more than delegating a few projects to individuals or groups.

Leadership in Turbulent Times

Effective leaders resolve tangled conflicts and calm turmoils.
                                          Tao Te Ching, **Chapter 56**

The translation of an ancient Chinese curse goes something like, "May you live in interesting times." Great uncertainty is, of course, more than just interesting. When the world seems to be changing around us, most people find that distressing—and often depressing, as well. What does leadership have to do with this? Everything.

Leaders reduce uncertainty. They make the world more clear and less ambiguous.[8] There are two basic ways to do this. One way is for the leader to tell people what to do (and what not to do), and to enforce those orders with rewards or sanctions. This may result in more predictable patterns of behavior by followers and, overall, less uncertainty in the organization. This strategy, however, relies on the leader to tell followers what is correct and what is not. Leaders must define for followers what actions are desirable and what actions to avoid. Finally, leaders have to define and administer consequences—rewards or punishments—for correct and incorrect, for desirable and undesirable, actions. This does make the situation less ambiguous—as long as the leader gives directions and ensures compliance.

Transformational leaders use a different approach to reduce uncertainty and make organizational situations less ambiguous. As we detailed in Chapter Nine, transformational leaders add certainty to the context by working to define clear, shared values, beliefs, and norms of behavior. That is, they construct organizational culture.

Values tell us what is right and wrong. Beliefs are summaries of cause and effect; that is, they remind us what is likely to happen when we act in certain ways. Norms simply state expected standards of overt behavior. When people have shared values to guide actions, commonly held beliefs that outline consequences of actions, and clear standards of behavior, the way they act will be far more predictable than when such values, beliefs, and norms are absent.

What's the difference between this approach and the first approach we described? Aren't they essentially similar? Not really. Transformational leaders don't have to tell followers what actions are "right" and "wrong" or "correct" and "incorrect." They work with followers to develop clear shared values. It is those values that guide behavior, not the leader's orders. Transformational leaders don't simply impose the values that define an organization's culture. They derive values collaboratively, with followers, and with recognition of the organizational context.

To make this work, though, followers must not only share the values, beliefs, and norms that determine correct action. Followers must be empowered to act. So, rather than leaders monitoring followers' actions and then rewarding correct actions and punishing wrong actions, followers become responsible for their actions.

The approach transformational leaders take to reduce uncertainty is more efficient than the other "command and control" approach we described. The transformational leader does not have to be a constant monitor and enforcer. The approach is also more effective. This is because much uncertainty arises from external events and from pressures outside an organization. Within an organization, systems can be designed to prevent undesired variability. This is the essence of "total quality management."[9] Well-designed technical control systems can, for example, monitor and correct undesired technical variation. External change is another matter. Such variability is often difficult to predict and sometimes impossible to control.

Leaders using the first approach we defined, giving and enforcing orders, must constantly be alert to factors outside the organization that could require major change. Competitors may develop new and more effective marketing strategies that have to be countered. New technological innovations may make current processes less efficient and more costly than what competitors are doing. Technological advances may even make products obsolete before you know it. It's asking a lot for a leader—or even a few people at the top—to attend to all these changes and determine what to do.

Transformational leaders have a clear advantage over those using other leadership approaches. That's because everyone in the organization, not just the leader or a small top-level group, can attend to external change and its effects. People are likely to come to similar conclusions because shared values and beliefs guide them. They can figure out for themselves what the right actions are; they don't need to be told. And they are likely to take those actions because they have been empowered to do so.

Transformational leadership is about dealing with and reducing uncertainty. Its aim is to decrease the ambiguity of life in organizations. It is, then, easy to see why transformational leadership matters.

Transformational Leadership and Globalization

We are all part of the same one world; we may appear separate but it's an illusion.

Tao Te Ching, **Chapter 39**

More than thirty years ago, the influential media analyst Marshall McLuhan observed that we live in a "global village." The truth and importance of that observation are only now becoming evident.[10] Events occurring halfway around the world—in Afghanistan, for example—can have direct impact on the lives of ordinary people in New York City. Thomas Friedman has said,

"What is new today is the degree and intensity with which the world is being tied together into a single globalized marketplace and village."[11]

Friedman argues that this is happening as a direct consequence of three specific "processes of democratization." What he means is that people throughout the world have, today, much greater access to three crucial resources: information, finance, and technology. We will define each of these processes. Then we will explain how they relate to transformational leadership.

Democratization of Information

In the global economy information is cheap, widely available, and cannot be limited or easily controlled by governments. In Afghanistan the former Taliban government did control information, but only by destroying all satellite dishes and killing those who had them. This was a draconian control method, but no other methods work anymore. People can no longer be kept in ignorance without resorting to truly extreme methods.

This is an important lesson for transformational leadership because such leadership is based on empowerment and the first key to empowerment is access to information. The global process of democratization of information is an important force supporting the spread of transformational leadership, leadership that by design empowers people. Democratization of information also makes transformational leadership even more effective within an organization.

Democratization of Finance

Markets have become far more open, globally. In the past many people, groups, and even nations were excluded from participating in markets because they could not get financing; they were considered poor risks. Now, however, they are able to become active players on the world economic stage. Friedman points out that, today, anyone with a credit card can start a new company almost overnight, at low cost, and be a global competitor.

The democratization of finance is relevant to transformational leaders not only because it allows them to found new companies. This process also gives leaders the opportunity to obtain funding for organizational activities that might not have been possible otherwise.

Aaron Feuerstein heads Malden Mills, manufacturer of PolarTec, a high-quality insulating fleece used in outdoor clothing. We interviewed him in depth a few years ago and concluded that he is an excellent example of a transformational leader. A dramatic illustration of this is what he did when his plant burned down several years ago. Feuerstein could have taken the insurance money, retired, and closed down, living out the rest of his life as a multimillionaire. But Malden Mills is the most important employer in the town of Lawrence, Massachusetts. So here is what Feuerstein did.

First, he kept all employees on the payroll for months, as plans were made for rebuilding. (We noted this in Chapter Three, as an example of one specific type of transformational leadership behavior: caring.) Malden Mills was a family owned firm. In past times it might have been difficult or impossible to obtain the financing needed to rebuild. The new economy, however, made it relatively easy for Feuerstein to obtain financing from firms such as GE Capital (now one of the largest financial organizations in the world), and he built an expanded plant.

Recently, due to a variety of economic factors, Malden Mills was pushed to the wall. Sales were down because a number of pre-fire customers had found new suppliers while the plant was closed, and never came back to Malden Mills. The company was unable to meet its debts. The lenders, however, did not foreclose. Instead, they called for organizational restructuring, under Feuerstein's leadership, and offered additional financing.

Democratization of Technology

Like information, advanced technology has become very cheap. And like financing, it is easily accessible. The inexpensive computer used by a schoolchild today is more powerful than the most powerful computer that existed twenty years ago. Many home computers can manage the information system needs of a large organization. Small and relatively poor organizations throughout the world are no longer at as great a disadvantage in comparison to large, rich firms in the United States.

Friedman points out that with a single computer, plus a credit card (financing) and a phone line (access to information), anyone can start a business just about anywhere and be competitive with industry giants. But, from our perspective, it is not just the entrepreneurial leader for whom democratization of technology is important. Cheap and available technology gives transformational leaders the ability to better use information within their organizations. Cheap and accessible advanced technology enables transformational leaders to empower organization members more effectively than ever.

Transformational Leadership in the Global Economy

Friedman identified three democratizations: democratization of information, finance, and technology. They are important for transformational leaders because they enable organizations to more easily compete in the global marketplace. The research we reviewed in Chapter Eleven showed that organizations with more transformational leaders are also more effective than organizations with leaders who are less transformational. Thus, the processes of democratization in the global economy should make it more likely that such organizations will be among the winners in global competition.

An underlying reason that the three democratizations are important for transformational leaders is that these changes enable such leaders to use information more effectively to empower people in the organization. The three democratizations transform the way information can be accessed and used. Thus they are an important new source of support for transformational leaders.

Research has demonstrated that organizations can have more or less total influence. In other words, influence is not a "fixed pie" to be divided. Instead, influence can expand—or contract—throughout an organization.[12] Organizations with more influence are, overall, more productive. Transformational leaders empower organization members, giving everyone in the organization more influence and say over operations. As a result, transformational leaders make their organizations more effective, that is, more productive and more profitable.

Summary

In this chapter we've raised several important issues. We have shown how transformational leadership, leadership that matters, addresses or relates to each of these issues. For the most part, though, more thought and action is needed with respect to each of the issues we've discussed.

There are, for example, implications that must be further developed about ways to better use women's transformational leadership abilities. Empowerment, which is at the core of transformational leadership, is more complex than has been thought. Developing a sense of empowerment on the part of women leaders may mean finding ways to make more women owners as well as executives.

Developing a sense of empowerment among followers requires more than just delegating responsibility. Transformational leaders must create opportunities for followers to learn that they can successfully deal with challenges. Making empowerment work also requires certain empowering structures. Globalization and democratization of information, finance, and technology give transformational leaders new tools for empowering followers. Empowering followers is the ultimate tool for managing in an uncertain world and reducing uncertainty to tolerable levels within the organization.

Research tells us that organizations do not need transformational leadership to survive, although organizations with transformational leaders are more likely to survive. Organizations can be productive and profitable without transformational leaders—but organizations with transformational leaders are likely to be far more profitable and productive.[13] The issues and related changes that we have described in this chapter may further increase the relative advantage and benefit of transformational leadership. Transformational leadership may, then, become even more important a factor for organizational productivity, performance, and perhaps even survival.

THIRTEEN

Leadership That Matters: A New Synthesis

When people forget the principle of how things work they are faced with paradoxes. . . . Understanding the way things happen resolves paradoxes.

Tao Te Ching, Chapters 18 and 21

Although we have only begun our journey of a thousand miles, we believe that we've taken several important beginning steps. Those who write about leadership, researchers and scholars as well as popular authors and consultants, have many disagreements. These quarrels are sometimes vehement. However, we see most such differences as superficial. Our understanding of leadership points to a fundamental, underlying agreement, which we've called the "new paradigm" of transformational leadership.

In Chapter Three we expressed dissatisfaction with the notion of transformational leadership as a set of behavioral skills. As we looked for other answers, we began to see more of the underlying nature of transformational leadership. Our explorations led us to examine the personal characteristics of the leader (Chapters Four, Five, Six, and Seven). We then added to our approach an understanding of the situation, of leadership in context (Chapter Eight).

In Chapter Nine we examined how leaders transform followers. This line of reasoning helped us begin to understand how, as Lao Tzu observed, leadership is mainly about knowing how to follow.[1] That is, leadership and followership are two aspects of a single relationship. Organizational psychologist Edwin Hollander, among others, has noted that leadership is but one side of the leader-follower relationship.[2] One can't really understand leadership without understanding followership.

Are we alone in "discovering" what transformational leadership is really about? Are the behaviors and personal characteristics that are its elements our unique insights? Has no one else noticed the way transformational leadership works organizationally, that is, by constructing culture? Of course not. We based our ideas about transformational leadership behaviors on the research of Bennis and Nanus, and of Kouzes and Posner. We identified transformational leaders' personal characteristics in the work of McClelland, House, Bandura, Rotter, Seligman, Jaques, and Streufert. Our ideas about culture derive from classical sociological theory—Weber and Parsons—as well as from the more recent organizational applications of Schein and others.

In Chapter One we quoted Bennis and Nanus, who said, "Multiple interpretations of leadership exist, each providing a sliver of insight but each remaining an incomplete and wholly inadequate explanation." In personal discussion with us, Bennis once commented that each leadership scholar tries to hold his or her sliver close. Each pretends that it is all there is to know. Each insists that it is all one need know about leadership. However, when we looked across the various theories and approaches, we could see the parts that completed the picture. What's more, we could see the overlaps and common elements. Let's briefly review the major approaches and their elements. We'll then look for common themes.

Approaches to Transformational Leadership

McClelland's "Leader Motive Pattern" and House's "Charismatic Leadership"

We devoted considerable attention in Chapters Four and Five to the work of David McClelland on the leader's high *need for power.* We used and expanded his framework on the stages of power need development. McClelland also observed that the "leadership motive pattern" included a high degree of "impulse control." Effective leaders are able to postpone their desire for immediate gratification of needs.[3] One reason for this ability is that they typically have a long-term time perspective. That suggested to us the work of Jaques and others on cognitive capability, a factor not considered by McClelland or House. McClelland did not develop his work into a full-blown leadership approach; his focus was always on power.

House, however—and later his associate Boas Shamir—did develop a formal theory of leadership. They based their approach partly on the earlier work of McClelland and his associates. Like McClelland, House pointed to the transformational leader's high power need. House also noted these leaders' high self-confidence and development of a vision. Later, Shamir formally added the idea of self-efficacy to the theory. However, neither House nor Shamir, nor their associates, formally incorporated the notion of a leader's cognitive ability into their approaches.

House did identify some specific behaviors used by transformational leaders. This includes exceptional and striking communication by the leader, to arouse followers' motivation to carry out a common vision. Transformational leaders also model self-sacrifice that is aimed at attaining the vision. They express clear, specific, and high expectations of followers. At the same time, they show confidence in followers' ability to achieve those goals and empower followers to do so. And, overall, transformational leaders are careful to model behavior that is consistent with the vision.[4]

McClelland and his associates found that effective leaders know how to use power and influence in positive, "prosocial" ways. They use power to empower others to achieve exceptional results. House and his associates didn't disagree. They recognized how important the leader's personal character is, that is, the leader's need for power. But they also focused on leaders' behavior.

House and his colleagues focused on how leaders effectively motivate followers. For example, when action is needed to confront and battle a competitor, effective leaders arouse followers' need for power. And when followers must exert exceptional efforts to attain difficult goals, leaders instead arouse followers' need for achievement.

In later work with Shamir, House and others added a focus on leaders' development of followers. Transformational leaders develop followers' self-concept through followers' internalization of values and increased self-efficacy.[5]

Like McClelland before them, House and his associates didn't include the leader's cognitive ability in their approach. In their theory, "vision" is simply an ideal organizational goal or condition. They didn't relate vision to the leader's thinking skill or cognitive ability. Neither did they incorporate a focus on the organizational context of leadership or the leader's role in constructing that context.

More than a quarter-century ago McClelland presented strong research evidence to show that the leadership motive pattern is associated with high performance. The research of House and his associates is equally well designed but involves many more measures. The results are generally supportive but complex.

Key Concepts
Behaviors
- communication: defining a "vision"
- creating empowering opportunities

Characteristics
- self-efficacy/self-confidence
- empowerment (need for power)

Bennis and Nanus: The Strategies for Taking Charge

In an article published before their book, Bennis identified five "competencies" or behaviors of transformational leaders. These are: management of attention, management of communication, management of trust, management of respect, and management of risk. In their book, Bennis and Nanus revised these into four "strategies." The strategies are: attention through vision; meaning through communication; trust through positioning (actions that implement the vision); and, deployment of self (knowing and nurturing one's strengths and making sure they fit with the organization's needs).

Their fourth strategy, deployment of self, also involves positive self-regard (or self-confidence) and willingness to risk success (as opposed to fearing failure). Bennis and Nanus said that empowerment is the central focus and aim of transformational leadership. That is, transformational leaders empower followers to realize the vision. All of this is worked out as leaders design and construct what Bennis and Nanus called "social architecture" and others refer to as "culture."

Bennis and Nanus developed their model on the basis of in-depth interviews with exceptional leaders. Thus, there is an obvious association between their approach and leadership effectiveness. They have not, however, conducted research designed to test their model.

Key Concepts
Behaviors
- communication
- trust
- respect/caring for others
- creating opportunities through "risk"

Characteristics
- self-confidence
- empowerment
- vision

Context
- culture

Bass and Associates: Performance Beyond Expectations

This approach is the most widely known among leadership researchers (although Kouzes and Posner's model is probably more popular among practitioners). Bass' theory centers on a measure these researchers used to call charisma but now term "idealized influence." The three other elements of transformational leadership defined by Bass and his colleagues are: individualized consideration (caring for followers personally); inspiration (inspiring communication of a vision); and, intellectual stimulation (leaders' actions to stimulate followers' thinking). According to this approach, leaders strive to motivate followers to perform beyond expectations. Bass also considered good management (transactional leadership) to be important, and included measures of it in his model.

Bass' approach emphasizes the charismatic leader's skill at creating a charismatic impression among followers.[6] Bass' approach does not, however, include the behavioral skills identified by Bennis and Nanus, Kouzes and Posner, or ourselves. Bass' theory does not, for example, include behaviors such as consistency to develop trust, or creating empowering opportunities.

Despite the apparent inconsistency between Bass' and various other approaches, there are some important similarities. Communication of a vision, for example, is included, as it is in other theories and models. So is the expression of personal concern for followers, which Bass called "individualized consideration."

Bass' approach has guided extensive research, much of which is supportive of the model. There is strong evidence that leaders who score higher on Bass' Multifactor Leadership Questionnaire (MLQ), which measures his four key dimensions, achieve higher performance outcomes. (In many of those studies, however, the measure of performance was the subjective report of those who rated the leader.)

Key Concepts
Behaviors
- actions that produce feelings of charisma (toward the leader) in followers
- inspiring communication of a vision
- individual consideration (caring)
- intellectual stimulation

Jaques' "Stratified Systems Theory" and Streufert's "Cognitive Complexity"— Leadership as Cognitive Capacity

These researchers have not worked together, but their work is similar, focused on the nature of vision, and is mutually supportive.[7] Both researchers included in their definitions of vision the ability to think through and understand complex cause-and-effect chains over time. Jaques uses the term *cognitive capability* to refer to this concept, while Streufert calls it *cognitive capability*. A high degree of this sort of thinking ability is crucial for leaders.

Without high cognitive complexity, leaders could not develop practical long-term plans of action that involve various parts of a large organization. This does not mean having a step-by-step blueprint. Effective leaders don't get locked into a fixed course of action, because they can manage a lot of information and quickly grasp relationships among rapidly changing events. According to Daniel Goleman (who coined the term *emotional intelligence*), Streufert describes executives with a low degree of cognitive complexity as individuals who see problems in isolation from each other. They may, for example, hold rigidly to a single overriding goal (such as profit), to the detriment of other important goals.[8]

Executives with greater cognitive complexity are able to confront the complexities that exist even in small problems. They plan extensively and make connections among decisions. Sometimes they even orchestrate an entire set and sequence of decisions, toward a single crucial action. Streufert called this "multidimensional thinking." This means not only considering the long-term consequences of actions but seeing multiple connections among actions.[9] Multidimensional thinking is especially important when the environment is very uncertain. It can also be crucial at the top levels of an organization, where the leader's decisions can make a great difference.[10]

Jaques' approach differs from Streufert's primarily in that Jaques put forth a comprehensive theory and model of the organization, which he called "stratified systems theory." Jaques pointed out that leaders at each level of the hierarchy must have a degree of cognitive capability that matches the complexity requirement of their position. Like Streufert, Jaques noted that because positions at higher levels are increasingly complex, they call for leaders with greater cognitive capability.

Streufert gave evidence that individuals with higher cognitive complexity make better decisions. Jaques took this further by showing that leaders whose cognitive capability matches the requirements of their organizational position are more effective.

It is not fair to consider Streufert's approach as a complete theory of leadership, as Jaques' approach is. However, while Jaques' theory is comprehensive, it neglects the emotional aspect of leadership (emphasized by McClelland and by House) that centers on power and empowerment. Jaques considered emotion and affect irrelevant for leaders. (Similarly, House saw the cognitive aspect of leadership as relatively unimportant.) Although Jaques did note that various behavioral skills are useful, his approach gives such skills a minor role. He did not emphasize the transformational behaviors identified by ourselves and others.

Jaques' model is based on extensive organizational research. Substantial data obtained in British government organizations support his approach.

Key Concept
Characteristic
  • vision (cognitive ability)

Conger and Kanungo: Charismatic Leadership Behavior

Conger and Kanungo asserted that transformational leaders engage in a set of behaviors designed to produce charismatic feelings in followers. They defined charisma as transformational leadership seen from the followers' viewpoint. When leaders are seen as charismatic, Conger and Kanungo believe followers will be more likely to act in ways consistent with the leader's vision.[11]

They constructed the C-K questionnaire to identify and reliably measure a set of leadership behaviors they believe result in charismatic feelings on the part of followers. It measures six dimensions of leadership behavior. They are: articulation of a vision; environmental sensitivity; unconventional behavior; taking risks; sensitivity to followers' needs; and, actions against the status quo. The questionnaire is relatively well developed, in terms of reliability and internal consistency. There has, however, been little research to test whether leaders who score high (on the questionnaire) achieve exceptional performance outcomes.

Key Concepts
Behaviors
    • articulation of a vision (communication)
    • going against the status quo
    • taking risks
    • unconventional behavior
    • sensitivity to followers' needs (caring)
Characteristic
    • sensitivity to factors in the environment

Kouzes and Posner: The Leadership Challenge

These researchers analyzed hundreds of "best practices" cases prepared by managers, to identify specific best practices. They developed a questionnaire, the Leadership Practices Inventory, to assess the five practices they found characteristic of exceptionally effective leadership. Each practice is composed of two leadership behaviors.[12]

The first practice is called "challenging the process." It consists of (a) searching for opportunities and (b) taking sensible risks. Second is "inspiring a shared vision." This is made up of (a) constructing a future vision and (b) building follower support. The third practice is "enabling others to act." It includes (a) fostering collaboration and (b) supporting followers' personal development. Fourth is "modeling the way." Leaders do this by (a) setting examples and (b) focusing on accomplishments. The fifth practice is "encouraging the heart." This means (a) recognizing followers' contributions and (b) celebrating their achievements.

Kouzes and Posner developed their approach out of empirical case data provided by leaders. Its great strength is in its concrete basis of evidence. The weakness of their approach, however, is that despite clear behavioral detail there is no equally clear theory base. That is, "The Leadership Challenge" offers no framework within which we can understand transformational leadership.

There has been some research on Kouzes and Posner's approach, using their assessment questionnaire. Results seem mixed, though at least somewhat supportive of the conclusion that use of the five practices is associated with high performance outcomes.

Key Concepts
Behaviors
- searching for opportunities
- taking sensible risks
- communicating the vision
- empowering followers
- developing followers
- modeling
- recognizing accomplishments
Characteristic
- vision

Kotter and Heskett: Leadership and Culture

These researchers studied more than 200 organizations, focusing on public records of profit and performance. They concluded that leadership associated with high performance outcomes is based on leaders' influence on organizational culture.[13] Kotter and Heskett identified four "action strategies" leaders use to construct culture.

These are: creating a need for change; developing a direction-setting vision; communication of the vision; and, encouraging subordinate managers to take leadership action to implement the leader's vision.

Kotter and Heskett used extensive data to identify the strategies and link them to organizational culture. However, they conducted no further research to test their model.

Key Concepts
  Behaviors
  - energizing followers with a need for change
  - including followers' needs in the vision
  - challenging the status quo
  - communicating the vision
  - modeling the vision
  - empowering followers to act
  Characteristic
  - vision

Common Elements Among Transformational Approaches

We have listed above the key concepts in the seven approaches to transformational leadership that we briefly reviewed. Table 13-1 shows how these approaches and elements fit with our own model of *Leadership That Matters*. That is, in Table 13-1 we identify common elements across the approaches.

As you can see, our approach draws together elements of each of the seven approaches. But only two of them—Bennis and Nanus, and Kotter and Heskett—have elements in all three of the key areas of behavior, personal characteristics, and organizational context (culture). And, of these two, only Bennis and Nanus cover all eight of the themes central to our approach, *Leadership That Matters.*They include our four behaviors (though not always with exactly the same definitions), our three personal characteristics, and our focus on the organizational context.

Of course, this is not all that surprising; after all, our own approach is grounded in the work of Bennis and Nanus. However, heeding their advice, we have drawn on many other approaches and incorporated elements of those approaches into our own. Our

TABLE 13-1	Elements Common to Various Approaches							
	Leadership That Matters	1	2	3	4	5	6	7
Behaviors	Communication	X	X	X		X	X	X
	Trust		X				X	
	Caring		X	X		X	X	
	Creating Opportunities ("risk")		X			X	X	X
Characteristics	Self-Confidence	X	X				X	
	Empowerment Orientation	X	X				X	X
	Vision (Cognitive Capability)	X	X	X	X	X	X	X
	Organizational Context (culture)		X					X

[1]House/McClelland   [5]Conger & Kanungo
[2]Bennis & Nanus   [6]Kouzes & Posner
[3]Bass   [7]Kotter & Heskett
[4]Jaques/Streufert

Note: An "x" indicates that the numbered approach in that column includes the element of *Leadership That Matters* in that row.

description of empowerment, for example, unlike that of Bennis and Nanus, is based on the work of McClelland, and our discussion of vision draws on the research of Jaques and of Streufert.

Transformational Leadership: A New Synthesis

Table 13-1 shows that, taken together, the seven transformational leadership approaches briefly reviewed in this chapter include many of the eight elements that are important parts of our own model of *Leadership That Matters*. All seven approaches deal in one way or another with "vision." The term is, of course, defined in somewhat different ways in these seven approaches. Even so, vision is clearly an important and perhaps basic element of any transformational leadership approach.

Two other elements of *Leadership That Matters,* elements that we've called personal characteristics of transformational leaders, are self-confidence and an orientation toward empowering others. Each of these characteristics is included in at least three of the approaches in Table 13-1. This suggests that these two elements are considered to be important by several transformational leadership theorists. In fact, it's clear that all three of the personal characteristics are common elements of transformational leadership, as various scholars and researchers see it.

Three of our four behaviors are also represented in more that half the transformational leadership approaches. The most common element is "communication," included in six of the seven approaches. What is more interesting is that the element that centers on creating opportunities for followers to take charge themselves is included in four of the seven approaches. This behavior directly reflects the leader's orientation toward empowering followers. And "caring," the leader's feeling of respect toward and concern for followers, is in three of the seven approaches. Only one of the behaviors central to our own approach, developing trust, is included in just two of the seven approaches we reviewed.

Several things are clear from this analysis. First is the importance of vision and empowerment, across the various approaches to transformational leadership. Second, our two categories of transformational leadership characteristics and transformational leadership behaviors seem to be useful ways to organize our understanding of transformational leadership. Finally, it is especially interesting that only two of the seven approaches deal explicitly with the organization's culture.

This review of various transformational leadership approaches confirms that our own approach, *Leadership That Matters,* draws on many of the most commonly recognized elements of transformational leadership. The added value in our approach is that it brings these elements together in a new synthesis. This new integration shows how the personal characteristics of the leader guide transformational leaders' actions. Transformational leaders involve organization members and work with them to construct a new cultural context.

Organizational culture is not just the context for transformational leadership; it is the essence of what leaders try to construct or transform. Yet most approaches to transformational leadership focus primarily—and often only—on the leader-follower relationship. We think that in such approaches the role of the leader is really regarded as it has been in the theories of leadership we reviewed in Chapters One and Two. That is, the traditional role of the transactional leader is to motivate followers to do what they're told to do. This is one reason leadership scholar Joseph Rost argued that the "new paradigm" of transformational leadership is nothing more than old wine in a new bottle.[14]

Transformational leadership matters because it is about changing people and organizations for the better, not just about getting higher levels of productivity. The aim is not to motivate but to instill *self*-motivation. Thirty years ago, Frederick Herzberg argued that proper design of jobs could do this.[15] Herzberg proposed that jobs should be designed to be inherently, intrinsically motivating. This could be done, he said, by providing opportunities for completion of a task and achievement of a goal. The job should also permit employees to control much of what they do, to become their own "managers."[16] These principles of good job design still hold true. But in this new century we have come to recognize that there is more to leadership.

The leader-follower relationship is surely central to any theory of leadership. Our view of leadership is based on—but goes beyond—the leader-follower pair. We look beyond empowerment of individual workers through job design, to take in the larger organizational context. We believe that transformational leadership is about constructing a culture to empower people, in groups and teams, throughout an organization.

Transformational leaders build organizational cultures that not only drive high performance—they sustain high-performance. And they sustain people, as well. Leaders do this by giving people the opportunity and capability to make meaning for themselves.

Conclusion

We have repeatedly noted that we relied on a wide range of other approaches to transformational leadership as the basis for our own. We did not develop our approach by looking at all the others we've sketched in this chapter and finding the common elements. However, there are common elements, as this chapter shows, and they fit reasonably well with our visionary leadership theory and the approach we call *Leadership That Matters.*

We began this journey by asking why leadership matters. One reason leadership matters is because leaders help reduce the uncertainty and clear up some of the ambiguities of organizational life. Even more important is the leader's role in creating a context in which individuals are able to determine for themselves what is really important, what is *meaningful* to them. More than twenty-five years ago, a respected scholar said that "leadership is a language game."[17] He meant that leadership is about defining meaning, determining what is meaningful on a personal level. But leaders cannot make meaning for us; they can only make it possible for us to do it for ourselves.[18]

Making our own meaning is difficult, even frightening. It is easier to avoid, to, as singer/songwriter Paul Simon says, "do our work, collect our pay," all the while not noticing that our lives are "slip-sliding away." We think, however, that making our own meaning is at least partly what James McGregor Burns meant when he said that through transformational leadership, leaders and followers raise one another to "new heights of achievement and moral development."

It isn't necessary for people to define meaning in their lives. Nor need organizations make that possible. We can live out our lives, including our work lives, without a clue.[19] Organizations in which people are not encouraged to make meaning need not be unsuccessful. Such organizations may not be dramatically successful or effective, but they can last for a long time and can be reasonably profitable.[20] The fact that transformational leadership seems to be in rather short supply gives evidence for these assertions. Creating organizations that are extremely effective, both in terms of the bottom line and benefits to employees, is difficult. But organizations of the sort we have described in this book, with cultures built by transformational leaders, do more than achieve sustained and outstanding performance. They sustain people in their life-long effort to define and construct meaning in their work-lives. Ultimately, this is why leadership matters.

Bibliography

This bibliography is divided into three sections. The first includes reports published in books and conference proceedings. Only reports that were subject to peer review and accepted for publication by referees and/or editors are listed.

Section Two lists papers presented at professional, scholarly meetings. Again, only papers that were accepted for presentation after being subjected to peer review are listed.

The third section lists doctoral dissertations investigating Visionary Leadership Theory.

Section One: Publications

Endeman, J.L. (1993) Visionary superintendents and their districts. In M. Sashkin and H.J. Walberg (Eds.), *Educational leadership and school culture* (pp. 146–162). Berkeley, CA: McCutchan.

Sashkin, M. (1988) The visionary leader: A new theory of organizational leadership. In J.A. Conger and R.N. Kanungo (Eds.), *Charismatic leadership: The elusive factor in organizational effectiveness* (pp. 120–160). San Francisco: Jossey-Bass.

Sashkin, M. (1992) Strategic leadership competencies: What are they? How do they operate? What can be done to develop them? In R.L. Phillips and J.G. Hunt (Eds.), *Leadership: A multiorganizational-level perspective* (pp. 139–160). New York: Quorum Books.

Sashkin, M., & Burke, W.W. (1990) Understanding and assessing organizational leadership. In K.E. Clark and M.B. Clark (Eds.), *Measures of leadership* (pp. 297–325). West Orange, NJ: Leadership Library of America (A Center for Creative Leadership Book).

Sashkin, M., & Fulmer, R.M. 1988. Toward an organizational leadership theory. In J.G. Hunt, B.R. Baliga, H.P. Dachler, & C.A. Schreisheim (Eds.), *Emerging leadership vistas* (pp. 51–65). Lexington, MA: Lexington Books.

Sashkin, M., & Rosenbach, W.E. (2001) A new vision of leadership. In W.E. Rosenbach and R.L. Taylor (Eds.), *Contemporary issues in leadership* (5th ed., pp. 19–41). Boulder, CO: Westview Press.

Sashkin, M., & Sashkin, M.G. (1993) Principals and their school cultures: Understandings from quantitative and qualitative research. In M. Sashkin and H.J. Walberg (Eds.), *Educational leadership and school culture* (pp. 100–123). Berkeley, CA: McCutchan.

Sashkin, M., & Walberg, H. (Eds.) (1993) *Educational leadership and school culture.* Berkeley, CA: McCutchan.

Sashkin, M., Rosenbach, W.E., & Sashkin, M.G. (1997) Development of the power need and its expression in leadership and management with a focus on leader-follower relations. In L.S. Estabrook (Ed.), *Leadership as legacy: Proceedings of the Twelfth Scientific Meeting of the A.K. Rice Institute* (pp. 15–25). Jupiter, FL: A.K. Rice Institute.

Sashkin, M., Rosenbach, W.E., & Sashkin, M.G. (1997) Development of the power need and its expression in leadership and management with a focus on leader-follower relations. In D. H. Kent (Ed.), *Managing in a global economy VII—Europe towards the 21st century: Convergence and divergence. Proceedings of the Seventh International Conference* (pp. 379–383). Bowling Green, OH: Eastern Academy of Management.

Sashkin, M., Rosenbach, W.E., Deal, T.E., & Peterson, K.D. (1992) Assessing transformational leadership and its impact. In K.E. Clark, M.B. Clark, & D.P. Campbell (Eds.), *Impact of leadership* (pp. 131–148). Greensboro, NC: Center for Creative Leadership.

Section Two: Presentations

Axelrod, R.H., & Sashkin, M. (2000, August) Outcome measurement in a leadership development program. Paper presented at the annual meeting of the Academy of Management, Toronto.

Colyer, S.L. (1997, August) An empirical investigation of the relationship between visionary leadership and organizational performance: consequences of self-other agreement. Paper presented at the annual meeting of the Academy of Management, Boston.

Lafferty, B.D. (1997, August) Investigation of a leadership program at the U.S. Air Force Air Command and Staff College. Paper presented at the annual meeting of the Academy of Management, Boston.

Sashkin, M. (1987, May) A theory of organizational leadership. Paper presented at the McGill International Symposium on Charismatic Leadership in Management, Montreal.

Sashkin, M. (1987, April) Explaining excellence in leadership in light of Parsonian theory. Paper presented as part of a symposium at the annual meeting of the American Educational Research Association, Washington, DC.

Sashkin, M. (1991, February) Strategic leadership competencies. Paper presented at the Invitational Symposium on Strategic Leadership, Army War College, Carlisle Barracks, PA.

Sashkin, M., & Fulmer, R.M. (1985) A new framework for leadership. Paper presented at the Biennial Leadership Symposium, Texas Tech University, Lubbock.

Sashkin, M., & Sashkin, M.G. (1990, August) Leadership and culture building in schools: Quantitative and qualitative understandings. Paper presented at the annual meeting of the American Educational Research Association, as part of a Division A refereed symposium, "Leadership and culture: Qualitative and quantitative research approaches and results," Boston.

Sashkin, M., Rosenbach, W.E., & Mueller, R. (1994) Leadership, culture, and performance: An exploration of relationships. Paper presented at the international meeting of the Western Academy of Management, Brisbane, Australia.

Sashkin, M., Rosenbach, W.E., & Sashkin, M.G. (1995, May) Development of the power need and its expression in leadership and management with a focus on leader-follower relations. Paper presented at the 12th Scientific Meeting of the A.K. Rice Institute, Washington, DC.

Sashkin, M., Rosenbach, W.E., & Sashkin, M.G. (1997, June) Development of the power need and its expression in leadership and management with a focus on leader-follower relations. Paper presented at the international meeting of the Eastern Academy of Management, Dublin, Ireland.

Sashkin, M., Rosenbach, W.E., & Sashkin, M.G. (1997, August) The leadership profile: Psychometric development of a leadership assessment tool and its use in leadership development. Paper presented at the annual meeting of the Academy of Management, Boston.

Section Three: Doctoral Dissertations

Adkins, D.S. (1990) *The relationship between visionary leadership and instructional leadership behavior of secondary school principals: Regression analysis and hermeneutic interpretation.* Doctoral dissertation, West Virginia University.

Colyer, S.L. (1996) *An empirical investigation of self and other perceptions of visionary leadership as related to organizational performance.* Doctoral dissertation, The George Washington University, Washington, DC.

Dixon, D.L. (1998) *The relationship between chief executive leadership (transactional and transformational) and hospital effectiveness.* Doctoral dissertation, The George Washington University, Washington, DC.

Endeman, J.L. (1990) *Visionary leadership in superintendents and its effect on organizational outcomes.* Doctoral dissertation, University of La Verne, California.

Ernst, L. (1997) *Transformational leadership of male and female executives as related to a measure of gender role orientation: Further development of a measure of leadership.* Doctoral dissertation, Graduate School of Education and Human Development, The George Washington University, Washington, DC.

Hall, C.A. (1999) *The relationship between leader behavior and characteristics and school culture.* Doctoral dissertation, University of Florida, Gainesville.

Harter, E.S. (1999) *The quest for sustainable leadership: The importance of connecting leadership principles to concepts of organizational sustainability.* Doctoral dissertation, Case Western Reserve University, Cleveland, OH.

Higgins, C.C. (1998) *Transactional and transformational leadership: An examination of the relationship between leadership orientation and perceptions of organizational effectiveness.* Doctoral dissertation, The George Washington University, Washington, DC.

Lafferty, B.D. (1998) *An empirical investigation of a leadership development program.* Doctoral dissertation, The George Washington University, Washington, DC.

Major, K. (1988) *Dogmatism, visionary leadership and effectiveness of secondary principals.* Doctoral dissertation, University of La Verne, California.

McElreath, J. (1999) *Development of a biodata measure of leadership skills.* Doctoral disseration, Wayne State University, Detroit, MI.

Palmer, D.V. (1999) *Leadership: Does it make a difference in a high technology career? An empirical investigation within high technology firms.* Doctoral dissertation, The George Washington University, Washington, DC.

Sawner, T.E. (1999) *An empirical investigation of the relationship between organizational culture and organizational performance in a large public sector organization.* Doctoral dissertation, The George Washington University, Washington, DC.

Silver, S.R. (1999) *Perception of empowerment in engineering workgroups: The linkage to transformational leadership and performance.* Doctoral dissertation, The George Washington University, Washington, DC.

Stoner, M.J. (1988) *Visionary leadership, management, and high performing work units: An analysis of workers' perceptions.* Doctoral dissertation, University of Massachusetts, Amherst.

Tibus, C.A. (1997) *Leadership and ownership: An investigation of leadership among women business owners and women business executives.* Doctoral dissertation, The George Washington University, Washington, DC.

Vona, M.K. (1997) *The relationship between visionary leadership and climates of innovation in organizational work units.* Doctoral dissertation, Graduate School of Education and Human Development, The George Washington University, Washington, DC.

Weese, W.J. (1991) *Visionary leadership and the development and penetration of organizational culture within campus recreation programs.* Doctoral dissertation, The Ohio State University, Columbus.

TWO

Development of
The Leadership Profile[1]

Our primary measure of leadership that matters is a question-naire that asks about a leader's behavior. It is usually completed by the leader and by several observers. The first version, published in 1984, assessed behaviors in five areas. It also measured followers' feelings of charisma toward the leader. Five items measured each of the five behavior dimensions. There were a total of six scales and thirty items. We expanded this questionnaire to ten scales, adding scales to assess four dimensions of leadership defined by Bowers and Seashore.[2] This fifty-item leadership assessment was published in 1985 as the Leader Behavior Questionnaire (LBQ).

Over the next ten years we continued to develop and refine our questionnaire. We dropped some measures (the four Bowers-Seashore dimensions of leadership, for example) and added others (measures of character and culture building). In 1995, we made three major revisions to the LBQ. First, we reduced the behavior scales from five to four. The first two scales both dealt with communication, so we combined them into a single measure. Second, we combined the two culture-building scales into a single measure. Finally, we added two scales to assess transactional leadership. Because our research has, since then, been based on use of this new assessment questionnaire, The Leadership Profile (TLP), the psychometric properties of earlier versions won't be reviewed here. We'll define and give examples of items from each scale of the TLP.

The Ten TLP Dimensions

The TLP has ten scales. Each is composed of five items. Respondents rate how well each item describes their behavior, or the behavior of the person they have been asked about. A five-point rating is used, from "to a very great extent" through "to a moderate extent" to "to little or no extent."

Scale 1: Capable Management. This scale measures how well the leader accomplishes the day-to-day basic administrative or managerial tasks that are necessary for any group or organization to function well in the short term. Capable managers make sure that people have the knowledge, skills, and resources they need to get the job done right.

Sample Item: This person makes sure people have the resources they need to do a good job.

Scale 2: Reward Equity. Effective managers find out what followers want. They promise followers what they want in exchange for good performance, and they deliver on their promises. This scale measures the degree to which transactional leaders make clear and explicit their goals and performance expectations. It also assesses how well they deliver on the rewards they promise for good performance and goal accomplishment.

Sample Item: This person recognizes good performance with rewards people value.

Scale 3: Communication Leadership. This scale assesses the ability to manage and direct the attention of others through clear and focused interpersonal communication. Transformational leaders listen and pay close attention to those with whom they are communicating. They focus on key issues and help followers to understand those issues. These leaders also pay attention to and appreciate followers' feelings. They use metaphors and analogies that make abstract ideas clear and vivid. In this way, they are able to get complicated ideas across clearly.

Sample Item: This person grabs people's attention, focusing on the important issue in a discussion.

Scale 4: Credible Leadership. This scale deals with a leader's perceived integrity. Is the leader reliable, keeping commitments and promises? Are the leader's words consistent with her or his actions? Effective leaders "walk the talk." They establish trust by acting consistently over time and with what they say. Because they trust others, they are themselves trusted.

Sample Item: This person acts in ways consistent with her or his words.

Scale 5: Caring Leadership. This scale measures the degree to which a leader demonstrates respect and concern for others. Transformational leaders consistently and constantly express concern for others. They respect other people's feelings, which reinforces others' positive self-regard. Transformational leaders also value people's differences and let people know it. They see how individuals' unique qualities and abilities can be used to the benefit of the group or organization.

Sample Item: This person respects people's differences.

Scale 6: Creative Leadership. Some would say that effective leadership involves a willingness to take risks. Transformational leaders, however, do not take undue risks—they *create opportunities.* Although their actions might appear to an outsider to be risky, they are actually based on careful thought. Transformational leaders carefully assess the ability of followers to perform and succeed. Transformational leaders empower followers by encouraging and allowing them to accept challenges. However, they don't just leave it at that. They do everything possible to make sure that followers succeed. What they don't do is spend a lot of time and energy worrying about failure. Of course, even effective leaders may at times experience failure. When that happens, they use the experience to learn how to do better the next time.

Sample Item: This person designs situations that permit people to achieve their goals.

Scale 7: Confident Leadership. Transformational leaders have a basic sense of self-assurance. They believe that they can personally make a difference and have an impact on people, events, and group achievements. Henry Ford said, "If you think you can . . .

or think you can't . . . you're probably right." Effective leaders believe they control their own fate. This scale measures the extent to which the leader possesses and displays this sort of self-confidence. To the extent that she or he does, the leader will be able to instill the same self-confidence in followers.

Sample Item: This person makes a difference.

Scale 8: Follower-Centered Leadership. Transformational leaders don't seek power and influence because they enjoy exercising power over others. Rather, they realize it is through the positive use of power and influence that they can achieve group and organizational goals. Transformational leaders use power by sharing it with followers. They empower followers to take an active role in achieving group goals. This scale measures the degree to which the leader sees followers as empowered partners rather than as pawns to be manipulated.

Sample Item: This person seeks power and influence to attain goals people agree on.

Scale 9: Visionary Leadership.   This scale measures a leader's ability to define and clearly express an idea about the future for the group or organization, both in concept and in action. Such long-term goals are based on shared values and beliefs. Transformational leaders derive these values, as well as organizational goals, from followers, at least in part. Groups and organizations that perform well have leaders with the perspective needed to deal with ambiguity and complexity. Such leaders know what actions are necessary to achieve desired outcomes. They develop plans that extend beyond the present into the long-range future. They also involve followers in the planning process.

Sample Item: This person has plans that extend over a period of several years or longer.

Scale 10: Principled Leadership.   An effective transformational leader helps develop and support certain shared values and beliefs among group members; that is what this scale measures. These values and beliefs reflect the important and fundamental issues faced by people in groups and organizations. Certain values about change will help the organization adapt more effectively. Beliefs about the type of goals that are appropriate and how to define them will facilitate performance. Values about how people should work together will determine whether internal coordination is effective. Finally, consensus on the values and beliefs that should guide action will aid in sustaining organizational stability. By defining and supporting appropriate values and beliefs—principles— transformational leaders build effective organizational cultures.

Sample Item: This person encourages others to act according to the values and beliefs we share.

TLP Reliability

Test-Retest Reliability

A reliable measure gives the same results each time it is used to measure the same thing. The simplest way to determine reliability is to measure the same thing twice and get a correlation between the two results. This becomes more difficult when we try to measure peoples' attitudes and observations. Because most people try to be consistent, it's important to have a reasonable time between the two measurements. That way people won't just reproduce their earlier responses from memory.

A correlation goes from –1.00 to +1.00. A negative correlation means that as one measure goes up, the other goes down. Because we are using the same measurement tool two times, the correlation is not likely to be negative. The correlation might, however, be close to zero. As the correlation approaches 1.00, the measure is said to be more reliable.

This "test-retest reliability" procedure is the strongest proof of reliability. We've done this in several large-scale studies, each involving hundreds of people who completed the TLP on two separate occasions. Some results are shown in Table 1, below. All of the results in Table 1 are based on data obtained from U.S. Air Force officers who attended a ten-month residential leadership development program.

For Group IIa and Group III, the TLP was completed at the beginning of the course and at its conclusion ten months later. For Group I and Group IIb, the time interval was a full year.

TABLE 1	Test-Retest Reliability Correlations	A	B	C
Group I. One year to two years after training program ($N = 189$)		.485**	.379**	.402**
Group IIa. Pretraining to posttraining ($N = 505$)		.533**	.502**	.519**
Group IIb. Posttraining to one year after training		.460**	.217*	.615**
Group III. Pretraining to posttraining ($N = 341$)		.532**	.231**	.490**

A. Transactional Leadership (sum of Scales 1 and 2)
B. Transformational Leadership Behavior (sum of Scales 3 through 6)
C. Transformational Leadership Characteristics (sum of Scales 7 through 9)

$**p < .01$ $*p < .05$

Therefore, it's very unlikely that the positive correlations, all of which are statistically significant, are due to individuals' remembering exactly the way they filled out the TLP the first time (ten months to a year earlier).

Although all of the correlations in Table 1 are statistically significant, some are clearly stronger than others. Correlations of .40 to .50 are generally considered moderately strong, and correlations above .50 are typically thought of as very strong. Correlations between .20 and .30 are weak, even when statistically significant.

In Table 1, all of the test-retest correlations for transformational leadership behavior (column B) are smaller than for transactional behavior (column A) or transformational characteristics (column C). It's not really surprising that the measures of transformational behavior appear to be changeable. For one thing, the program these officers were enrolled in was designed to develop their transformational leadership skills. In contrast, one's orientation toward transactional leadership, and a leader's personal characteristics, are probably more stable over time. This is one explanation for higher reliability of the transactional and transformational characteristics scales. Nonetheless, all ten TLP scales are reliable.

Internal Scale Reliability

Yet another type of reliability measures the degree to which the items (questions) that make up a scale "hang together." A statistic called "Cronbach's alpha" assesses the degree to which the items are intercorrelated. This statistic is interpreted much like a correlation. However, very high alphas—about .90 and above—are not only unlikely, they are not really desirable. That's because a correlation at or near 1.00 means that you might as well have asked just one question instead of several. That is, some items are probably highly redundant and a waste of time and effort.

Table 2 shows internal scale reliabilities (Cronbach's alpha) for each TLP scale, in seven separate studies. A scale with an alpha much below about .60 is not considered reliable. That is, the items don't seem to be measuring the same thing. Alphas above .70 are good and those at .80 or higher are excellent.

Table 2 shows that all of the TLP scales are good to excellent in terms of internal reliability, with two exceptions. Scale 8 shows consistently low and unacceptable internal reliability. However, this is because Scale 8 is actually composed of two separate and independent subscales. One measures prosocial power, the other personalized power (see Chapters Four and Five). When we separate the items into these two subscales, alphas for each are above .70.[3]

Scale 9 also shows alphas lower than desirable. Closer examination of the data led us to identify one of the five items that make up this scale as the problem. After revising this item, the alphas for Scale 9 also reach .70 and above.

Summary

Overall, the various reliability tests have shown that the ten TLP scales are reliable. Examination of test-retest reliability coefficients showed that the TLP yields consistent results over time. With the minor revision noted in Scale 9, and when we view Scale 8 correctly as two independent subscales, we see that all ten scales have internal scale reliability scores (Cronbach alphas) of .60 or better, usually much better. These results strongly support our belief in the reliability of The Leadership Profile.

TABLE 2	Cronbach's Alphas for the Ten TLP Scales						
	Group						
Scale	**A**	**B**	**C**	**D**	**E**	**F**	**G**
1. Capable Management	.769	.767	794	.822	.804	.780	.900
2. Reward Equity	.801	.801	.805	.890	.866	.900	.930
3. Communication Leadership	.647	.668	.682	.800	.654	.790	.890
4. Credible Leadership	.857	.785	.847	.892	.778	.890	.940
5. Caring Leadership	.764	.771	.790	.900	.822	.900	.940
6. Creative Leadership	.804	.814	.795	.844	.839	.840	.910
7. Confident Leadership	.764	.740	.768	.747	.812	.830	.870
8. Follower-Centered Leadership	.213	.334	.208	.366	.401	.440	.510
9. Visionary Leadership	.562	.589	.419	.568	.592	.640	.520
10. Principled Leadership	.596	.597	.572	.714	.674	.710	.780

Key Groups A, B, and C: U.S. Air Force officers, as in Table 1.
Group D: Audit team members in a national "Big 6" accounting firm reporting about their leaders; $N = 149$.
Group E: Engineers in several different high-technology firms in Northern Virginia; $N = 68$.
Group F: Design engineers in a major U.S. high-technology organization; $N = 300$ (TLP—other).
Group G: Florida public school teachers and principals; $N = 1466$.

TLP Validity

The results reported above show that the TLP is a reliable measure. The question remains whether it is also a "true," or valid, measure of leadership. There are several ways to assess validity. Most have been applied to test our Visionary Leadership Theory and its measure, The Leadership Profile.

Criterion Validity

We presented evidence in Chapter Eleven to show that transformational leadership, as measured by the TLP, is significantly related to performance outcomes. This sort of validity, called "criterion validity," is considered the strongest possible support for any theory. Thus, in terms of criterion validity, both our approach (Visionary Leadership Theory, *Leadership That Matters*) and the TLP measure are strongly supported. One may still ask, however, whether the TLP actually measures what it claims to.

Content Validity

One answer is to look at the questions that make up the TLP. By examining their content, one can see if the five questions that comprise a scale describe what that scale purports to measure. Examination of the TLP items gives evidence of content validity.

Construct Validity

We can develop additional support for validity of our ideas and measures by showing that data support the existence of the essential concepts, the "constructs" on which visionary leadership theory is built. If we can show that these constructs can be identified in the data collected using the TLP, this will add to the evidence for the validity of the measure and the approach. One method for doing this is a statistical procedure called "factor analysis."

Factor analysis requires a reasonably large amount of data. A 50-item assessment such as the TLP must have at least 250 responses, to do a reliable factor analysis. The data are mathematically condensed into a set of separate dimensions. The technical procedures are complex, but they involve the same sort of correlations used to assess reliability. All of the questions and responses are, in essence, tossed into n-dimensional space and correlated. This goes on until a final set of independent dimensions is defined, within pre-set parameters.[4]

The most recently developed factor analytic procedure is called "confirmatory factor analysis." This means defining the dimensions in advance and testing whether factor analysis supports them. To do this, however, requires defining so many parameters, that we believe (based on our experience) that proving whatever one wishes to prove is too easy. For this reason, we use traditional, or "exploratory," factor analysis, which simply takes the data and determines what dimensions are formed.

Data for analysis. We had available three large data sets that could be used for exploratory factor analytic studies. We obtained the first data set as part of a study sponsored by the American Management Association. This data set included 517 male and 434 female executives and CEOs, 951 in all. These individuals completed the TLP about themselves.

Our second data set consisted of U.S. Air Force officers, enrolled in the Air Command Staff College, a military postgraduate college operated by the U.S. Air Force in Montgomery, Alabama. We obtained data from 505 officers before the course. The data were TLP self-reports.

The third large data set consisted of 202 participants in courses at the National Fire Academy. The NFA is a federally funded management and executive development center for fire service professionals from throughout the United States. The data, here, were from observers of the participants, totaling 1378 responses.

American Management Association data. We obtained this first data set as part of an AMA-sponsored study of leadership and gender.[5] We used a random sample from the American Management Association's list of senior executive members in small to moderate-sized organizations. They mailed TLP assessments to 4000 male and 4000 female senior executives. We received usable responses from about equal numbers, 705 females and 820 males. Note that these are self-reports; reports from others were not collected. Our final sample for this data analysis involved 517 male and 434 female respondents, totaling 951 observations. These numbers are more than adequate for the analyses we performed.

We performed exploratory factor analyses separately on the male and female samples. Because there were no significant differences in results, we combined the samples.[6] There were twelve independent factors.

Factor 1. All five of the items comprising Scale 5, Caring Leadership Behavior, are strongly associated with this factor. Three other items from three different scales also appear in this factor. Overall, this result supports the construct validity of this scale.

Factor 2. Three items from each of two of the Leadership Characteristics scales, Scale 7 (Confident Leadership) and Scale 9 (Visionary Leadership) were most strongly associated with this factor. Two items from Scale 10 (Principled Leadership, which measures the leader's culture-building efforts) were also associated with this factor. Although this second factor is, therefore, mixed, all of the items are from scales that assess Transformational Leadership Characteristics. This result, then, does provide support for the construct validity, that is, the existence of such characteristics.

Factor 3. This factor includes four of the five items that assess Scale 4, Credible Leadership Behavior. No other items were strongly associated with this factor. Therefore, this result strongly supports the construct validity of Scale 4.

Factor 4. The two items that assess the personalized power aspect of Scale 8, Follower-Centered Leadership, were strongly associated with this factor, which contains no other items. This subscale of Scale 8, personalized power, has strong construct validity.

Factor 5. This factor contains two items each from Scale 9 (Visionary leadership) and Scale 10 (Principled Leadership—the building of cultural values). Two more items, from different scales, were also strongly associated with this factor. This factor is, then, a mixture of items from several scales. However, if we were to give it a label we might call this factor "vision and values."

Factor 6. All five items from Scale 2, designed to assess that aspect of transactional leadership centered on rewarding followers (Reward Equity), are found on this factor. This result strongly supports the construct validity of Scale 2.

Factor 7. This factor includes a mix of two items from each of two scales. Represented are Scale 6, Creative Leadership, which refers to leadership actions aimed at empowering followers by involving them; and Scale 7, Confident Leadership. Although there is a logical link between the two scales, the presence of only one item from each does not provide much support for the construct validity of either.

Factor 8. This factor contains three items from three different scales and is not interpretable (we couldn't figure out any sensible meaning).

Factor 9. The remaining three items from Scale 8 (Follower-Centered Leadership), assessing the leader's prosocial power need, are most strongly associated with this factor. As noted earlier, this subscale of Scale 8 is an independent factor and this result strongly supports its construct validity.

Factor 10. Three items from Scale 1, Capable Management, are most strongly associated with this factor. This supports the construct validity of Scale 1.

Factor 11. Four of the five items assessing Communication Leadership, Scale 3, are strongly associated with this factor. This result strongly supports the construct validity of Scale 3.

Factor 12. Two of the culture-building items from Scale 10 (Principled Leadership) were strongly associated with this factor, though not as strongly as two other items from two different scales. This factor does not, therefore, provide much support for the construct validity of Scale 10.

A second factor analysis was performed using a forced ten-factor solution. That is, we required the program to fit the data to ten factors. The results were quite similar to those just described, except that the uninterpretable factor and one other that included a mix of items from several scales were missing.

Air University data.   These data were obtained from 505 individuals at the start of a ten-month residential leadership development program at Air Command Staff College (ACSC) of Air University, a military postgraduate college operated by the U.S. Air Force in Montgomery, Alabama.[7] The data are part of a longitudinal study that followed these individuals through several years of their military careers.

To analyze the ACSC data sample, we used a varimax rotation and set the eigenvalue to 1.00, as we had done for the AMA data factor analysis. This produced a ten-factor solution, but the ten TLP scales did not map precisely onto the ten factors.

Factor 1. This first factor contains thirteen items. Three are Scale 7 (Confident Leadership) items and three are from

Scale 9 (Visionary Leadership). Less strongly associated are three items from Scale 3 (Communication Leadership). The factor also includes two of the three prosocial power items from Scale 8 (Follower-Centered Leadership). Finally, two of the Scale 10 (Principled Leadership) items, which refer to the leader's culture-building actions, are also included.

Although this might seem a polyglot factor, we can interpret it as representing the Transformational Leadership Character-istics area. Recall that this area consists of Scales 7 (Confident Leadership), 8 (Follower-Centered Leadership, or empowered leadership), and 9 (Visionary Leadership), along with Scale 10, which assesses culture building. The communicati.on items can be seen as the "how"—that is, they reflect the leader behavior used to build culture.

Factor 2. Three of the items from Scale 5 (Caring Leadership) form this factor, along with one item from Scale 3. This factor supports Scale 5.

Factor 3. The two items of Scale 8 (Follower-Centered Leader-ship) reflecting personalized power are the only items on this factor. This is consistent with past results, in which Scale 8 fac-tors clearly into two separate factors, one representing person-alized power, the other prosocial power.

Factor 4. All five items from Scale 4 (Credible Leadership) are included in this factor. No other items fit Factor 4. These results strongly support the construct validity of the scale mea-suring Credible Leadership.

Factor 5. Four of the items on Scale 1 (Capable Management) loaded high on this scale, as did three of the items from Scale 6 (Creative Leadership). The latter assess the transformational leadership behavior of empowering and involving followers. The behaviors assessed by these two scales are not necessarily inconsistent. However, the fact that they are mixed into a single factor does not support the construct validity of either.

Factor 6. This factor contains the remaining two items from Scale 7 (Confident Leadership).

Factors 7, 8, and 9. These factors each contain just one item (two unrelated items in the case of Factor 7) and are not interpretable.

Factor 10. Several items from Scales 1 and 2, the Transactional Leadership scales, are moderately strongly associated with this factor. Most of these items, however, are also associated with other factors. It is, therefore, a stretch to argue that this factor represents transactional leadership or provides construct validity evidence.

Overall, the results of this factor analysis provide some support for the construct validity of the TLP. Factor 1 suggests a constellation of Transformational Leadership Characteristics, incorporating Scale 7, 8, and 9. This is similar to what we saw in the AMA data. Factor 2 clearly represents Scale 5, (Caring Leadership). Factor 3 and Factor 6 relate clearly to Scale 8 (Follower-Centered Leadership). Factor 4 supports the construct validity of Scale 4 (Credible Leadership). However, the transactional scales do not appear as a clear separate construct. Moreover, the results support the construct validity of just two of the four transformational leadership behavior scales (4 and 5).

National Fire Academy data.   The prior two data sets included only TLP self-assessment reports. Unlike the previous two data sets, this one provides a sample of 1378 responses from *observers* of leaders. This number is far more than required for factor analysis.

As with the above factor analyses, a varimax rotation was required, with eigenvalue set as greater than or equal to 1.00. The result was somewhat surprising: a five-factor solution, organized as follows.

Factor 1. This factor incorporates three scales. All five items from Scale 7 (Confident Leadership) appear. So do four of the Scale 9 (Visionary Leadership) items. Also included are three items from Scale 3 (Communication Leadership). This result is similar to that we obtained for the AMA data set (which, recall, consists of self-report data only). Factor 2 in that analysis combined confidence, vision, and culture. The present result is nearly identical with Factor 1 obtained for the Air University data set, which included items from Scales 3, 7, and 9.

Factor 2. All five of the items on Scale 5 (Caring Leadership) were strongly associated with this factor. In addition, three items from Scale 2 (Reward Equity), were most strongly associated with this factor. This combination of a Transformational

Behavior scale (5) with a Transactional scale (2) does not support the construct validity of the TLP.

Factor 3. Four of the five items on Scale 8 (Follower-Centered Leadership) were most strongly associated with this factor. These items typically form two separate factors. Here they are combined into a single factor.

Factor 4. All five of the Scale 4 (Credible Leadership) items were most strongly associated with this factor; no other items were strongly associated with this factor. This result strongly supports the construct validity of Scale 4.

Factor 5. We have seen factors similar to this one in the above analyses. We earlier said we might label this factor "empowering management," because it includes three of the five items from Scale 1 (Capable Management) and two items from Scale 6 (Creative Management).

This factor analysis, using observers' reports rather than self-assessment data, is generally consistent with the previous two analyses. We see a grouping of the transformational leadership characteristics assessed by Scale 7 (Confident Leadership) and Scale 9 (Visionary Leadership) in a single factor. The transformational characteristic of Scale 8 (Follower-Centered Leadership), which assesses the degree of a person's prosocial power orientation) appears as a separate factor. The transformational behavior of Scale 4 (Credible Leadership, or trust building) is represented as a single clear factor. Two other transformational behaviors, Scale 5 (Caring Leadership) and Scale 6 (Creative Leadership) also appear as separate factors, though each is combined with one of the transactional behaviors. Overall, these results provide some support for the construct validity of the TLP assessment and of our visionary leadership theory.

Construct Validity: Relationships to Other Assessments

Another way to demonstrate construct validity is to show that a measure is significantly related to another measure that has been independently validated. One recent study did this by correlating our earlier assessment measure, the Leader Behavior Questionnaire (LBQ),[8] with two other widely used transformational leadership assessments.[9]

The Leader Behavior Questionnaire was correlated with each of two other well-known measures of transformational leadership. These are Kouzes and Posner's Leadership Practices Inventory (LPI) and Bass' Multifactor Leadership Questionnaire (MLQ)[10]. There were substantial and statistically significant relationships between each of the three LBQ scale groups (transformational behavior, transformational characteristics, and transformational culture-building) and each of the five LPI scales.[11] Relationships between LPI scales and the LBQ Culture Building scales were, however, smaller than correlations between LPI scales and each of the other two LBQ areas.

These results support the conclusion that the LPI and LBQ Behavior scales are quite similar. The results also indicate some overlap between LPI scales and the LBQ Transformational Leadership Characteristics scales. The weaker relationships between LPI scales and LBQ Culture Building scales is logical, since the LPI does not address culture building directly. Overall, the two assessments showed consistent relationships of the sort that we would logically expect, though they were developed through independent research efforts.

In contrast, the correlations between the set of MLQ transformational scales and the three LBQ areas, while statistically significant, were distinctly smaller (.31 to .42) than the LPI-LBQ correlations. This is consistent with the different theoretical basis for these two instruments (though both address transformational leadership).

The same study also found large, statistically significant relationships between a standard measure of self-efficacy and each of the three LBQ areas.[12] Overall, these results add to the construct validity of the theory that underpins both the LBQ and its current version, The Leadership Profile.

Summary

Various studies show that the TLP is a reliable assessment tool with strong criterion validity (demonstrated by the research reviewed in Chapter Eleven). The factor analyses described above support the construct validity of the two transactional leadership scales. Of the four transformational behavior scales, our results strongly support the construct validity of three: Communication Leadership (Scale 3), Credible Leadership (Scale 4), and Caring Leadership (Scale 5). However, Scale 6, Creative Leadership, links to the leadership characteristic of self-confidence (Scale 7) as well as to Scale 1, which was designed as a measure of good management (transactional leadership).

We observed repeatedly how the three Transformational Leadership Characteristics (along with Scale 10, Principled Leadership) clustered together. This supports the construct validity of the category of Transformational Leadership Characteristics.

The fact that a clear and independent factor does not define each of the ten TLP scales is neither surprising nor troubling to us. Our view is that in real-world leadership action the TLP behavior scales are necessarily intertwined and statistically interrelated. Although some behavior scales (e.g., trust) cohere in a single factor more clearly than do others, the six behaviors (including the two transactional behaviors) are interrelated in action. That is, they are interrelated aspects of the everyday actions of transformational leaders. Even so, the three areas of leadership assessed—transactional, transformational behavior, and transformational characteristics—do sort into relatively clear and separate factor groupings.

Overall, these results provide construct validity support for the three domains of Transactional Leadership, Transformational Leadership Behavior, and Transformational Leadership Characteristics. The results also support the construct validity of the two transactional scales and three of the four transformational behavior scales. Based on these results, we conclude that Visionary Leadership Theory—*Leadership That Matters*—is well supported and that the TLP assessment tool has good reliability and validity.

Notes

Introduction

1. Quoted from "Review of Soame Jenyns, 'A Free Enquiry into the Nature and Origin of Evil.'" (http://andromeda.rutgers.edu/~jlynch/Texts/jenys.html) In this somewhat lengthy critique Dr. Johnson goes on to observe, ". . . how will either of those [better enjoying life or better enduring it] be put more in our power by him who tells us that we are puppets of which some creature, not much wiser than ourselves, manages the wires!" One important aspect of leadership, in our approach, is the leader's self-confidence—belief that he or she can have an impact, rather than being a puppet of others—and the leader's capacity to develop such self-confidence in followers.

2. The Center for Creative Leadership, in Greensboro, North Carolina, is considered by many (including us) to be one of the premier leadership research and training organizations in the U.S. For more information about CCL, see their website: ccl.org

Chapter One

1. This quotation is from *The Tao of Leadership* by John Heider (New York: Bantam Books, 1986, p. 113). That book, and the quotations we use to introduce chapters and key concepts in this book, is based on the *Tao Te Ching*. The *Tao* is about 2,500 years old and is traditionally ascribed to Lao Tzu, considered the founder of Taoism, one of the major religions of the East.

Scholars disagree as to whether or not the *Tao* was written by a single person at a single time in history. "Lao Tzu," translated literally, means "Old Man" and scholars also disagree as to whether Lao Tzu was a real historical figure. There is, however, reason to believe that Lao Tzu was a real person. That is, there is strong evidence that Lao Tzu actually met with Confucius, and historians do agree that Confucius was an actual historical figure.

We do not read Chinese and have developed our versions of the quotations we used after reviewing several translations. We have been most influenced by Heider's leadership-centered interpretations in *The Tao of Leadership.* However, except for the quote used to introduce this chapter, which is from Heider, we have used our own words and made our own interpretations.

The *Tao* is composed of eighty-one short sections, or chapters. The quotation used to begin our book is from John Heider's version of Chapter 57. In the following chapters of the present book we have sometimes combined elements from more than one chapter of the *Tao*.

As does Heider, we recommend Arthur Waley's classic *The Way and Its Power* (New York: Grove Press, 1958) as one of the very best translations. However, a more recent and much easier to follow translation is John Wu's *Tao Teh Ching* (Boston: Shambala, 1995). Red Pine's *Lao-tzu's Taoteching* (San Francisco: Mercury House, 1996) is especially useful because he presents each line of the Chinese with a parallel English translation and includes details of the most important commentaries to each chapter written over the past two thousand years.

2. Meindl, J.R., Ehrlich, S.B., & Dukerich, J.M. (1985) The romance of leadership. *Administrative Science Quarterly, 30,* 78-102.

3. In his book *Leadership* (New York: Harper, 1978), James McGregor Burns uses Gandhi as an exemplar of leadership. See also:

Keshavan, N. (1997) *A higher standard of leadership: Lessons from the life of Gandhi* (2nd ed.). San Francisco: Berrett-Koehler.

4. Bennis, W.G., & Nanus, B. (1985) *Leaders: The strategies for taking charge.* New York: Harper & Row.

Chapter Two

1. Zaleznik, A. (1977) Mangers and leaders: Are they different? *Harvard Business Review, 55*(3), 67–78.

2. In his 1928 text on aptitude testing, the psychologist Clark Hull notes that at the outbreak of World War I, J.L. Otis, an industrial psychologist, gave the U.S. Army his work on selection tests for leaders, resulting in the Army Alpha test.

3. Stogdill, R.M. (1948) Personal factors associated with leadership: A survey of the literature. *Journal of Psychology, 25,* 35–71.

4. Katz, D., Maccoby, N., Gurin, G., & Floor, L. (1951) *Productivity, supervision, and morale among railroad workers.* Ann Arbor, MI: Survey Research Center, Institute for Social Research, The University of Michigan.

Katz, D., Maccoby, N., & Morse, N.C. (1950) *Productivity, supervision and morale in an office situation.* Ann Arbor, MI: Survey Research Center, Institute for Social Research, The University of Michigan.

5. Stogdill, R.M., & Coons, A.E. (1957) *Leader behavior: Its description and measurement.* Columbus, OH: Bureau of Business Research, Ohio State University.

6. Blake, R.R., & Mouton, J.S. (1964) *The managerial grid.* Houston, TX: Gulf.

Blake, R.R., & Mouton, J.S. (1995) *The leadership grid.* Houston, TX: Gulf.

7. Bales, R.F. (1958) Task roles and social roles in problem-solving groups. In E.E. Maccoby, T.M. Newcomb, & E.L. Hartley (Eds.), *Readings in social psychology.* New York: Holt.

Bales, R.F. (1950) *Interaction process analysis.* Reading, MA: Addison-Wesley.

8. Fleishman, E.A., & Harris, E.F. (1962) Patterns of leadership behavior related to employee grievances and turnover. *Personnel Psychology, 15,* 43–56.

9. Evans, M.G. (1970) The effects of supervisory behavior on the path-goal relationship. *Organizational Behavior and Human Performance, 5,* 277–298.

House, R.J. (1971) A path-goal theory of leader effectiveness. *Administrative Science Quarterly, 16,* 321–338.

10. House, R.J., & Dessler, G. (1974) The path-goal theory of leadership: Some post hoc and a priori tests. In J.G. Hunt and L.L. Larson (Eds.), *Contingency approaches to leadership* (pp. 29–55). Carbondale, IL: Southern Illinois University Press.

House, R.J., & Mitchell, T.R. (1974) Path-goal theory of leadership. *Contemporary Journal of Business, 3*(Fall), 81–98.

11. House, R.J. (1996) Path-goal theory of leadership: Lessons, legacy, and a reformulated theory. *Leadership Quarterly, 7,* 323–352.

12. Hersey, P., & Blanchard, K.H. (1969) Life cycle theory of leadership. *Training and Development Journal, 23,* 26–34.

13. Hersey, P., & Blanchard, K.H. (1982) *Management of organizational behavior* (4th ed.). Englewood Cliffs, NJ: Prentice-Hall.

14. Ken Blanchard is, of course, best known today for his popular "One Minute Manager" books. After he and Hersey parted, each continued to put forth his own version of situational leadership and both are still used today.

15. Complex statistical analyses of more than a hundred path-goal theory research studies showed that while the situational context may have an effect on what leadership approach is most effective, no clear conclusions could be drawn due to problems in research design and conduct [Wofford, J.C., & Liska, L.Z. (1993) Path-goal theories of leadership: A meta-analysis. *Journal of Management, 19,* 857–877].

Mixed findings also characterize the research on Hersey and Blanchard's approach. While some research on the Hersey-Blanchard approach has been supportive, there have been relatively few published studies [Hersey, P., Angelini, A.L., & Carakushansky, S. (1982) The impact of situational leadership and classroom structure on learning effectiveness. *Group & Organization Studies, 7,* 216–224].

16. Leana, C.R. (1986) Predictors and consequences of delegation. *Academy of Management Journal, 29,* 754–774.

17. Jung, C.G. (1923) *Psychological types.* New York: Harcourt Brace.

Myers, I.B., with Myers, P.B. (1980) *Gifts differing.* Palo Alto, CA: Consulting Psychologists Press.

The MBTI is an assessment questionnaire based on the theories of Carl Jung. Early work on the MBTI was initiated during the late nineteenth century by Katherine Briggs and continued through the twentieth century by her daughter, Isabel Briggs Myers. It is one of the most popular assessment tools in use, proposing that individuals' personalities can be understood in terms of development of preferences on four bipolar dimensions. This leads to a categorization system comprised of sixteen basic personality types.

18. McCauley, M.H. (1990) The Myers-Briggs Type Indicator and leadership. In K.E. Clark and M.B. Clark (Eds.), *Measures of leadership* (pp. 381–418). West Orange, NJ: Leadership Library of America (A Center for Creative Leadership Book).

McCauley notes, "All 16 types may become presidents or chief executive officers but [our data] indicate that some types are more likely to reach these heights than others" (p. 411). McCauley also comments that, in an early undated and unpublished paper, Myers asserts that to be effective a leader must be capable of applying all of the dimensional preferences. Myers says that while this is difficult a well-developed individual, one who has learned the strengths and weaknesses of his or her own natural preferences, can learn to do so.

19. Digman, J.M. (1990) Personality structure: Emergence of the five-factor model. *Annual Review of Psychology (Volume 4)* (pp. 417–440). Palo Alto, CA: Annual Reviews.

20. McCall, M.W., Jr., Lombardo, M.M., & Morrison, A.M. (1988) *The lessons of experience: How successful executives develop on the job.* New York: Lexington Books.

McCall, M.W., Jr., & Lombardo, M.M. (1983) *Off the track: Why and how successful executives get derailed* (Technical Report No. 21). Greensboro, NC: Center for Creative Leadership.

21. Stogdill, R.M. (1963) *Manual for the Leader Behavior Description Questionnaire— Form XII.* Columbus, OH: Ohio State University, Bureau of Business Research.

A quick search of doctoral dissertations of the past few years (especially in the field of education) will easily confirm that many current dissertations continue to study the dimensions of task and relationship leadership behavior using the LBDQ. Although Stogdill's final version expanded the LBDQ, adding ten new scales, most dissertation research uses only the two task and relationship scales.

22. Fleishman, E.A. (1989) *Examiner's manual for the Supervisory Behavior Description (SBD) Questionnaire (Revised).* Chicago: Science Research Associates.

23. Graen, G.B., & Cashman, J. (1975) A role-making model of leadership in formal organizations: A developmental approach. In J.G. Hunt and L.L. Larson (Eds.), *Leadership frontiers* (pp. 143–165). Kent, OH: Kent State University Press.

24. Graen, G.B., & Uhl-Bien, M. (1995) Relationship-based approach to leadership: Development of leader-member exchange (LMX) theory of leadership over 25 years: Applying a multi-level-multi-domain perspective. *Leadership Quarterly, 6,* 219–247.

25. Dansereau, F., Alutto, J.A., Markham, S.E., & Dumas, M. (1982) Multiplexed supervision and leadership: An application of within and between analysis. In J.G. Hunt, U. Sekaran, and C.A. Schriescheim (Eds.), *Leadership: Beyond establishment views* (pp. 81–103). Carbondale, IL: Southern Illinois University Press.

Graen, G.B., Novak, M.A., & Sommerkamp, P. (1982) The effects of leader-member exchange and job design on productivity and job satisfaction: Testing a dual attachment model. *Organizational Behavior and Human Performance, 30,* 109–131.

26. Burns, J.M. (1978) *Leadership.* New York: Harpers.

27. Kuhn, T.S. (1996) *The structure of scientific revolutions* (3rd ed.). Chicago: University of Chicago Press.

28. Burns, op. cit., p.4.

29. Hollander, E.P. (1980) Leadership and social exchange processes. In K.J. Gergen, M.S. Greenberg, and R.H. Willis (Eds.), *Social exchange: Advances in theory and research* (pp. 103–118). New York: Plenum Press.

Hollander, E.P. (1993) Legitimacy, power, and influence: A perspective on relational features of leadership. In M.M. Chemers and R. Ayman (Eds.), *Leadership theory and research: Perspectives and directions* (pp. 29–47). New York: Academic Press.

30. Sergiovanni, T.J. (1984) Leadership and excellence in schooling. *Educational Leadership, 41* (February), 4–13.

Sergiovanni, T.J. (1992) *Moral leadership.* San Francisco: Jossey-Bass.

Sergiovanni, T.J. (2000) *The lifeworld of leadership.* San Francisco: Jossey-Bass.

31. Bennis, W.G. (1984) The four competencies of leadership. *Training and Development Journal, 38*(8), 14–19.

32. House, R.J. (1977) A 1976 theory of charismatic leadership. In J.G. Hunt and L.L. Larson (Eds.), *Leadership: The cutting edge* (pp. 189-207). Carbondale, IL: Southern Illinois University Press. House originally called his approach a "charismatic leadership theory" but has recently preferred the term "value-based leadership."

33. Bass, B.M. (1985) *Leadership and performance beyond expectations.* New York: Free Press.

Bass' theory and research have dominated the study of the new paradigm. We believe, however, that the measure he and his associates developed, the Multifactor Leadership Questionnaire, has serious psychometric flaws. In particular, the MLQ appears to us to assess a single global dimension that we would call "charismatic feelings of followers toward a leader." (Bass originally called this dimension "charisma" but has renamed it "idealized influence.") The other three dimensions of the MLQ do focus more on actual leader behaviors. These three appear related to behavioral dimensions found in other theories, such as Bennis and Nanus', Conger and Kanungo's, or Kouzes and Posner's approach. For example, Kouzes and Posner speak of "encouraging the heart" while Bass refers to "individualized consideration." However, Bass' three behaviors—inspiration, individualized consideration, and intellectual stimulation—explain only a tiny proportion of the leader's behavior compared to the charisma dimension, which explains over 60% of the perceptions of leadership behavior.

Finally, we think that Bass' approach continues the old paradigm focus on the leader-follower relationship as a one-to-one dynamic. That approach fails to adequately take into account teams and, in particular, the organizational context. The latter is crucial for a meaningful understanding of transformational leadership.

Despite these problems we believe that Bass and his colleagues have made important and significant contributions to the study of transformational leadership. They were among the first to formally study leadership in terms of Burns' ideas. Moreover, their work has stimulated many others to focus on researching and understanding the new paradigm.

34. Bennis, W.G. (1984) The four competencies of leadership. *Training and Development Journal, 38*(8), 14–19.

Bennis, W.G., & Nanus, B. (1985) *Leaders: The strategies for taking charge.* New York: Harper & Row.

35. Kouzes, J.M., & Posner, B.Z. (1987) *The leadership challenge* (2nd ed., 1995; 3rd ed., 2002). San Francisco: Jossey-Bass.

Posner, B.Z., & Kouzes, J.M. (1988) Development and validation of the Leadership Practices Inventory. *Educational and Psychological Measurement, 48*(2), 483–496.

Posner, B.Z., & Kouzes, J.M. (1993) Psychometric properties of the Leadership Practices Inventory—Updated. *Educational and Psychological Measurement, 53*(1), 191–199.

Chapter Three

1. Bennis, W.G., & Nanus, B. (1985) *Leaders: The strategies for taking charge.* New York: Harper & Row.

2. Kouzes, J.M., & Posner, B.Z. (1987) *The leadership challenge* (2nd ed., 1995; 3rd ed., 2002). San Francisco: Jossey-Bass.

3. Bennis & Nanus, op. cit.; Kouzes & Posner, op. cit.

4. Sashkin, M. (1984) *Leader Behavior Questionnaire: The Visionary Leader.* Bryn Mawr, PA: Organization Design and Development.

Sashkin, M. (1985) *Trainer guide: Leader Behavior Questionnaire.* Bryn Mawr, PA: Organization Design and Development.

Sashkin, M. (1996) *The Visionary Leader: Leader Behavior Questionnaire.* (3rd ed.). Amherst, MA: Human Resource Development Press.

Sashkin, M. (1996) *The Visionary Leader: Leader Behavior Questionnaire. Trainer guide* (Rev. ed.). Amherst, MA: Human Resource Development Press.

The latest version of the *LBQ,* now published by HRD Press (800/822-2801 or www. hrdpress.com) is currently available as a hand-scored booklet designed for use in leadership development seminars. Both self-report and other-report versions are available, to provide an opportunity for full "360-degree" feedback. The *LBQ* has been used by more than 100,000 managers and executives and is available in Spanish and other languages from HRD Press and various international distributors of materials for use in human resource development.

Appendix Two describes the development of the *LBQ* and its most recent revision, *The Leadership Profile.*

5. Sashkin, M., & Rosenbach, W.E. (1996) *The Leadership Profile.* Seabrook, MD: Ducochon Press.

This latest version of our leadership questionnaire measures several dimensions of leadership in addition to the four behaviors. These additional dimensions will be discussed in detail in the chapters that follow. The *TLP* is available as an optical scan form that is used to generate individual numerical/graphic assessment reports for use in leadership development seminars that involve full "360-degree" feedback. For information contact Ducochon Press (301/552-9523 or www.ducochonpress.com).

Appendix Two describes the development of the *TLP* and gives a summary of research evidence demonstrating its reliability and validity.

6. This research centered on identifying and developing a valid measure of organizational trust based on the two dimensions of consistency and credibility. This research is reported in detail in the following:

Levin, S.L. (1999) *Development of an instrument to measure organizational trust.* Doctoral dissertation, The George Washington University, Washington, DC.

Sashkin, M., & Levin, S.L. (2001, April) Development of an instrument to measure organizational trust. Paper presented at the annual meeting of the Society for Industrial and Organizational Psychology, San Diego, California.

7. As quoted in *Fortune* magazine, September 1986.

8. Major, K. (1988) *Dogmatism, visionary leadership, and effectiveness of secondary principals.* Doctoral dissertation, University of La Verne, California.

9. Endeman, J.L. (1990) *Visionary leadership in superintendents and its effect on organizational outcomes.* Doctoral dissertation, University of La Verne, California.

Endeman, J.L. (1993) Visionary superintendents and their districts. In M. Sashkin and H.J. Walberg (Eds.), *Educational leadership and school culture* (pp. 146–162). Berkeley, CA: McCutchen.

10. The Organizational Culture Assessment Questionnaire (OCAQ) was developed by Marshall Sashkin to measure the extent to which an organization's culture is based on values and beliefs that support the effective operation of the four crucial functions defined by Talcott Parsons: adapting to change; achieving goals; coordinating the work activities of individuals and teams; and maintaining these patterns of action through shared values and beliefs. For details see:

Parsons, T. (1960) *Structure and process in modern societies.* New York: Free Press.

Sashkin, M. (1990) *Organizational Culture Assessment Questionnaire.* Seabrook, MD: Ducochon Press.

Sawner, T., & Sashkin, M. (2001, April) An empirical investigation of the relationship between organizational culture and organizational performance in a large public service organization. Paper presented at the annual meeting of the Society for Industrial and Organizational Psychology, San Diego, California.

11. Sashkin, M., Rosenbach, W.E., & Mueller, R. (1994, June) Leadership, culture, and performance: An exploration of relationships. Paper presented at the international meeting of the Western Management Association, Brisbane, Australia.

12. Colyer, S.L. (1996) *An empirical investigation of self and other perceptions of visionary leadership as related to organizational performance.* Doctoral dissertation, The George Washington University, Washington, DC.

Colyer, S.L. (1997, August) An empirical investigation of the relationship between visionary leadership and organizational performance: Consequences of self-other agreement. Paper presented at the annual meeting of the Academy of Management, Boston.

Chapter Four

1. This is quoted directly from John Heider's *The Tao of Leadership* (New York: Bantam, 1985), p. 77. Heider takes considerable liberty in his interpretation but generally has it right. This chapter says, essentially, that to be effective leaders must really be humble (like a servant) as well as (and in order to) be high and noble (and, therefore, well-served). That is, they can't just feign humility but must actually practice it. Fake humility will not ring true. It will, moreover, demonstrate the leader's lack of real power.

2. House, R.J. (1977) A 1976 theory of charismatic leadership. In J.G. Hunt and L.L. Larson (Eds.), *Leadership: The cutting edge* (pp. 189–207). Carbondale, IL: Southern Illinois University Press.

3. Weber, M. (1922/1963) *The sociology of religion.* Beacon, NY: Beacon Press.

4. Weber, M. (1924/1947) *The theory of social and economic organization* (T. Parsons, Translator). New York: Free Press.

5. Most of the biographical information presented here is found in the excellent biography of Max Weber published as the introduction to the translated essays and papers, *From Max Weber,* by Hans Gerth and C. Wright Mills (New York: Oxford University Press, 1946).

6. Durkheim, E. (1897) *Le suicide.* Paris: F. Alcan.

7. Weber, M. (1924/1963) *The sociology of religion.* Beacon, NY: Beacon Press.

8. Helmsley went to prison not because she abused employees but because she tried to take business tax deductions for the materials and labor expended on her personal residence.

9. Weber's writings on bureaucracy are complex and not clearly organized in a single volume. Definitions of bureaucracy are presented in his classic work, *Wirtschaft und Gesellschaft,* which was only published (in German) after Weber's death and was first translated into English by an American sociologist, Talcott Parsons, and published in 1947 as *The Theory of Social and Economic Organization* (New York: Free Press). Weber's description of bureaucracy is probably most accessible in the set of excerpts and essays *From Max Weber,* translated and edited by Hans Gerth and C. Wright Mills (New York: Oxford University Press, 1946). Weber defines three primary elements of bureaucracy: (1) authority to carry out defined job duties in specific areas, according to rules and regulations; (2) a clear hierarchy of authority; (3) written records.

10. House, R.J. (1977) A 1976 theory of charismatic leadership. In J.G. Hunt and L.L. Larson (Eds.), *Leadership: The cutting edge* (pp. 189–207). Carbondale, IL: Southern Illinois University Press.

11. McClelland's work is compiled in his comprehensive text, *Human motivation* (New York: Cambridge University Press, 1987).

12. McClelland, D.C. (1965) N achievement and entrepreneurship: A longitudinal study. *Journal of Personality and Social Psychology, 1,* 389–392.

13. McClelland, D.C., & Winter, D.G. (1969) *Motivating economic achievement.* New York: Free Press.

14. This definition was actually developed by McClelland's student, David Winter, in his 1973 book, *The Power Motive* (New York: Free Press). McClelland credits Winter and uses this definition in his own comprehensive text published in 1987, *Human Motivation* (New York: Cambridge University Press, p. 271).

We use McClelland's definition but interpret it more explicitly to mean a concern with control over one's own life, in the sense of survival. In this sense we see the power need as related to Maslow's most basic needs for survival, expressed in his classic "hierarchy of needs" concept. Both Maslow and McClelland were deeply influenced by Freudian psychological theory, which places survival as the most basic human need. For further discussion see the following works by Maslow:

Maslow, A.H. (1943) A theory of human motivation. *Psychological Review, 50,* 370–396.

Maslow, A.H. (1967) A theory of metamotivation: The biological rooting of the value of life. *Journal of Humanistic Psychology, 7,* 93–127.

Maslow, A.H. (1998) *Maslow on management* (D.C. Stephens and G. Heil, Eds.). New York: Wiley.

15. McClelland, D.C., & Burnham, D.H. (1976) Power is the great motivator. *Harvard Business Review, 54*(2), 100–110.

16. Tannenbaum, A.S. (Ed.) (1968) *Control in organizations.* NY: McGraw-Hill.

17. McClelland, D.C., & Winter, D.G. (1969) *Motivating economic achievement.* New York: Free Press.

18. McClelland, D.C. (1977) The impact of power motivation training on alcoholics. *Journal of Studies on Alcohol, 38*(1), 142–144.

19. Conger, J.A. (1992) *The charismatic leader.* San Francisco: Jossey-Bass.

20. This chart is based on but not identical with McClelland's model as presented in his 1987 book, *Human motivation* (New York: Cambridge University Press).

Chapter Five

1. Conger, J.A., & Kanungo, R.N., (Eds.) (1988) *Charismatic leadership: The elusive factor in organizational effectiveness.* San Francisco: Jossey-Bass.

Conger, J.A. (1989) *The charismatic leader: Behind the mystique of exceptional leadership.* San Francisco: Jossey-Bass.

2. Kelman, H.C. (1958) Compliance, identification, and internalization: Three processes of attitude change. *Journal of Conflict Resolution, 2,* 51–60.

3. Sashkin, M., & Fulmer, R.M. (1985) A new framework for leadership. Paper presented at the Biennial Leadership Symposium, Texas Tech University, Lubbock.

Sashkin, M., & Fulmer, R.M. (1988) Toward an organizational leadership theory. In J.G. Hunt, B.R. Baliga, H.P. Dachler, and C.A. Schreischeim (Eds.), *Emerging leadership vistas* (pp. 51–65). Lexington, MA: Lexington Books.

4. Post, J.M. (1986) Narcissism and the charismatic leader-follower relationship. *Political Psychology, 7*(4), 675–687.

5. Post, op. cit.

6. Post, op. cit.

7. Bion, W. (1961) *Experiences in groups.* New York: Basic Books.

8. Quoted by Joshua O. Haberman in *The God I Believe In* (New York: Free Press, 1994, pp. 154–155), from the edited transcript of his conversation with Ozick on February 2, 1992.

9. Letter from David McClelland to Marshall Sashkin, August 17, 1995.

10. Comment to us by Harry Levinson (May, 2001), noting that the concept of identification is important for transformational as well as charismatic leadership.

11. Maccoby, M. (2000) Narcissistic leaders. *Harvard Business Review, 78*(1), 68–77.

12. Observation made by Robert J. House, in conversation with Marshall Sashkin.

Chapter Six

1. Many of these studies are described in detail in the following two references: Maier, S.F., & Seligman, M.E.P. (1976) Learned helplessness: Theory and evidence. *Journal of Experimental Psychology: General, 105,* 3–46.

Seligman, M.E.P. (1993) *Helplessness: On depression, development, and death.* San Francisco: Freeman.

Some specific studies we referred to are:

Lee, R.K., & Maier, S.F. (1988) Inescapable shock and attention to internal versus external cues in a water discrimination escape task. *Journal of Experimental Psychology: Animal Behavior Processes, 14,* 302–310.

Overmier, J.B., & Seligman, M.E.P. (1967) Effects of inescapable shock upon subsequent escape and avoidance learning. *Journal of Comparative and Physiological Psychology, 63,* 28–33.

Seligman, M.E.P., & Beagley, G. (1975) Learned helplessness in the rat. *Journal of Comparative and Physiological Psychology, 88,* 534–541.

2. Skinner, B.F. (1938) *The behavior of organisms.* New York: Appleton Century Crofts.

Skinner, B.F. (1974) *About behaviorism.* New York: Knopf.

The first reference above is Skinner's classic textbook on behaviorism (which is out of print). The second was written at the end of his long career and is directed at the general reader.

3. Will Smith related this story to Charlie Rose on *The Charlie Rose Show*, broadcast on PBS on March 13, 2002.

4. Merton, R.K. (1948) The self-fulfilling prophecy. *Antioch Review, 8,* 193–210.

5. Rosenthal, R. (1964) Experimenter outcome orientation and the results of the psychological experiment. *Psychological Bulletin, 61,* 405–412.

Rosenthal, R., & Jacobson, L. (1968) *Pygmalion in the classroom: Teacher expectation and pupils' intellectual development.* New York: Holt, Rinehart and Winston.

6. Bandura, A. (1977) *Social learning theory.* Englewood Cliffs, NJ: Prentice-Hall.

Bandura, A. (1982) Self-efficacy mechanism in human agency. *American Psychologist, 37,* 122–147.

7. Kogan, N., & Wallach, M.A. (1964) *Risk taking.* New York: Holt.

8. Sashkin, M. (2001) *Tough Choices: The managerial decision-making assessment inventory* (Rev. ed.). Seabrook, MD: Ducochon Press.

9. We administered Tough Choices to a group of mid-level managers and another group of clerical employees. As we had expected, the managers were, in general, willing to take more risks than the clericals, who were generally more conservative about risk-taking. However, when we compared the two groups on the stories about the heart operation and the hostage, we found that the clerks were more conservative than the managers in their willingness to risk escaping but were willing to take a greater risk than were the managers with regard to undergoing the heart operation.

10. Bennis, W.G., & Nanus, B. (1985) *Leaders: The strategies for taking charge.* New York: Harper & Row.

11. In Chapter Four of his book, *The Optimistic Child* (Boston: Houghton Mifflin, 1995), Martin E.P. Seligman castigates the "self-esteem movement" in schools. This approach is designed to convince children that they are worthwhile and "special," regardless of their actions. Seligman, however, argues that such an approach actually *damages* children's self-confidence. He says that efforts to bolster self-esteem may even increase the incidence of childhood depression. This happens when children exposed to self-esteem–inducing praise find that their actions are not successful and that their "esteem" is not tied to the outcomes of their actions.

Chapter Seven

1. Streufert, S. & Swezey, R.W. (1986) *Complexity, managers, and organizations.* Orlando, FL: Academic Press.

Streufert, S., & Streufert, S.J. (1978) *Behavior in the complex environment.* New York: Halsted.

Streufert, S., Pogash, R.M., & Piasecki, M.T. (1988). Simulation-based assessment of managerial competence. *Personnel Psychology, 41,* 537–555.

2. We draw on two primary sources for our concept of vision as a personal characteristic based on the capacity of a leader for complex thinking over long time periods. These are

Jaques, E. (1986) The development of intellectual capacity. *Journal of Applied Behavioral Science, 22,* 361-383.

Streufert, S., & Swezey, R.W. (1986) *Complexity, managers, and organizations.* Orlando, FL: Academic Press.

We rely more on the work of Jaques and his colleagues because they have developed a comprehensive theory of executive leadership centered on their concept of "cognitive capability." Streufert and his associates, however, add a practical focus to the measurement and development of what they call "cognitive complexity." They are more clear than Jaques in describing how effective executives think and plan actions in terms of complex and interactive sequences of cause and effect.

3. Jaques, E. (1986) The development of intellectual capacity. *Journal of Applied Behavioral Science, 22,* 361–383.

Jaques, E. (1976) *A general theory of bureaucracy.* London: Heinemann.

Jaques, E. (1979) Taking time seriously in evaluating jobs. *Harvard Business Review, 57*(5), 124–132.

Jaques, E., & Clement, S.D. (1991) *Executive leadership: A practical guide to managing complexity.* Arlington, VA: Cason-Hall.

Jaques, E., & Cason, K. (1998) *Human capability.* Alexandria, VA: Cason-Hall.

4. Jaques has used a variety of labels for this idea, including "cognitive capability." The term he uses currently is "cognitive power," but we prefer to avoid this term so as not to confuse it with our earlier discussion of the need for power.

5. In Jaques' theory, cognitive power is considered as a genetically defined trait. Individuals are born at a particular "stratum" and, while their actual cognitive power develops with age and maturity, it will always be within the range limits for that stratum. We disagree with this view and put greater weight on the views of Streufert and his associates. They believe, as we do, that cognitive complexity (their term for cognitive power) can be developed, although there may be a limit to what any particular individual may achieve. That is, with enough practice (and determination) almost anyone can learn to play the piano, even if not very well. Most people, again with practice and motivation, can probably learn to play well enough that others will find their music inoffensive, if not pleasant. But very few people, no matter how hard they try or how long they practice, will achieve results comparable to those of a great classical pianist such as Vladimir Horowitz.

6. Table 7-1 is based on Jaques' theory and data reported in Jaques (1986), op. cit.

7. Jaques, E. (1978) *A general theory of bureaucracy.* Exeter, NH: Heinemann.
Jaques, E. (1989) *Requisite organization.* Arlington, VA: Cason-Hall.

8. Sashkin, M. (1986, May) True vision in leadership. *Training and Development Journal, 40*(5), 58–61.
This presentation of the four cognitive skills of visioning is based almost entirely on the work of Elliott Jaques (op. cit.). Jaques uses different terminology, but the four skill elements presented here are essentially the same as his.

9. James, W. (1890) *Principles of psychology.* New York: Henry Holt.
See also:
James, W. (1880) Great men, great thoughts, and their environment. *Atlantic Monthly, 46,* 441–459.

10. Maslow, A.H. (1943) A theory of human motivation. *Psychological Review, 50,* 370–396.
Sashkin, M. (1996) *The MbM Questionnaire: Managing by motivation* (3rd ed.). Amherst, MA: HRD Press.

11. Kouzes, J.M., & Posner, B.Z. (1987) *The leadership challenge.* San Francisco: Jossey-Bass (2nd ed., 1995; 3rd ed., 2002).

12. Hymowitz, C. (1988, May 2) Five main reasons why managers fail. *The Wall Street Journal.*
McCall, M.W., Jr., & Lombardo, M.M. (1983) Off the track: Why and how successful executives get derailed. Technical report No. 21. Greensboro, NC: Center for Creative Leadership.
McCall, M.W., Jr., Lombardo, M.M., & Morrison, A.M. (1988) *The lessons of experience.* New York: Lexington Books.

13. For example, the approach developed by House and his associates centers on the power need while neglecting efficacy and cognition. See the following:
House, R.J. (1977) A 1976 theory of charismatic leadership. In J.G. Hunt and L.L. Larson (Eds.), *Leadership: The cutting edge* (pp. 189–204). Carbondale, IL: Southern Illinois University Press.
House, R.J., Spangler, D., & Wyocke, J. (1991) Personality and charisma in the U.S. Presidency: A psychological theory of leadership effectiveness. *Administrative Science Quarterly, 36,* 364–396.

14. Lewin, K. (1948) *Resolving social conflicts.* New York: Harper.

Chapter Eight

1. Lewin, K. (1951) *Field theory in social science* (D. Cartwright, Ed.). New York: Harper & Row.

2. House, R.J. (1971) A path-goal theory of leader effectiveness. *Administrative Science Quarterly, 12,* 556–571.
    Hersey, P., & Blanchard, K. (1969) Life cycle theory of leadership. *Training & Development Journal, 23,* 26–34.

3. Weber, M. (1947) *The theory of social and economic organization* (A.M. Henderson & Talcott Parsons, Translators, Talcott Parsons, Ed.). New York: Free Press, pp. 94–96.

4. Fayol, H. 1916. *Administration industrielle et generale.* Paris: Dunod.

5. Mooney, J.D., & Reiley, A.C. (1931) *Onward industry: The principles of organization and their significance to modern industry.* New York: Harper.

6. This is essentially the point made by Parsons in his introduction to his and Henderson's translation of Weber's *The Theory of Social and Economic Organization* (New York: Free Press, 1947).

7. Parsons, again, raises this issue of the "incomplete" nature of Weber's formulation in his introduction to *The Theory of Social and Economic Organization* (op. cit.), referring the reader to Parsons' own classic work, *The Structure of Social Action* (New York: Free Press, 1937).

8. Parsons, T. (1951) *The social system.* New York: Free Press.
    Parsons, T. (1960) *Structure and process in modern societies.* New York: Free Press.
    Parsons, T., & Shils, E.A. (Eds.) (1959) *Toward a general theory of action.* Cambridge, MA: Harvard University Press.

9. von Bertalanffy, L. (1968) *General system theory.* New York: George Braziller.

10. Hersh, S.M. (2001, July 9) The price of oil; what was Mobil up to in Kazakhstan and Russia? *The New Yorker, 77*(18), 48–65.

11. Blau, P.M. (1974) *Exchange and power in social life.* New York: Wiley.

Chapter Nine

1. Schein, E.H. (1985) *Organizational culture and leadership* (2nd ed., 1992). San Francisco: Jossey-Bass.

2. The person behind the Tylenol murders was never caught. No similar cases have occurred since, although several people have tried to make the killing of a particular individual look like a Tylenol "copycat" murder.

3. We don't mean to denigrate team-building. Such interventions can be quite valuable, in building the skills people need to work together effectively. However, real cooperation must arise out of the working relationships themselves, that is, out of the values and beliefs that define organizational culture and guide action.

4. Sashkin, M., & Sashkin, M.G. (1993) Principals and their school cultures: Understandings from quantitative and qualitative research. In M. Sashkin and H.J. Walberg (Eds.), *Educational leadership and school culture* (pp. 100–123). Berkeley, CA: McCutchan.

Chapter Ten

1. In their book *Leaders* (New York: Harper & Row, 1985) Warren Bennis and Bert Nanus cite the case of Karl Wallenda and "The Flying Wallendas" to point out the disastrous consequences that can result when a leader concentrates solely on not failing rather than on successfully attaining a goal. (Wallenda fell to his death from the tightwire.) Our point here, however, is not the problem of fearing failure so much that it becomes a self-fulfilling prophecy. Rather, we were impressed by the observation of Wallenda's wife that for the first time Wallenda felt he had to personally supervise all equipment set-up and check it all himself, "something he had never even thought of doing before" (p. 70).

2. Senge, P.M. (1990, Fall) The leader's new work: Building the learning organization. *Sloan Management Review, 32*(1), 7–23.

3. M.E.P. Seligman, former president of the American Psychological Association, makes this quite clear in his scathing critique of the self-esteem movement in U.S. education, contained in Chapter 4 of his book *The Optimistic Child* (Boston: Houghton Mifflin, 1995).

4. Senge, op. cit. The concept of leadership as stewardship is generally credited to Robert Greenleaf, author of *Servant Leadership* (New York: Paulist Press, 1977). More recently, Peter Block elaborated on this idea in his book *Stewardship* (San Francisco: Berrett-Koehler, 1993).

5. Randolph, W.A., & Sashkin, M. (2002) Can organizational empowerment work in multinational settings? *Academy of Management Executive, 16,* 102–115.

6. Lafferty, B.D. (1997, August) Investigation of a leadership program at the U.S. Air Force Air Command and Staff College. Paper presented at the annual meeting of the Academy of Management, Boston.

Lafferty, B.D. (1998) *An empirical investigation of a leadership development program.* Doctoral dissertation, The George Washington University, Washington, DC.

7. What makes this different from other pre-post non-experimental tests is that we did this for several years, and also re-administered the TLP to the past graduates each year. Thus we could show that there were no differences between a group starting in one year and any group starting in another year. We could also look for consistent changes that appeared again and again, for each class. And, we could see whether changes held up over time. What we did is called a "quasi-experimental" research design. It is not as rigorous as a true experiment, in which we would have randomly assigned people to the group to get the training or to a control group that got no training, and then tested each group after the training to see if the leadership training had any effects. But, our quasi-experiment permits us to draw conclusions that are almost as definitive as a true experiment and has the additional value of providing data over several years, to track program graduates.

8. A follow-up study recently completed by another doctoral student, Lynne Thompson, showed that certain on-the-job experiences are associated with continued development of transformational leadership. The most potent factor was the challenge of increased responsibility.

9. Axelrod, R.H., & Sashkin, M. (2000, August) Outcome measurement in a leadership development program. Paper presented at the annual meeting of the Academy of Management, Toronto.

10. Goleman, D. (1995) *Emotional intelligence.* New York: Bantam Books.

11. Colyer, S.L. (1996) *An empirical investigation of self and other perceptions of visionary leadership as related to organizational performance.* Doctoral dissertation, The George Washington University, Washington, DC.

Colyer, S.L. (1997, August) An empirical investigation of the relationship between visionary leadership and organizational performance: Consequences of self-other agreement. Paper presented at the annual meeting of the Academy of Management, Boston.

12. Stryker, J. (2000) *The effects of 360 degree feedback: A field experiment.* Doctoral dissertation, The George Washington University, Washington, DC.

13. Conger, J.A. (1992) *Learning to lead: The art of transforming managers into leaders.* San Francisco: Jossey-Bass.

Chapter Eleven

1. The results of our research, as well as research we have guided, have been published in a number of books and journals and presented at various professional meetings. A reference list is provided in Appendix One.

2. Appendix Two gives a brief presentation of the technical background of **The Leadership Profile.**

3. One study was conducted by one of the authors and two of his colleagues. Four were done under that author's supervision by his doctoral students at The George Washingtion University. The remaining two studies were conducted at other universities, with Marshall Sashkin serving as an informal outside advisor.

4. Higgins, C.C. (1998) *Transactional and transformational leadership: An examination of the relationship between leadership orientation and perceptions of organizational effectiveness.* Doctoral dissertation, The George Washington University, Washington, DC.

5. Major, K. (1988) *Dogmatism, visionary leadership and effectiveness of secondary principals.* Doctoral dissertation, University of La Verne, California.

6. Sashkin, M., Rosenbach, W.E., & Mueller, R. (1994, June) Leadership, culture, and performance: An exploration of relationships. Paper presented at the international meeting of the Western Academy of Management, Brisbane, Australia.

7. Sashkin, M. (1988) *The Organizational Culture Assessment Questionnaire.* Seabrook, MD: Ducochon Press.

The *OCAQ* was shown to be significantly related to performance measures in 53 wings of the U.S. Air National Guard, including inspection ratings, turnover, and ground safety incidents (accidents). See:

Sawner, T.E. (1999) *An empirical investigation of the relationship between organizational culture and organizational performance in a large public sector organization.* Doctoral dissertation, The George Washington University.

Sawner, T.E., & Sashkin, M. (2001, April) An empirical investigation of the relationship between organizational culture and organizational performance in a large public sector organization. Paper presented at the annual meeting of the Society for Industrial and Organizational Psychology, San Diego.

8. Colyer, S.L. (1997, August) An empirical investigation of the relationship between visionary leadership and organizational performance: Consequences of self-other agreement. Paper presented at the annual meeting of the Academy of Management, Boston.

Colyer, S.L. (1998) *An empirical investigation of self and other perceptions of visionary leadership as related to organizational performance.* Doctoral dissertation, The George Washington University, Washington, DC.

9. Goleman, D. (1995) *Emotional intelligence.* New York: Bantam Books.

10. Dixon, D.L. (1998) *The relationship between chief executive leadership (transactional and transformational) and hospital effectiveness.* Doctoral dissertation, The George Washington University, Washington, DC.

11. Scholars often criticize results based on one or a few cases as unreliable and unproven. Some scholars also incorrectly criticize rigorous research that uses statistical tests on a relatively small number of cases. The fact is, when a result is statistically significant that means that it is very unlikely to be a mere chance outcome. A statistically significant result means that there is a real relationship between the measures studied. The limitation of small numbers, however, is real. That is, the results cannot be said to generalize to other cases and contexts. The results hold only for the specific group of organizations in the study.

12. Silver, S.R. (1999) *Perception of empowerment in engineering workgroups: The linkage to transformational leadership and performance.* Doctoral dissertation, The George Washington University, Washington, DC.

Sashkin, M., Silver, S.R., & Scott-Lennon, F. (1998, June) Organizational empowerment and the individual. Paper presented at the annual meeting of the International Federation of Training and Development Organizations, Dublin, Ireland.

13. De Pree, M. (1989) *Leadership Is an Art.* New York: Doubleday.

Chapter Twelve

1. Friedman, T.L. (2000) *The Lexus and the olive tree.* New York: Anchor Books.

2. Ernst, L. (1997) *Transformational leadership of male and female executives as related to a measure of gender role orientation: Further development of a measure of leadership.* Doctoral dissertation, The George Washington University, Washington, DC.

3. Bennis, W.G., & Nanus, B. (1985) *Leaders: The strategies for taking charge.* New York: Harper & Row.

4. Helgesen, S. (1990) *The female advantage: Women's ways of leadership.* New York: Doubleday.

5. Tibus, C.A. (1997) *Leadership and ownership: An investigation of leadership among women business owners and women business executives.* Doctoral dissertation, The George Washington University, Washington, DC.

6. Silver, S.R. (1999) *Perception of empowerment in engineering workgroups: The linkage to transformational leadership and performance.* Doctoral dissertation, The George Washington University, Washington, DC.

7. Blanchard, K.H., Carlos, J.P., & Randolph, W.A. (1996) *Empowerment takes more than a minute.* San Francisco: Berrett-Koehler.

Blanchard, K.H., Carlos, J.P., & Randolph, W.A. (1999) *The 3 keys to empowerment: Release the power within people for astonishing results.* San Francisco: Berrett-Koehler.

8. Cohen, D., & March, J.G. (1974) *Leadership and ambiguity.* New York: McGraw-Hill.

9. Sashkin, M., & Kiser, K.J. (1993) *Putting total quality management to work.* San Francisco: Berrett-Koehler.

10. McLuhan, M., & Fiore, Q. (1968) *War and peace in the global village: An inventory of some of the current spastic situations that could be eliminated by more feedforward.* New York: McGraw-Hill.

McLuhan, M., & Powers, B.R. (1989) *Global village: Transformations in world life and media in the 21st century.* New York: Oxford University Press.

11. Friedman, op. cit.

12. Tannenbaum, A.S. (Ed.) (1968) *Control in organizations.* New York: McGraw-Hill.

13. Kotter, J.P., & Heskett, J.L. (1992) *Corporate culture and performance.* New York: Free Press.

Chapter Thirteen

1. We began Chapter One with this quote from Lao Tzu's *Tao Te Ching,* the "book of the way things work." In this final chapter we will provide references primarily for new information. When names are given without a note, they have been referenced fully in earlier chapters.

2. Hollander, E.P. (1992) The essential interdependence of leadership and followership. *Current Directions in Psychological Science, 1*(2), 71-75.

Hollander, E.P. (1992) Leadership, followership, self, and others. *Leadership Quarterly, 3*(1), 43–54.

3. McClelland, D.C., & Boyatzis, R.E. (1982) Leadership motive pattern and long-term success in management. *Journal of Applied Psychology, 67*(6), 737–743.

Jacobs, R.L., & McClelland, D.C. (1994) Moving up the corporate ladder: A longitudinal study of the leadership motive pattern and managerial success in women and men. *Consulting Psychology Journal: Practice and Research, 46*(1), 32–41.

4. House, R.J. (1995, June) Value based leadership. *Personalführung,* 476–479.

5. House, R.J., & Shamir, B. (1993) Toward the integration of transformational, charismatic, and visionary theories. In M.M. Chemers and R. Ayman (Eds.), *Leadership theory and research: Perspectives and directions* (pp. 81–107). New York: Academic Press.

Shamir, B. (1991) Meaning, self, and motivation in organizations. *Organization Studies, 12,* 405–424.

Shamir, B., House, R.J., & Arthur, M.B. (1993) The motivational effects of charismatic leadership: A self-concept based theory. *Organization Science, 4,* 1–14.

6. Neither Bass nor most other leadership scholars agree with us that charismatic leadership is generally fraught with problems and is very different from transformational leadership.

7. Jaques, E. (1986) The development of intellectual capacity. *Journal of Applied Behavioral Science, 22,* 361–383.

Jaques, E., & Clement, S.D. (1991) *Executive leadership.* Arlington, VA: Cason Hall.

Streufert, S., & Swezey, R.W. (1986) *Complexity, managers, and organizations.* Orlando, FL: Academic Press.

8. Goleman, D. (1994, July 31) Successful executives rely on own kind of intelligence. *The New York Times (Science Times)*, pp. C1, C11.

9. Streufert, S. (1991) The art of multidimensional management. *Clinical Laboratory Management Review, 5*(2), 106–113.

10. Streufert, S. (1986) How top managers think and decide. *Executive Excellence, 8,* 7–9.

11. Conger, J.A., & Kanungo, R.N. (1994) Charismatic leadership in organizations: Perceived behavioral attributes and their measurement. *Journal of Organizational Behavior, 15,* 439–452.

Conger, J.A., & Kanungo, R.N. (1998) *Charismatic leadership in organizations.* Thousand Oaks, CA: Sage.

12. Kouzes, J.M., & Posner, B.Z. (1987) *The leadership challenge* (2nd ed., 1995; 3rd ed., 2002). San Francisco: Jossey-Bass.

13. Kotter, J.P., & Heskett, J.L. (1992) *Corporate culture and performance.* New York: Free Press.

14. Rost, J.C. (1991) *Leadership for the twenty-first century.* New York: Praeger.

15. Herzberg, F., Mausner, B., & Snyderman, B.B. (1959) *The motivation to work.* New York: Wiley.

16. Myers, M.S. (1981) *Every employee a manager* (2nd ed.). New York: McGraw-Hill.

17. Pondy, L. R. (1977) Leadership is a language game. In M. McCall and M. Lombardo (Eds.), *Leadership: Where else do we go?* Durham, NC: Duke University Press.

Pondy was, of course, echoing the twentieth-century philosopher Ludwig Wittgenstein, who asserted that philosophy is a language game. Wittgenstein argued that all philosophical problems can be resolved by clearly defining the meaning of the terms being used. He asserted that such definitional clarity could resolve all philosophical questions, since all such questions really center on defining what we mean. Thus, the term "language game" refers to the use of language to define meaning. This technique has been widely applied in many fields and is one reason that Wittgenstein is considered one of the most influential philosophers of the twentieth century.

18. Sievers, B. (1994) *Work, death, and life itself: Essays on management and organization.* Berlin: Walter de Gruyter.

19. Lao Tzu seems to recognize this in Chapter 62 of the *Tao.* In that chapter he points out that people who are not aware of the meaning of things—of Tao—are not "bad" or "wrong." However, he notes that being aware of Tao, of meaning and the way things work, is a very useful capability.

20. Collins, J.C., & Porras, J.I. (1994) *Built to last: Successful habits of visionary companies.* New York: HarperBusiness.

Collins, J.C. (2002) *Good to great.* New York: HarperBusiness.

Appendix Two

1. The research described here is taken from the following reports:

Sashkin, M., Rosenbach, W.E., & Sashkin, M.G. (1997, August) The Leadership Profile: Psychometric development of a leadership assessment tool and its use in leadership development. Paper presented at the annual meeting of the Academy of Management, Boston.

Sashkin, M. (2002) Visionary leadership theory: The research evidence. Working paper, Center for the Study of Learning, Graduate School of Education and Human Development, The George Washington University.

2. Palmer, D. (1999) *Leadership: Does it make a difference in a high technology career?* Doctoral dissertation, The George Washington University, Washington, DC.

3. The final set of dimensions is never completely independent. That would be impossible, since many things are at least a little bit interrelated. What factor analysis does is try to find the most independent set of dimensions possible. The items (questions) are all tossed together and intercorrelated repeatedly to identify the strongest sets of interrelationships. These sets of most strongly interrelated items form a "factor." Most of the other items are also related to the items central to a factor, but those relationships are generally very small, so they are disregarded.

The factors in the final result don't come with a name or label. Based on the items that make up the factor it is up to the researcher to figure out a name for the factor, that is, to determine what the factor really measures in content.

4. We are grateful to the American Management Association and to Eric Rolfe Greenberg, Director of Research, for their support. More extensive details of this study can be found in a doctoral dissertation conducted under our supervision by Dr. Lynn Ernst:

Ernst, L. (1997) *Transformational leadership of male and female executives as related to a measure of gender role orientation: Further development of a measure of leadership.* Doctoral dissertation, The George Washington University, Washington, DC.

5. A varimax rotation has the factor analysis program try to get the most independent factors possible without specifying exactly how independent they have to be. Eigenvalues are parameters that are set to define how "important" a factor must be to be called a factor. The most common setting for the eigenvalue is 1.00. This produces factors that are not of such minor importance as to be practically irrelevant. The percent of variance accounted for is a quantitative measure of a factor's importance. Ideally, a factor analysis should "account for" (predict) a large proportion of the variance—the variability in the total score. At the same time, each factor should account for about the same amount of variance. This means that no one factor is by far the most important.

Using our data we conducted a factor analysis, with a varimax rotation and eigenvalue set to be greater than 1.00. The result was a 12 factor solution, explaining 54% of the total variance. Individual factors accounted for from 7.4% to 2.9% of the variance; no one or few factors dominated the analysis.

6. Lafferty, B.D. (1998) *An empirical investigation of a leadership development program.* Doctoral dissertation, The George Washington University, Washington, DC.

Lafferty, B.D. (1997, August) Investigation of a leadership program at the U.S. Air Force Air Command and Staff College. Paper presented at the annual meeting of the Academy of Management, Boston.

7. Sashkin, M. (1996) *The Leader Behavior Questionnaire: The Visionary Leader* (Rev. ed.). Amherst, MA: Human Resource Development Press.

8. McElreath, J. (1999) *Development of a biodata measure of leadership skills.* Doctoral dissertation, Wayne State University, Detroit, MI.

9. Bass, B.M. (1985) *Leadership and performance beyond expectations.* New York: Free Press.

Kouzes, J., & Posner, B.Z. (1987) *The leadership challenge* (2nd ed., 1995; 3rd ed., 2002). San Francisco: Jossey-Bass.

The ten *LBQ* scales were not separately correlated with the other measures. Only the total scores for the three areas were used by McElreath.

10. The correlations ranged from .47 to .54. These are moderate to strong correlations. All were statistically significant. That is, the odds of finding these correlations by chance alone are less than one in one hundred.

11. These correlations ranged from .53 to .64. These are strong correlations, all statistically significant to the extent that the odds of finding any by chance alone are less than one in one hundred.

Index

About the Authors

Marshall Sashkin is professor of human resource development at The George Washington University, where he teaches leadership, consulting skills, organizational diagnosis, and research methods. He holds a doctorate in organizational psychology from the University of Michigan. Prior to his current appointment he was professor of industrial and organizational psychology at the University of Maryland and Senior Associate in the U.S. Department of Education's Office of Educational Research and Improvement, where he developed and guided applied research aimed at improving leadership in schools. He has consulted with private firms (such as GE Capital and American Express–Corporate) and public organizations (including the U.S. Army and the Michigan Region of the American Red Cross), as well as school systems. More than fifty of his research papers on leadership, participation, and organizational change have been published in academic journals, and he is author or coauthor of more than a dozen books and monographs. He is coauthor of the best-selling business book *Putting Total Quality Management to Work*.

Molly G. Sashkin holds two master's degrees, the first in secondary education and the second in guidance and personnel services. She has teaching and counseling experience at every level of the educational system, from preschool through elementary, secondary, and college levels. She has been an educational advisor for the U.S. Navy, counseling individuals and administering academic programs, and has worked as a test development specialist and psychometrician for the U.S. Army Engineers, constructing and validating job qualification tests. She has extensive experience in career development. She has worked as a career development specialist at the U.S. Department of Commerce, advising personnel from entry-level clerical staff to members of the Senior Executive Service. Since 1985 she has been president of Ducochon Press, a publishing firm specializing in assessment and training materials for management and organization development. She has conducted research on leadership and culture and coauthored (with Marshall Sashkin), *The New Teamwork,* a guide to cross-functional teamwork published by the American Management Association.

Berrett-Koehler Publishers

Berrett-Koehler is an independent publisher of books and other publications at the leading edge of new thinking and innovative practice on work, business, management, leadership, stewardship, career development, human resources, entrepreneurship, and global sustainability.

Since the company's founding in 1992, we have been committed to creating a world that works for all by publishing books that help us to integrate our values with our work and work lives, and to create more humane and effective organizations.

We have chosen to focus on the areas of work, business, and organizations, because these are central elements in many people's lives today. Furthermore, the work world is going through tumultuous changes, from the decline of job security to the rise of new structures for organizing people and work. We believe that change is needed at all levels—individual, organizational, community, and global—and our publications address each of these levels.

To find out about our new books,
special offers,
free excerpts,
and much more,
subscribe to our free monthly eNewsletter at

www.bkconnection.com

Berrett-Koehler books and audios are available at quantity discounts for orders of 10 or more copies.

Leadership that Matters

The Critical Factors for Making a Difference in People's Lives and Organizations' Success

Marshall Sashkin and Molly G. Sashkin

]Paperback, 200 pages
ISBN 1-57675-193-7
Item #51937-415 $22.95

To find out about discounts on orders of 10 or more copies for individuals, corporations, institutions, and organizations, please call us toll-free at (800) 929-2929.

To find out about our discount programs for resellers, please contact our Special Sales department at (415) 288-0260; Fax: (415) 362-2512. Or email us at bkpub@bkpub.com.

Berrett-Koehler Publishers
PO Box 565, Williston, VT 05495-9900
Call toll-free! **800-929-2929** 7 am-9 pm Eastern Standard Time
Or fax your order to 802-864-7627
For fastest service order online: **www.bkconnection.com**